Central Europe
phrasebook

Chris Andrews
James Jenkin
Koronczi Katalin
Richard Nebeský
Katarina Steiner
Sally Steward

Central Europe phrasebook
    1st edition

Published by
   Lonely Planet Publications
   Head Office: PO Box 617, Hawthorn, Vic, 3122, Australia
   Branches: 155 Filbert Street, Suite 251, Oakland, CA 94607, USA
                   10 Barley Mow Passage, Chiswick, London W4 4PH, UK
                   71 bis rue du Cardinal Lemoine, 75005 Paris, France

Printed by
   Colorcraft Ltd, Hong Kong

Published
   January 1995

Cover Photo
   Freudenberg, Germany (The Image Bank - Hans Wolf)

National Library of Australia Cataloguing in Publication Data
Central Europe phrasebook
   1st ed.
   ISBN 0 86442 259 8.

   1. Indo-European languages - Conversation and phrase books - English. 2.
   Hungarian language - Conversation and phrase books - English 3. Slovak
   language - Conversation and phrase books - English 4. Central Europe - Languages - Conversation and phrase books - English I. Nebesky, Richard. (Series:
   Lonely Planet language survival kit).

409.43

text © Lonely Planet Publications Pty Ltd 1994
cover photo © photographer as indicated 1994

Contents

Acknowledgements

The Czech chapter was written by Richard Nebeský, with assistance from his parents. The French chapter was written by Chris Andrews and proofread by Adrienne Costanzo. James Jenkin wrote the German chapter. The Hungarian chapter was written by Koronczi Katalin, with assistance from James Stewart. Sally Steward wrote the Italian chapter, with assistance from Adrienne Costanzo and Stefania Salamon. Katarina Steiner wrote the Slovak section.

The book was edited by Sally Steward. Valerie Tellini was responsible for design and cover design.

From the Publisher

In this book Lonely Planet uses a simplified phonetic transcription, based on the International Phonetic Alphabet. While this can only approximate the exact sounds of each language, it serves as the most useful guide for readers attempting to say the various words and phrases. As you spend time in a country, listening to native speakers and following the rules offered here in the pronunciation sections, you should be able to read directly from the language itself.

Most of the languages in this book have masculine and feminine, and sometimes neuter, forms of words. The different forms are separated in the text by slashes and/or the bracketed abbreviations (m), (f) and (neut), when appropriate. Many words share the same form, in which case no indication of gender is required.

Each of the languages in this book has both formal and informal ways of speech, which means that for one word in English (especially 'you') you may find two in another language, one being the polite, formal word, and the other being more casual and informal. For the purposes of this book the formal way of speech has been adopted throughout, as this will ensure that at least you will not offend anyone by using a more intimate style. In instances where the informal is more appropriate, we have included it, indicated by the letters (inf).

CZECH

Czech

Introduction

The Czech language belongs to the Slavonic group of Indo-European languages, which is subdivided into East, West and South Slavonic groups. Czech, together with Slovak, Polish and Lusatian, is part of the West Slavonic group. It is the main language of the Czech Republic and is spoken by 10 million people.

Although Czech has several dialects, this phrasebook uses a standardised form of the language, literary Czech (*spisovná čeština*), which is based on the central Bohemian dialect. However, this is no longer associated with a particular social group or territory, and functions as a common language understood by all Czechs. Therefore, you won't have trouble communicating wherever you are in the country.

Some Czech sentences will be phrased differently depending on whether you are male or female, so both forms are given when applicable.

Pronunciation

Czech is spelt as it is spoken, and once you become familiar with the sounds, it can be read easily.

Vowels

An accent over a vowel indicates that it is lengthened.

a	as the 'ah' sound in 'cut'
á	as the 'a' in 'father'
e	as the 'eh' sound in 'bet'
é	as 'air'
ě	as the 'ye' in 'yet'
i/y	as the 'i' in 'bit'
í/ý	as the 'ee' in 'see'
o	as the 'o' in 'pot'
ó	as the 'aw' in 'saw'
u	as the 'u' in 'pull'
ú/ů	as the 'oo' in 'zoo'

Diphthongs

aj	as the 'i' in 'ice'
áj	like 'eye'
au	an 'ow' sound as in 'out'
ej	as the 'ay' in 'day'
ij/yj	a short 'eey' sound
íj/ýj	a long 'eey' sound
oj	as the 'oi' in 'void'
ou	as the 'o' in 'note', but both the 'o' and 'u' are more strongly pronounced than in English
uj	a short 'u' sound as in 'pull', followed by 'y'
új	a long 'oo' sound as in 'zoo', followed by 'y'

Consonants

c	as the 'ts' in 'lets'
č	as the 'ch' in 'chew'
ch	a 'kh' sound, as in the Scottish 'loch', or German 'Buch'

g	a hard sound like the 'g' in 'get'
h	always pronounced, as the 'h' in 'hand'
j	as the 'y' in 'year'
r	a rolled 'r', made with the tip of the tongue
ř	'rzh'. It's the sound in the composer's name Dvořák – a rolled 'r' followed by the 's' in 'treasure'.
s	as the 's' in 'sit', not as in 'rose'
š	as the 'sh' in 'ship'
ž	a 'zh' sound, as the 's' in 'treasure'
ď, **ň** & **ť**	are very soft palatal sounds. There is a momentary contact between the tongue and the hard palate, as if a 'y' sound is added, as in the 'ny' in canyon. The same sound occurs with **d**, **n** and **t** followed by **i**, **í** & **ě**.

All other consonants are similar to English, apart from **k**, **p** and **t**, which are pronounced with no puff of breath after them.

Stress

In Czech the first syllable is usually stressed. Vowels are pronounced the same whether they are stressed or not – say each syllable clearly and distinctly.

Greetings & Civilities
Top 10 Useful Phrases

Hello./Goodbye.

dob-ree-dehn/   Dobrý den./
nah-skhleh-dah-noh   Na shledanou.

Yes./No.
  ah-no/neh   Ano./Ne.
Yes. (colloquial)
  yo   Jo.
Excuse me.
  zdo-vo-leh-nyeem   S dovolením.
May I? Do you mind?
  do-vol-teh-mi?   Dovolte mi?
Sorry. (excuse me,
  forgive me)
  pro-miny-teh   Promiňte.
Please.
  pro-seem   Prosím.
Thank you.
  dyeh-ku-yi   Děkuji.
Many thanks.
  mots-kraat dyeh-ku-yi   Mockrát děkuji.
That's fine. You're welcome.
  neh-nyee zahch. pro-   Není zač. Prosím.
  seem

Greetings
Good morning!
  dob-rair yit-ro (raa-no)!   Dobré jitro (ráno)!
Good afternoon!
  dob-rair ot-po-lehd-neh!   Dobré odpoledne!
Good evening/night!
  dob-ree veh-chehr!   Dobrý večer!
  dob-roh nots!   Dobrou noc!

How are you?
*yahk-seh **maa**-teh?*   Jak se máte?
Well, thanks.
*dyeh-ku-yi, **dob**-rzheh*   Děkuji, dobře.

Forms of Address

Madam/Mrs   *pah-nyee*   Paní
Sir/Mr   *pahn*   Pan
Miss   *slehch-nah*   Slečna
companion,   *przhee-tehl* (m)   přítel
   friend   *przhee-tehl-ki-nyeh* (f) přítelkyně

Small Talk
Meeting People

What is your name?
*yahk-seh **ymeh**-nu-yeh-teh?* Jak se jmenujete?
My name is ...
ymeh-nu-yi-seh ...   Jmenuji se ...
I'd like to introduce you
to ...
*mo-hu vaas **przheht**-*   Mohu vás představit ...
stah-vit ...
I'm pleased to meet you.
tye-shee mnyeh, zheh   Těší mně, že vás poznávám.
*vaas **po**-znaa-vaam*

I like ...
*mnyeh **seh**-to **lee**-bee ...*   Mně se to líbí ...

I don't like ...
   *mnyeh **seh**-to*   Mně se to nelíbí ...
   neh-lee-bee ...
How old are you?
   ***ko**-lik yeh vaam leht?*   Kolik je vám let?
I am ... years old.
   yeh mi ... let   Je mi ... let.

Nationalities
Where are you from?
   *od-kud **po**-khaa-zee-teh?*   Odkud pocházíte?

I am from ...
   ysehm ...   Jsem ...

Australia	*sow-**straa**-li-yeh*	z Austrálie
Canada	***skah**-nah-di*	z Kanady
England	***sahn**-gli-yeh*	z Anglie
Ireland	***sir**-skah*	z Irska
New Zealand	***sno**-vair-ho*	z Nového Zélandu
	*zair-**lahn**-du*	
Scotland	*zeh **skot**-skah*	ze Skotska
the USA	*zeh **spo**-yeh-neekh*	ze Spojených států
	***staa**-too*	
Wales	*z**vah**-leh-su*	z Walesu

Occupations
What do you do?
   *tso **dyeh**-laa-teh?*   Co děláte?
I am a/an ...
   ysehm ...   Jsem ...

artist	*u*-myeh-lehts (m)	umělec
	u-myehl-ki-nyeh (f)	umělkyně
business person	*op*-kho-dnyeek (m)	obchodník
	op-kho-dnyi-tseh (f)	obchodnice
doctor	*lair*-kahrzh (m)	lékař
	lair-kahrzh-kah (f)	lékařka
engineer	*in*-zheh-neer (m)	inženýr
	in-zheh-neer-kah (f)	inženýrka
farmer	*zeh*-myeh-dyeh-lehts (m)	zemědělec
	zeh-myeh-dyehl-ki-nyeh (f)	zemědělkyně
journalist	*no*-vi-naarzh (m)	novinár
	no-vi-naarzh-kah (f)	novinářka
lawyer	*praa*-vnyeek (m)	právník
	praa-vnyi-chkah (f)	právnička
manual worker	*dyehl*-nyeek (m)	dělník
	dyehl-nyi-tseh (f)	dělnice
mechanic	*ow*-to-meh-khah-nik (m)	automechanik
	ow-to-meh-khah-nich-kah (f)	automechanička
nurse	*o*-sheh-trzho-vah-tehl (m)	ošetřovatel
	o-sheh-trzho-vah-tehl-kah (f)	ošetřovatelka
office worker	*oo*-rzheh-dnyeek (m)	úředník
	oo-rzheh-dnyi-tseh (f)	úřednice
scientist	*vyeh*-dehts (m)	vědec
	vyeht-ki-nyeh (f)	vědkyně
student	*stu*-dehnt (m)	student
	stu-dehnt-kah (f)	studentka

teacher	*u*-chi-tehl (m)	učitel
	u-chi-tehl-kah (f)	učitelka
waiter	*chee*-shnyeek (m)	číšník
	chee-shnyi-tseh	číšnice
	(*sehr*-veer-kah) (f)	(servírka)
writer	*spi*-so-vah-tehl (m)	spisovatel
	spi-so-vah-tehl-kah (f)	spisovatelka

Religion

What is your religion?

yah-kair-ho ysteh	Jakého jste náboženského
naa-bo-zhehn-skair-ho	vyznání?
vi-znaa-nyee?	

I am not religious.

| ysehm behz *vi*-znaa-nyee | Jsem bez vyznání. |

I am ...

ysehm ...	Jsem ...
Buddhist	*bu*-dhi-stah (m)	buddhista
	bu-dhist-kah (f)	budhistka
Catholic	*kah*-to-leek (m)	katolík
	kah-to-li-chkah (f)	katolička
Christian	*krzheh*-styahny (m)	křesťan
	krzheh-styahny-	křesťanka
	kah (f)	
Hindu	*hin*-du	hindu
Jewish	zhid (m)	žid
	zhi-dof-kah (f)	židovka
Muslim	*mu*-slim (m)	muslim
	mu-slim-kah (f)	muslimka

Family

Are you married?
*ysteh **zheh**-nah-tee?* (m) Jste ženatý?
*ysteh **vdah**-naa?* (f) Jste vdaná?

I am single.
*ysehm **svo**-bo-dnee* (m) Jsem svobodný.
*ysehm **svo**-bo-dnaa* (f) Jsem svobodná.

I am married.
*ysehm **zheh**-nah-tee* (m) Jsem ženatý.
*ysehm **fdah**-naa* (f) Jsem vdaná.

How many children do you
have?
*ko-lik **maa**-teh dyeh-tyee?* Kolik máte dětí?

I don't have any children.
***neh**-maam **dyeh**-tyi* Nemám děti.

I have a daughter/a son.
***maam** si-nah/**tseh**-ru* Mám syna/dceru.

How many brothers/sisters
do you have?
*ko-lik **maa**-teh*
***brah**-troo/**sehs**-tehr?* Kolik máte bratrů/sester?

Is your husband here?
*yeh zdeh **vaash***
***mahn**-zhehl?* Je zde váš manžel?

Is your wife here?
*yeh zdeh **vah**-sheh***
***mahn**-zhehl-kah?* Je zde vaše manželka?

Do you have a boyfriend/
girlfriend?
   maa-teh znaa-most?   Máte známost?

brother	**brah**-tr	bratr
children	**dyeh**-tyi	děti
daughter	**tseh**-rah	dcera
family	**ro**-dyi-nah	rodina
father	**o**-tehts	otec
grandfather	**dyeh**-deh-chehk	dědeček
grandmother	**bah**-bi-chkah	babička
husband	**mahn**-zhehl	manžel
mother	**maht**-kah	matka
sister	**sehs**-trah	sestra
son	*sin*	syn
wife	**mahn**-zhehl-kah	manželka

Feelings
(I am ...)

angry	*hnyeh-vaam-seh*	Hněvám se.
cold	*yeh mi **zi**-mah*	Je mi zima.
happy	*ysehm **shtyahst**-nee* (m)	Jsem šťastný.
	*ysehm **shtyahst**-naa* (f)	Jsem šťastná.
hot	*yeh mi **hor**-ko*	Je mi horko.
hungry/thirsty	*maam hlaht/ **zhee**-zehny*	Mám hlad/žízeň.
in a hurry	**spyeh**-khaam	Spěchám.
right	*maam **prahf**-du*	Mám pravdu.

sad	*ysehm **smut**-nee* (m)	Jsem smutný.
	*ysehm **smut**-naa* (f)	Jsem smutná.
tired	*ysehm **u**-nah-veh-nee* (m)	Jsem unavený.
	*ysehm **u**-nah-veh-naa* (f)	Jsem unavená.
well	*mnyeh-yeh **dob**-rzheh*	Mně je dobře.
worried	*maahm **stah**-rost*	Mám starost.

I am sorry. (condolence)
   *u-przhee-mnoh **soh**-strahst* Upřímnou soustrast.
I am grateful.
   *ysehm vaam **vdyehch**-nee* (m) Jsem vám vděčný.
   *ysehm vam **vdyehch**-naa* (f) Jsem vám vděčná.

Language Difficulties

Do you speak English?
   *mlu-vee-teh **ahn**-glits-ki?* Mluvíte anglicky?
Does anyone speak English?
   *mlu-vee **nyeh**-gdo **ahn**-glits-ki?* Mluví někdo anglicky?
I speak a little ...
   *mlu-veem **tro**-khu ...* Mluvím trochu ...
I don't speak ...
   neh-mlu-veem ... Nemluvím ...
I understand.
   ***ro**-zu-meem* Rozumím.

I don't understand.
   neh-roh-zu-meem   Nerozumím.

Could you speak more
slowly please?
   moo-zheh-teh mlu-vit   Můžete mluvit pomaleji?
   po-mah-leh-yi?

Could you repeat that?
   moo-zheh-teh to   Můžete to opakovat?
   o-pah-ko-vaht?

How do you say ...?
   yahk-seh rzheh-kneh ...?   Jak se řekne ...?

What does ... mean?
   tso znah-meh-naa ...?   Co znamená ...?

I speak ...
   mlu-veem ...   Mluvím ...

Dutch	*ho-lahn-ski*	holandsky
English	*ahn-glits-ki*	anglicky
French	*frahn-tsoh-ski*	francouzsky
German	*nye-mehts-ki*	německy
Hungarian	*mah-dyahrs-ki*	maďarsky
Italian	*i-tahl-ski*	italsky
Russian	*rus-ki*	rusky
Spanish	*shpah-nyehl-ski*	španělsky

Some Useful Phrases

Sure.
   yi-styeh!   Jistě!

Just a minute.
   poch-kehy-teh khvee-li   Počkejte chvíli.

It's important.
toh-yeh **doo**-le-zhi-tair   To je důležité.

It's not important.
toh **neh**-nyi *doo-leh-*
zhi-tair   To neni důležité.

It's possible.
to-yeh **mo**-zhnair.   To je možné.

It's not possible.
to **neh**-nyi *mo-zhnair*   To neni možné.

Wait!
poch-kehy-teh!   Počkejte!

Good luck!
przheh-yu vaam   Přeju vám mnoho štěstí!
mno-ho **shtyeh**-styee!

Signs

BAGGAGE COUNTER	PODEJ ZAVAZADEL
CHECK-IN COUNTER	ODBAVENÍ
CUSTOMS	CELNICE
EMERGENCY EXIT	NOUZOVÝ VÝCHOD
ENTRANCE	VCHOD
EXIT	VÝCHOD
FREE ADMISSION	VSTUP VOLNÝ
HOT/COLD	HORKÁ/STUDENÁ
INFORMATION	INFORMACE
NO ENTRY	VSTUP ZAKÁZÁN
NO SMOKING	ZÁKAZ KOUŘENÍ
OPEN/CLOSED	OTEVŘENO/ZAVŘENO
PROHIBITED	ZAKÁZÁNO

RESERVED	ZADÁNO/RESERVOVÁNO
TELEPHONE	TELEFON
TOILETS	ZÁCHODY/WC/TOALETY

Emergencies

POLICE	POLICIE
POLICE STATION	POLICEJNÍ STANICE

Help!
po-mots Pomoc!
It's an emergency!
*to-yeh **nah**-lair-hah-vee
przhee-paht!* To je naléhavý případ!
There's been an accident!
*do-shlo **kneh**-ho-dyeh* Došlo k nehodě!
Call a doctor/ambulance/
police!
*zah-vo-lehy-teh **do**-kto-
rah/**sah**-nit-ku/**po**-li-tsi-yi!* Zavolejte doktora/sanitku/
policii!
Where is the police station?
***gdeh**-yeh po-li-tsehy-
nyee **stah**-nyi-tseh?* Kde je policejní stanice?

I've been raped.
*bi-lah ysehm **znaa**-sil-
nyeh-naa* Byla jsem znásilněná.

I've been robbed.
   ***bil** ysehm o-krah-dehn* (m)   Byl jsem okraden.
   ***bi**-lah ysehm o-krah-deh-*   Byla jsem okradená.
   naa (f)
Go away!
   ***byezh**-teh prich!*   Běžte pryč!
I'll call the police!
   ***zah**-vo-laam po-li-tsi-yi!*   Zavolám policii!
Thief!
   ***zlo**-dyehy!*   Zloděj!

I am ill.
   *ysehm **neh**-mo-tsnee* (m)   Jsem nemocný.
   *ysehm **neh**-mo-tsnaa* (f)   Jsem nemocná.
I am lost.
   ***zah**-bloh-dyil-sem* (m)   Zabloudil jsem.
   ***zah**-bloh-dyi-lah-sem* (f)   Zabloudila jsem.
Where are the toilets?
   ***gdeh-**ysoh **zaa**-kho-di?*   Kde jsou záchody?
Could you help me please?
   ***pro**-seem, **moo**-*   Prosím, můžete mi pomoci?
   zheh-teh mi po-mo-tsi?
Could I please use the
telephone?
   ***do**-vo-lee-teh, ah-bikh-si*   Dovolíte, abych si
   ***ah**-teh-leh-fo-no-vahl?* (m)   zatelefonoval?
   ***do**-vo-lee-teh, ah-bikh-si*   Dovolíte, abych si
   ***zah**-teh-leh-fo-no-vah-*   zatelefonovala?
   lah? (f)

I'm sorry. I apologise.
pro-miny-teh.   Promiňte.
o-mloh-vaam-seh.   Omlouvám se.
I didn't realise I was doing
anything wrong.
   neh-u-vyeh-do-mil   Neuvědomil jsem si
   ysehm-si zheh ysehm   že jsem udělal něco
   u-dyeh-lahl nyeh-tso   špatného.
   shpaht-nair-ho (m)
   neh-u-vyeh-do-mi-lah   Neuvědomila jsem si
   ysehm-si zheh ysehm   že jsem udělala něco
   u-dyeh-lah-lah nyeh-tso   špatného.
   shpaht-nair-ho (f)
I didn't do it.
   neh-u-dye-lahl   Neudělal jsem to.
   ysehm-to (m)
   neh-u-dye-lahl-lah   Neudělala jsem to.
   ysehm-to (f)
I wish to contact my
embassy/consulate.
   przheh-yu-si mlu-vit   Přeju si mluvit s mým
   zmeem vehl-vi-slah-   velvyslanectvím/konzulátem.
   nehts-tveem/
   kon-zu-laa-tehm

I have medical insurance.
   maam neh-mo-tsehns-koh   Mám nemocenskou pojistku.
   po-yist-ku
My possessions are insured.
   mo-yeh zah-vah-zah-dlah   Moje zavazadla
   ysou po-yi-shtyeh-naa   jsou pojištěná.

My ... was stolen.
 u-krah-dli myeh ...   Ukradli mě ..
I've lost ...
 strah-tyil ysehm ... (m)   Ztratil jsem ...
 strah-tyi-lah ysehm ... (f)   Ztratila jsem ...

my bags	*mo-yeh zah-vah-zah-dlah*	moje zavazadla
my handbag	*mo-yee kah-behl-ku*	moji kabelku
my money	*mo-yeh peh-nyee-zeh*	moje peníze
my travellers' cheques	*mo-yeh tsehs-to-vnyee sheh-ki*	moje cestovní šeky
my passport	*mooy pahs*	můj pas

Paperwork

name	*ymair-no*	Jméno.
address	*ah-dreh-sah*	Adresa.
date of birth	*dah-tum nah-ro-zeh-nyee*	Datum narození.
place of birth	*mees-to nah-ro-zeh-nyee*	Místo narození.
age	*vyehk*	Věk.
sex	*po-hlah-vee*	Pohlaví.
nationality	*staa-tynyee przhee-slush-nost*	Státní příslušnost.
next of kin	*nehy-blizh-shee przhee-bu-znee* (m)	Nejbližší příbuzný
	nehy-blizh-shee przhee-bu-znaa (f)	Nejbližší příbuzná

religion	*naa*-bo-zhehn-stvee	Náboženství.
reason for travel	*oo*-chehl *tsehs*-ti	Účel cesty.
profession	*po*-vo-laa-nyee	Povolání.
marital status	*mahn*-zhehl-skee stahf	Manželský stav.
passport	pahs	Pas.
passport number	*chee*-slo *pah*-su	Pas č. (číslo)
visa	*vee*-zum	Vízum.
identity card	*proo*-kahz *to*-to-zhno-styi	Průkaz totožnosti.
identification	*leh*-gi-ti-mah-tseh	Legitimacc.
birth certificate	*ro*-dnee list	Rodný list.
driver's licence	*rzhi*-dyich-skee *proo*-kahz	Řidičský průkaz.
car registration	*tehkh*-ni-tskee *proo*-kahz	Technický průkaz.
customs	tslo	Clo.
border	*hrah*-nyi-tseh	Hranice.

Getting Around

ARRIVALS	PŘÍJEZDY
BUS STOP	AUTOBUSOVÁ ZASTÁVKA
DEPARTURES	ODJEZDY
STATION	STANICE
SUBWAY	METRO
TICKET OFFICE	POKLADNA
TIMETABLE	JÍZDNÍ ŘÁD
TRAIN STATION	NÁDRAŽÍ

What time does ... leave/
arrive?

*gdi **ot**-yee-zhdyee/* *przhi-yee-zhdyee ...?*		Kdy odjíždí/přijíždí ...?
the boat	*lody*	loď
the bus (city)	*(**myehst**-skee)* *ow-to-bus*	(městský) autobus
the bus (intercity)	*(**meh**-zi-myehst-skee)* *ow-to-bus*	(meziměstský) autobus
the train	*vlahk*	vlak
the tram	***trahm**-vahy*	tramvaj

Directions

Where is ...?
    ***gdeh**-yeh ...?*   Kde je ...?

How do I get to ...?
    ***yahk**-seh **do**-stah-nu k ...?*   Jak se dostanu k ...?

Is it far from/near here?
    *yeh to **dah**-leh-ko/* *blees-ko?*   Je to daleko/blízko?

Can I walk there?
    do-stah-nu-seh *tahm **pyehsh**-ki?*   Dostanu se tam pěšky?

Can you show me (on
the map)?
    *moo-zheh-teh **mi**-to* *u-kaa-zaht (nah* ***mah**-pyeh)?*   Můžete mi to ukázat (na mapě)?

Are there other means of
getting there?
  mo-hu-seh tahm do-staht   Mohu se tam dostat jinak?
  yi-nahk?
I want to go to ...
  khtsi yeet ...   Chci jít ...

Go straight ahead.
  ydyeh-teh przhee-mo   Jděte přímo.
It's two blocks down.
  o dvyeh u-li-tseh daal   O dvě ulice dál.
Turn left ...
  zah-to-chteh vleh-vo ...   Zatočte vlevo ...
Turn right ...
  zah-toch-teh fprah-vo ... Zatočte vpravo ...
at the next corner
  nah przhee-shtyeem   na příštím rohu
  ro-hu
at the traffic lights
  u seh-mah-for-ru   u semaforu

behind	*zah*	za
in front of	*przhehd*	před
far	*dah-leh-ko*	daleko
near	*blees-ko*	blízko
opposite	*nah-pro-tyi*	naproti

Booking Tickets

Excuse me, where is the
ticket office?
    pro-seem, gdeh-yeh   Prosím, kde je pokladna?
    po-klah-dnah?

Where can I buy a ticket?
    gdeh-seh pro-daa-vah-   Kde se prodávají jízdenky?
    yee yeez-dehn-ki?

I want to go to ...
    khtsi yeht do ...   Chci jet do ...

Do I need to book?
    po-trzheh-bu-yi   Potřebuji místenku?
    mees-tehn-ku?

You need to book.
    po-trzheh-bu-yeh-teh   Potřebujete místenku.
    mee-stehn-ku?

I would like to book a seat to...
    pro-sil bikh mees-tehn-ku   Prosil bych místenku do ...
    do ... (m)
    pro-si-lah bikh mees-   Prosila bych místenku do ...
    tehn-ku do ... (f)

It is full.
    yeh o-psah-zeh-no   Je obsazeno.

Is it completely full?
    jeh oo-pl-nyeh   Je úplně obsazeno?
    o-psah-zeh-no?

I would like ...
    raad bikh ... (m)   Rád bych ...
    raa-dah bikh ... (f)   Ráda bych ...

a one-way ticket	
yeh-dno-smyehr-noh	jednosměrnou jízdenku
yeez-dehn-ku	
a return ticket	
spaa-teh-chnyee	zpáteční jízdenku
yeez-dehn-ku	
two tickets	
dvyeh yee-zdehn-ki	dvě jízdenky
tickets for all of us	
yeez-dehn-ki pro	jízdenky pro všechny
vshehkh-ni	
a student's fare	
stu-dehnts-koh	studentskou jízdenku
yeez-dehn-ku	
a child's fare	
dyets-koh yeez-dehn-ku	dětskou jízdenku
1st class	
pr-vnyee trzhee-du	první třídu
2nd class	
dru-hoh trzhee-du	druhou třídu

Air

CHECKING IN	ODBAVENÍ
LUGGAGE PICKUP	VÝDEJ ZAVAZADEL
REGISTRATION	REGISTRACE

Is there a flight to ...?	
yeh leh-teh-tskair	Je letecké spojení do ...?
spo-yeh-nyee do ...?	

When is the next flight to ...?
   gdi-yeh *przhee*-shtyee   Kdy je příští let do ...?
   leht do ... ?
How long does the flight take?
   yahk dloh-ho *tr-vaa* leht?   Jak dlouho trvá let?
What is the flight number?
   yah-kair yeh chee-slo   Jaké je číslo letu?
   leh-tu?
You must check in at ...
   mu-see-teh-seh   Musíte se přihlásit ...
   przhi-hlaa-sit ...

airport tax	*leh-tyish-tnyee* *po-plah-tehk*	letištní poplatek
boarding pass	*pah-lub-nyee* *fstu-pehn-kah*	palubní vstupenka
customs	*tsehl-nyi-tseh*	celnice

Bus

BUS/TRAM STOP	AUTOBUSOVÁ/ TRAMVAJOVÁ ZASTÁVKA

Where is the bus/tram stop?
   gdeh-yeh stah-nyi-tseh   Kde je stanice autobusů/
   ow-to-bu-soo/trahm-vah-yee?   tramvají?

Which bus goes to ...?
   kteh-ree ow-to-bus   Který autobus jede do ...?
   yeh-deh do ...?

Does this bus go to ...?
   yeh-deh tehn-hleh   Jede tenhle autobus do ...?
   ow-to-bus do ...?

How often do buses pass by?
   yahk chahs-to tu-di   Jak často tudy jezdí autobus?
   yehz-dyee ow-to-bus?

Could you let me know when
we get to ...?
   mohl bi-steh-mi pro-seem   Mohl byste mi prosím říci,
   rzhee-tsi, gdi przhi-yeh-   kdy přijedeme do ...?
   deh-meh do ...? (m)
   moh-lah bi-steh-mi pro-   Mohla byste mi prosím říci,
   seem rzhee-tsi, gdi przhi-   kdy přijedeme do ...?
   yeh-deh-meh do ...? (f)

I want to get off!
   khtsi vi-stoh-pit!   Chci vystoupit!

What time is the ... bus?
   gdi yeh-deh ... ow-to-bus?   Kdy jede ... autobus?

next   *przheesh-tyee*   příští
first   *pr-vnyee*   první
last   *po-sleh-dnyee*   poslední

Metro

METRO/UNDERGROUND	METRO
THIS WAY TO	PŘÍCHOD
WAY OUT/WAY IN	VÝCHOD/VCHOD

Which line takes me to ...?
kteh-raa trah-sah
veh-deh do ...?

Která trasa vede do ...?

What is the next station?
yahk-seh ymeh-nu-yeh
przhee-shtyee stah-
nyi-tseh?

Jak se jmenuje příští stanice?

Train

PLATFORM NO	NÁSTUPIŠTĚ

Is this the right platform
for ...?
yeh-deh vlahk do ...
sto-ho-to
naa-stu-pi-shtyeh?

Jede vlak do ... z tohoto
nástupiště?

Passengers must change
trains to ...
tsehs-tu-yee-tsee do ...
mu-see przheh-stoh-pit f ...

Cestující do ... musí
přestoupit v ...

The train leaves from
platform ...
vlahk ot-yeezh-dyee
znaas-tu-pi-shtyeh ...

Vlak odjíždí z nástupiště ...

dining car	**_yee-dehl-nyee vooz_**	jídelní vůz
express	**_ri-khleek_**	rychlík
local	**_mees-tnyee_**	místní
sleeping car	**_spah-tsee vooz_**	spací vůz

Taxi

Can you take me to ...?
*moo-zheh-teh mnyeh
do-vairst do ...?*

Můžete mě dovést do ...?

Please take me to ...
*pro-seem, od-vehs-teh
mnyeh do ...?*

Prosím, odvezte mě do ...?

How much does it cost to
go to ...?
*ko-lik sto-yee tsehs-
tah do ...?*

Kolik stojí cesta do ...?

Instructions

Here is fine, thank you.
*zahs-tahf-teh zdeh,
pro-seem*

Zastavte zde, prosím.

The next corner, please.
*nah przheesh-tyeem
ro-hu, pro-seem*

Na příštím rohu, prosím.

Continue!
po-krah-chuy-teh!

Pokračujte!

The next street to the left/
right.
*przhee-shtyee u-li-tsi
vleh-vo/fprah-vo*

Příští ulici vlevo/vpravo.

Stop here!
zah-stahf-teh zdeh!

Zastavte zde!

Please slow down.
*yehty-teh po-mah-leh-yi,
pro-seem.*

Jeďte pomaleji, prosím.

Please wait here.
poch-*kehy-teh zdeh,*
pro-*seem*   Počkejte zde, prosím.

Some Useful Phrases
The train is cancelled.
vlahk yeh **zru**-*sheh-nee*   Vlak je zrušený.
The train is delayed.
vlahk maa **spozh**-   Vlak má zpoždění.
dyeh-nyee
How long will it be
delayed?
yah-*kair maa* **spozh**-   Jaké má zpoždění?
dyeh-nyee?
There is a delay of ... hours.
maa ... **ho**-*dyi-no-vair*   Má ... -hodinové zpoždění?
spozh-*dyeh-nyee?*
Can I reserve a place?
mo-*hu-si* **reh**-*zehr-vo-*   Mohu si reservovat místenku?
vaht **mee**-*stehn-ku?*
How long does the trip
take?
yahk **dloh**-*ho* **trvaa**   Jak dlouho trvá cesta?
tsehs-*tah?*
Is it a direct route?
yeh-to **przhee**-*maa*   Je to přímá cesta?
tsehs-*tah?*
Is that seat taken?
yeh **to**-*to* **mees**-*to*   Je toto místo obsazeno?
op-*sah-zeh-no?*

I want to get off at ...
    *khtsi **vis**-toh-pit f ...*   Chci vystoupit v ...
Excuse me.
    zdo-vo-leh-nyeem   S dovolením.
Where can I hire a bicycle?
    *gdeh-si **mo**-hu **pooy**-   Kde si mohu půjčit kolo?
    chit **ko**-lo?*

Car

DETOUR	OBJÍŽĎKA
FREEWAY	DÁLNICE
GARAGE	BENZÍNOVÁ PUMPA
GIVE WAY	DEJ PŘEDNOST V JÍZDĚ
MECHANIC	AUTOMECHANIK
NO ENTRY	ZÁKAZ VJEZDU
NO PARKING	ZÁKAZ PARKOVÁNÍ
NORMAL	STANDART
ONE WAY	JEDNOSMĚRNÝ PROVOZ
REPAIRS	AUTOOPRAVNA
SELF SERVICE	SAMOOBSLUHA
STOP	ZASTAVTE/STOP
SUPER	SUPER
UNLEADED	NATURAL

Where can I rent a car?
    *gdeh-si **mo**-hu*   Kde si mohu pronajmout
    ***pro**-nahy-moht **ow**-to?*   auto?

How much is it ...?
ko-*lik* **sto**-*yee* ...?   Kolik stojí ...?
daily/weekly
deh-*nyeh*/**tee**-*dnyeh*   denně/týdně
Does that include insurance/
mileage?
yeh **zah**-*hr-nu-tah* **ftseh**-   Je zahrnuta v ceně pojistka/
nyeh **po**-*yist-kah*/**po**-*plah*- poplatek za najeté kilometry?
tehk zah **nah**-*yeh-tair*
ki-*lo-meh-tri*?
Where's the next petrol
station?
gdeh-*yeh* **przheesh**-*tyee*   Kde je příští benzínová
behn-*zee-no-vaa*   pumpa?
pum-*pah*?
Please fill the tank.
pl-*noh* **naa**-*drzh*,   Plnou nádrž, prosím.
pro-*seem*
I want ... litres of petrol (gas).
po-*trzheh-bu-yi* ... **li**-*troo*   Potřebuji ... litrů benzínu.
behn-*zee*-*nu*
Please check the oil and water.
pro-*seem*-*vaas*,   Prosím vás zkontrolujte
skon-*tro-luy-teh*   ole ja vodu.
o-*lehy ah* **vo**-*du*
How long can I park here?
yahk **dloh**-*ho zdeh*   Jak dlouho zde mohu
mo-*hu* **pahr**-*ko-vaht*?   parkovat?
Does this road lead to ...?
veh-*deh* **tah**-*to*   Vede tato cesta do ...?
tsehs-*tah do* ...?

What make is it?
> *yah-kee yeh-to mo-dehl?*   Jaký je to model?

air (for tyres)	*vzdukh*	vzduch
battery	*bah-teh-ri-yeh*	baterie
brakes	*brz-di*	brzdy
clutch	*spoy-kah*	spojka
driver's licence	*rzhi-dyich-skee*	řidičský průkaz
	proo-kahz	
engine	*mo-tor*	motor
lights	*svyeh-tlah*	světla
oil	*o-lehy*	olej
puncture	*pee-khlaa*	píchlá pneumatika
	pneh-u-mah-ti-kah	
radiator	*khlah-dyich*	chladič
road map	*ow-to-mah-pah*	automapa
tyres	*pneh-u-mah-ti-ki*	pneumatiky
windscreen	*przheh-dnyee sklo*	přední sklo

Car Problems

I need a mechanic.
> *po-trzheh-bu-yi*   Potřebuji automechanika.
> *ow-to-meh-khah-ni-kah*

The battery is flat.
> *bah-tair-ri-eh yeh*   Baterie je vybitá.
> *vi-bi-taa*

The radiator is leaking.
> *khlah-dyich teh-cheh*   Chladič teče.

I have a flat tyre.
> *maam pee-khloh*   Mám píchlou pneumatiku.
> *pneh-u-mah-ti-ku*

It's overheating.
   mo-tor-seh
   przheh-hrzhee-vaa   Motor se přehřívá.
It's not working.
   neh-fun-gu-yeh-to   Nefunguje to.

Accommodation

CAMPING GROUND	STANOVÝ TÁBOR/ AUTOKEMP
GUEST HOUSE	PENZIÓN
HOTEL	HOTEL
MOTEL	MOTEL
PRIVATE ACCOMMODATION	ZIMMER FREI/PRIVÁT
STUDENT HOSTEL	STUDENTSKÁ NOCLEHÁRNA
YOUTH HOSTEL	MLÁDEŽNICKÁ UBYTOVNA/TURISTICKÁ UBYTOVNA

I am looking for ...
   hleh-daam ...   Hledám ...
Where is a ...?
   gdeh-yeh ...?   Kde je ...?

cheap hotel	*leh-vnee ho-tehl*	levný hotel
good hotel	*do-bree ho-tehl*	dobrý hotel

| nearby hotel | *bleez-kee **ho**-tehl* | blízký hotel |
| clean hotel | *chis-tee **ho**-tehl* | čistý hotel |

What is the address?
   *yah-kaa yeh **zdehy**-shee ah-dreh-sah?*   Jaká je zdejší adresa?
Could you write the address, please?
   *moo-zheh-teh mi **nah**-psaht ah-dreh-su, pro-seem?*   Můžete mi napsat adresu, prosím?

At the Hotel

Do you have any rooms available?
   *maa-teh **vol**-nair po-ko-yeh?*   Máte volné pokoje?

I would like ...
   przhaal bikh-si ... (m)   Přál bych si ...
   przhaa-lah bikh-si ... (f)   Přála bych si ...

a single room	*yeh-dno-loozh-ko-vee **po**-koy*	jednolůžkový pokoj
a double room	*dvoh-loozh-ko-vee **po**-koy*	dvoulůžkový pok
a room with a bathroom	*po-koy skoh-pehl-noh*	pokoj s koupelnou
a bed	*loozh-ko*	lůžko

I want a room ...
mo-hu meet po-koy ...	Mohu mít pokoj ...
with a bathroom	*skoh-pehl-noh*	s koupelnou
with a shower	*seh-spr-khoh*	se sprchou
with a television	*steh-leh-vi-zee*	s televizí
with a window	*so-knehm*	s oknem

I'm going to stay for ...
zoo-stah-nu ...	Zůstanu ...
one day	*yeh-dehn dehn*	jeden den
two days	*dvah dni*	dva dny
one week	*yeh-dehn tee-dehn*	jeden týden

Do you have passport/
identification?
   maa-teh pahs/
   o-so-bnyee proo-kahz?   Máte pas/osobní průkaz?
Your membership card,
please.
   maa-teh chlehn-skoh
   leh-gi-ti-ma-tsi, pro-seem   Máte člReenskou legitimaci,
                                    prosím.
Sorry, we're full.
   pro-miny-teh, neh-maa-
   meh vol-nair po-ko-yeh   Promiňte, nemáme volné
                                    pokoje.
How long will you be
staying?
   yah-kaa bu-deh dairl-
   kah vah-sheh-ho po-bi-tu?   Jaká bude délka vašeho
                                    pobytu?

How many nights?
ko-lik no-tsee? Kolik nocí?

It's ... per day/per person.
*sto-yee-to ... dehn-nyeh/
zah o-so-bu* Stojí to ... denně/za osobu.

How much is it per night?
*ko-lik sto-yee
yeh-dnah nots?* Kolik stojí jedna noc?

How much is it per
person?
*ko-lik to sto-yee zah
o-so-bu?* Kolik to stojí za osobu?

Can I see it?
*mo-hu-seh nah-nyey
po-dyee-vaht?* Mohu se na něj podívat?

Are there any others?
*neh-maa-teh yi-nee
po-koj?* Nemáte jiný pokoj?

Are there any cheaper
rooms?
*neh-maa-teh leh-
vnyeh-shee po-ko-yeh?* Nemáte levnější pokoje?

Can I see the bathroom?
*mo-hu-seh po-dyee-vaht
nah koh-pehl-nu?* Mohu se podívat na koupelnu?

Is there a reduction for
students/children?
*maa-teh sleh-vu pro
stu-dehn-ti/dyeh-tyi?* Máte slevu pro studenty/děti?

Does it include breakfast?
*yeh ftom **zah-hr**-nu-tah
snyee-dah-nyeh?*

Je v tom zahrnuta snídaně?

It's fine, I'll take it.
*to-yeh **fpo**-rzhaat-ku,
yaa ho **vehz**-mu*

To je v pořádku, já ho vezmu.

I'm not sure how long I'm
staying.
*nehy-sehm-si yist yahk
dloh-ho zdeh **zoos**-tah-nu*

Nejsem si jist jak dlouho zde
zůstanu.

Is there a lift?
*yeh tu **vee**-tah?*

Je tu výtah?

Where is the bathroom?
*gdeh-yeh **koh**-pehl-nah?*

Kde je koupelna?

Is there hot water all day?
*maa-teh-tu **hor**-koh
vo-du **tseh**-lee dehn?*

Máte tu horkou vodu celý
den?

Do you have a safe where I
can leave my valuables?
*maa-teh-tu **treh**-zor
gde-si **mo**-hu **u**-lo-zhit
tseh-no-styi?*

Máte tu trezor kde si mohu
uložit cennosti?

Is there somewhere to wash
clothes?
*gdeh-si **mo**-hu **vi**-praht
o-bleh-cheh-nyee?*

Kde si mohu vyprat oblečení?

Can I use the kitchen?
*mo-hu-si **u**-vah-rzhit
fku-khi-nyi?*

Mohu si uvařit v kuchyni?

Can I use the telephone?
>*mo-hu-si zah-teh-leh-*
>*fo-no-vaht?*

Mohu si zatelefonovat?

Requests & Complaints

Please wake me up at ...
>*pro-seem, vzbudy-teh-*
>*mnyeh v ...*

Prosím, vzbuďte mě v ...

The room needs to be
cleaned.
>*mooy po-koy*
>*po-trzheh-bu-yeh u-kli-dyit*

Můj pokoj potřebuje uklidit.

Please change the sheets.
>*pro-seem,*
>*przheh-vlair-knyeh-teh-*
>*mi lo-zhnyee praa-dlo*

Prosím, převlékněte mi ložní
prádlo.

I can't open/close the
window.
>*neh-mo-hu o-teh-vrzheet/*
>*zah-vrzheet o-kno*

Nemohu otevřít/zavřít okno.

I've locked myself out of
my room.
>*zah-klahp-nul* (m)/
>*zah-klahp-nu-lah* (f)
>*ysehm-si klee-cheh*
>*fmairm po-ko-yi*

Zaklapnul/Zaplapnula
jsem si klíče v mém pokoji.

The toilet won't flush.
>*zaa-khod neh-splah-*
>*khu-yeh*

Záchod nesplachuje.

I don't like this room.
> *po-koy seh mi neh-lee-bee*   Pokoj se mi nelíbí.

It's too small.
> *yeh przhee-lish mah-lee*   Je příliš malý.

It's noisy.
> *po-koy yeh hlu-chnee*   Pokoj je hlučný.

It's too dark.
> *yeh przhee-lish tmah-vee*   Je příliš tmavý.

It's expensive.
> *yeh przhee-lish drah-hee*   Je příliš drahý.

Some Useful Words & Phrases

I am/We are leaving ...
> *od-yeezh-dyeem ...*   Odjíždím ...
> *od-yeezh-dyee-meh ...*   Odjíždíme ...

now/tomorrow
> *tehdy/zee-trah*   teď/zítra

I would like to pay the bill.
> *raad bikh zah-plah-tyil*   Rád bych zaplatil účet.
> *oo-cheht* (m)
> *raa-dah bikh zah-plah-t*   Ráda bych zaplatila účet.
> *tyi-lah oo-cheht* (f)

name	*ymai -no*	jméno
surname	*przheey-myeh-nyee*	příjmění
room number	*chee-slo po-ko-yeh*	číslo pokoje
address	*ah-dreh-sah*	adresa
air-conditioned	*kli-mah-ti-zah-tseh*	klimatizace

balcony	*bahl*-kawn	balkón
bathroom	*koh*-pehl-nah	koupelna
bed	*loozh*-ko	lúžko
bill	*oo*-cheht	účet
blanket	*po*-kreef-kah	pokrývka
candle	*sveech*-kah	svíčka
chair	*zhi*-dleh	židle
clean	*chis*-tee	čistý
cupboard	*kreh*-dehnts	kredenc
dark	*tmah*-vee	tmavý
dirty	*shpi*-nah-vee	špinavý
double bed	*dvoh*-loozh-ko-vaa *po*-stehl	dvoulúžková postel
electricity	*eh*-lehk-trzhi-nah	elektřina
excluded	*neh*-nyi *zahhr*-nu-tah	neni zahrnuta
fan	*vyeh*-traak	větrák
included	*zah*-hr-nu-tair	zahrnuté
key	*kleech*	klíč
lift (elevator)	*vee*-tah	výtah
light bulb	*zhaa*-rof-kah	žárovka
lock (n)	*zaa*-mehk	zámek
mattress	*mah*-trah-tseh	matrace
mirror	*zr*-tsah-dlo	zrcadlo
padlock	*vi*-sah-tsee *zaa*-mehk	visací zámek
pillow	*pol*-shtaarzh	polštář
quiet	*tyi*-kho	ticho
room (in hotel)	*po*-koy	pokoj
sheet	*pro*-styeh-rah-dlo	prostěradlo
shower	*spr*-khah	sprcha
soap	*mee*-dlo	mýdlo

suitcase	*ku-fr*	kufr
swimming pool	*bah-zairn*	bazén
table	*stool*	stůl
toilet	*zaa-khod/vair-tsair*	záchod/WC
toilet paper	*toah-leh-tynyee pah-peer*	toaletní papír
towel	*ru-chnyeek*	ručník
water	*vo-dah*	voda
cold water	*stu-deh-naa vo-dah*	studená voda
hot water	*teh-plaa vo-dah*	teplá voda
window	*o-kno*	okno

Around Town

I'm looking for ...
hleh-daam ...   Hledám ...

the art gallery	*u-myeh-lehts-koh gah-lair-ri-i*	uměleckou galérii
a bank	*bahn-ku*	banku
the church	*ko-stehl*	kostel
the city centre	*strzhehd myehs-tah (tsehn-trum)*	střed města (centrum)
the ... embassy	*vehl-vi-slah-nehts-vee* ...	velvyslanectví ...
my hotel	*muy ho-tehl*	muj hotel
the market	*tr-zhi-shtyeh*	tržiště
the museum	*mu-seh-um*	museum
the police	*po-li-tsi-yi*	policii
the post office	*posh-tu*	poštu
a public toilet	*veh-rzhehy-nair zaa-kho-di*	veřejné záchody

| the telephone centre | *teh*-leh-fo-nyee *oo*-strzheh-dnu | telefonní ústřednu |
| the tourist information office | *in*-for-mah-chnyee *kahn*-tse-laarzh pro *tu*-ri-sti | informační kancelář pro turisty |

What time does it open?
fko-lik *ho*-dyin *o*-teh-vee-rah-yee? V kolik hodin otevírají?

What time does it close?
fko-lik *ho*-dyin *zah*-vee-rah-yee? V kolik hodin zavírají?

What ... is this?
yahk-seh *ymeh*-nu-yeh *tah*-hleh ...? Jak se jmenuje tahle ...?

| street | *u*-li-tseh | ulice |
| suburb | *chtvrty* | čtvrť |

For directions, see the Getting Around section, page 26-27.

At the Post Office

I would like some stamps.
raad (m)/*raa*-dah (f) *bikh* *nyeh*-yah-kair *znaam*-ki Rád/Ráda bych nějaké známky.

How much is the postage?
ko-lik *sto*-yee *posh*-to-vnair? Kolik stojí poštovné?

How much does it cost to
send ... to ...?
> *ko*-lik *sto*-yee *po*-slaht ...   Kolik stojí poslat ... do ...?
> *do* ...?

I would like to send ...
> *khtyehł bikh pos-laht* ... (m)   Chtěl bych poslat ...
> *khtyeh*-lah bikh
> *pos-laht* ... (f)   Chtěla bych poslat ...

a letter	*do*-pis	dopis
a postcard	*po*-hlehd	pohled
a telegram	*teh*-leh-grahm	telegram

an aerogram	*ah-eh*-ro-grahm	aerogram
air mail	*leh*-teh-tski	letecky
envelope	*o*-baal-kah	obálka
mail box	*po*-shto-vnyee	poštovní schránka
	skhraan-kah	
parcel	*bah*-leek	balík
registered mail	*do*-po-ru-cheh-nyeh	doporučeně
surface mail	*o*-bi-chehy-noh	obyčejnou poštou
	posh-toh	

Telephone

I want to ring ...
> *raad bikh-si zah-teh-leh-*
> *fo-no-vahl* ... (m)   Rád bych si zatelefonoval ...
> *raa-dah bikh-si zah-teh-*
> *leh-fo-no-vah-lah* ... (f)   Ráda bych si zatelefonovala ...

The number is ...
chees-lo yeh ...

Číslo je ...

I want to speak for three
minutes.
*raad bikh mlu-vil
trzhi mi-nu-ti* (m)
*raa-dah bikh mlu-vi-lah
trzhi mi-nu-ti* (f)

Rád bych mluvil tři minuty.

Ráda bykh mluvila tři minuty.

How much does a three-
minute call cost?
*ko-lik sto-yee trzhee
mi-nu-to-vee roz-ho-vor?*

Kolik stojí tří minutový
rozhovor?

How much does each extra
minute cost?
*ko-lik sto-yee kazh-daa
dahl-shee mi-nu-tah?*

Kolik stojí každá další
minuta?

I would like to speak to
Mr Perez.
*khtyehl bikh mlu-vit
spah-nehm Peh-rehz* (m)
*khtyeh-lah bikh mlu-vit
spah-nehm Peh-rehz* (f)

Chtěl bych mluvit s panem
Perez.

Chtěla bych mluvit s panem
Perez.

I want to make a reverse-
charges phone call.
*raad bikh zah-vo-lal nah
oo-cheht vo-lah-nair-
ho* (m)
*raa-dah bikh zah-vo-la-
lah nah oo-cheht vo-lah-
nair-ho* (f)

Rád bych zavolal
na účet volaného.

Ráda bykh zavolala
na účet volaného.

It's engaged.
yeh op-sah-zeh-no

Je obsazeno.

I've been cut off.

*bil ysehm **przheh**-ru-shehn* (m)   Byl jsem přerušen.

*bi-lah ysehm **przheh**-ru-sheh-nah* (f)   Byla jsem přerušena.

At the Bank

I want to exchange some
money/travellers' cheques.

*khtyehl bikh **vi**-mnyeh-nyit **peh**-nyee-zeh/**tsehs**-tov-nyee **sheh**-ki* (m)   Chtěl bych vyměnit peníze/cestovňí šeky.

*khtyeh-lah bikh **vi**-mnyeh-nyit peh-nyee-zeh/**tsehs**-tov-nyee **sheh**-ki* (f)   Chtěla bych vyměnit peníze/cestovňí šeky.

What is the exchange rate?

*yah-kee yeh **vee**-mnyeh-nee **kurs**?*   Jaký je výměnný kurs?

How many crowns are there
per US dollar?

*ko-lik ko-run do-stah-nu zah **yeh**-dehn ah-meh-ri-tskee do-lahr?*   Kolik korun dostanu za jeden americký dolar?

Can I have money transferred
here from my bank?

*mo-hoh **mair** peh-nyee-zeh beet **przheh**-veh-deh-ni **smair**-ho kon-tah ... **bahn**-ki do **zdehy**-shee **bahn**-ki?*   Mohou mé peníze být převedeny z mého konta ... (name of bank) banky do zdejší banky?

How long will it take to arrive?

*yahk **dloh**-ho **bu**-deh **tr**-vaht nehzh **zdeh bu**-doh?*

Jak dlouho bude trvat než zde budou?

Has my money arrived yet?

przhi-shli-mi mo-yeh peh-nyee-zeh?

Přišly mi moje peníze?

bankdraft	**bahn**-ko-vnyee **smnyehn**-kah	bankovní směnka
bank notes	**bahn**-kof-ki	bankovky
cashier	**po**-klah-dnyeek	pokladník
coins	**min**-tseh	mince
credit card	**oo**-vyeh-ro-vaa **kahr**-tah	úvěrová karta
exchange	**smyeh**-naar-nah	směnárna
signature	**pot**-pis	podpis

Sightseeing

Do you have a guidebook/ local map?

maa-teh proo-vot-tseh/ mah-pu o-ko-lee?

Máte průvodce/mapu okolí?

What are the main attractions?

yah-kair ysoh zdehy-shee po-zo-ru-ho-dno-styi?

Jaké jsou zdejší pozoruhodnosti?

What is that?

tso-yeh to?

Co je to?

How old is it?

yahk-yeh to stuh-rair?

Jak je to staré?

Can I take photographs?
*yeh zdeh **po**-vo-leh-no
fo-to-grah-fo-vaht?*

Je zde povoleno fotografovat?

What time does it open/
close?
*f**ko**-lik **ho**-dyin o-teh-vee-
rah-yee/**za**-vee-rah-yee?*

V kolik hodin otevírají/
zavírají?

ancient	***stah**-ro-vyeh-kee*	staroveký
archaeological	***ahr**-kheh-o-lo-gits-kair*	archeologické
beach	*plaazh*	pláž
building	***bu**-do-vah*	budova
castle	*hrahd/**zaa**-mehk*	hrad/zámek
cathedral	***kah**-teh-draa-lah*	katedrála
church	***ko**-stehl*	kostel
concert hall	***kon**-tsehrt-nyee seeny*	koncertní síň
library	***knyi**-ho-vnah*	knihovna
main square	***hla**-vnyee **naa**-myeh-styee*	hlavní náměstí
market	*trh*	trh
monastery	***klaash**-tehr*	klášter
monument	***pah**-maa-tyneek/**po**-mnyeek*	památník/pomník
mosque	***meh**-shi-tah*	mešita
old city	***stah**-rair **myehs**-to*	staré město
palace	***pah**-laats*	palác
opera house	*o-**peh**-rah*	opera
ruins	*z**rzhee**-tseh-nyi-ni*	zříceniny

stadium	*stah*-di-awn	stadión
statues	*so*-khi	sochy
synagogue	*si*-nah-gaw-gah	synagóga
temple	*khraam*	chrám
university	*u*-ni-vehr-si-tah	universita

Entertainment

What's there to do in the evenings?
   kahm-seh-tu daa *veh-chehr yeet?*   Kam se tu dá večer jít?

Are there any discos?
   *ysoh zdeh **dis**-ko-tair-ki?*   Jsou zde diskotéky?

Are there places where you can hear local folk music?
   hrah-yee *nyeh*-gdeh *li-do-voh* **hud**-bu?   Hrají někde lidovou hudbu?

How much is it to get in?
   ko-lik yeh **fstu**-pnair?   Kolik je vstupné?

cinema	*ki*-no	kino
concert	*kon*-tsehrt	koncert
discotheque	*dis*-ko-tair-kah	diskotéka
theatre	*dyi*-vah-dlo	divadlo

In the Country
Weather

What's the weather like?
   yah-kair yeh **po**-chah-see?   Jaké je počasí?

Will it be ... tomorrow?

bu-deh zee-trah ...?   Bude zítra ...?

cloudy	*zah-tah-zheh-no*	zataženo
cold	*khlah-dno*	chladno
foggy	*ml-hah-vo*	mlhavo
frosty	*mraaz*	mráz
hot	*hor-ko*	horko
sunny	*slu-neh-chno*	slunečno
windy	*vyeh-tr-no*	větrno
It's raining.	*pr-shee*	Prší.
It's snowing.	*snyeh-zhee*	Sněží.

Camping

Am I allowed to camp here?

mo-hu zdeh stah-no-vaht? Mohu zde stanovat?

Is there a campsite nearby?

yeh fo-ko-lee *taa-bo-rzhi-shtyeh?*   Je v okolí tábořiště?

backpack	*bah-tyoh*	baťoh
can opener	*o-tvee-rahch kon-zehrf*	otvírač konzerv
compass	*kom-pahs*	kompas
crampons	*mah-chki*	mačky
firewood	*drzheh-vo*	dřevo
gas cartridge	*pli-no-vaa bom-bi-chkah*	plynová bombička
hammock	*ha-mahk*	hamak
ice axe	*tseh-peen*	cepín
mattress	*mah-trah-tseh*	matrace

penknife	*kah-peh-snyee noozh*	kapesní nůž
rope	*pro-vahz*	provaz
tent	*stahn*	stan
tent pegs	*stah-no-vair ko-lee-ki*	stanové kolíky
torch (flashlight)	*bah-tehr-kah*	baterka
sleeping bag	*spah-tsee pi-tehl*	spací pytel
stove	*vah-rzhich*	vařič
water bottle	*pol-nyee laa-hehf*	polní láhev

Food

breakfast	*snyee-dah-nyeh*	snídaně
lunch	*o-byehd*	oběd
dinner	*veh-cheh-rzheh*	večeře

Table for ..., please.
   stool pro ..., pro-seem   Stůl pro ..., prosím.

May I have the menu please?
   yee-dehl-nyee lee-stehk,   Jídelní lístek, prosím.
   pro-seem

I would like today's special.
   mo-hu-si o-byeh-dnaht   Mohu si objednat
   speh-tsi-ah-li-tu dneh   specialitu dne.

What is today's special?
   yah-kaa yeh speh-tsi-   Jaká je specialita dne?
   ah-li-tah dneh?

Is service included in the
bill?
   yeh to fcheh-tnyeh   Je to včetně obsluhy?
   op-slu-hi?

Not too spicy.
> *neh **przhee**-lish*   Ne příliš kořeněné.
> ***ko**-rzheh-nyeh-nair*

ashtray	***po**-pehl-nyeek*	popelník
the bill	***oo**-cheht*	účet
Bon appétit.	***do**-broh khuty*	Dobrou chuť.
Cheers!	***nah**-zdrah-vee*	Na zdraví!
a cup	***shaa**-lehk*	šálek
dessert	***moh**-chnyeek*	moučník
a drink	***pi**-tyee*	pití
a fork	***vi**-dli-chkah*	vidlička
fresh	***chehr**-stvee*	čerstvý
a glass	***skleh**-nyi-tseh*	sklenice
a knife	*noozh*	nůž
off/spoiled	***skah**-zheh-nee*	zkažený
a plate	***tah**-leerzh*	talíř
spicy	***ko**-rzheh-nyeh-nee*	kořeněný
a spoon	***lzhee**-tseh*	lžice
stale	*o-ko-rah-lee*	okoralý
sweet	***slaht**-kee*	sladký
teaspoon	***lzhi**-chkah*	lžička
toothpick	***paa**-raat-ko*	párátko

Vegetarian Meals

I am a vegetarian.
> *ysehm **veh**-geh-tah-ri-aan* (m)   Jsem vegetarián.
> *ysehm **veh**-geh-tah-ri-aan-kah* (f)   Jsem vegetariánka.

I don't eat meat.
  neh-yeem **mah**-so   Nejím maso.
I don't eat chicken/fish/ham.
  neh-yeem **ku**-rzheh/   Nejím kuře/rybu/šunku.
  ri-bu/**shun**-ku

Staple Foods & Condiments

à la carte	*Jídla na objednávku*
bread	*Chléb*
butter	*Máslo*
cabbage, similar to saurkraut	*Zelí*
cheese	*Sýr*
chips	*Hranolky*
(bread) dumplings	*Houskové knedlíky*
(potato) dumplings	*Bramborové knedlíky*
eggs	*Vejce*
fish	*Ryba*
fruit	*Ovoce*
ham	*Šunka*
honey	*Med*
horseradish	*Křen*
kidneys	*Ledvinky*
liver	*Játra*
long roll	*Rohlík*
meat	*Maso*
mustard	*Hořčice*
pastry	*Pečivo*
pepper	*Pepř*
pickled cabbage/vegetables	*Sterilizované zelí/zelenina*
potatoes	*Brambory*

rice	*Rýže*
roll	*Houska*
salt	*Sůl*
sugar	*Cukr*
tartare sauce	*Tatarská omáčka*
vegetable	*Zelenina*
vinegar	*Ocet*
water	*Voda*

Breakfast Menu

eggs	*Vejce*
bacon and eggs	*Vejce se slaninou*
boiled eggs	*Vařená vejce*
fried eggs	*Smažená vejce*
ham and eggs	*Vejce se šunkou*
omelette	*Omeleta*
scrambled eggs	*Míchaná vejce*
soft/hard-boiled eggs	*Vejce na měkko/tvrdo*
jam	*Džem/Marmeláda*
type of croissant	*Loupáček*

Starters & Buffet Meals

Klobásy
   Mild or spicy sausages.
Langoše
   A Hungarian snack made of fried pastry coated in garlic, cheese, butter or jam.
Obložené chlebíčky
   Open sandwiches.

Párky
Frankfurt or wiener-type sausages.
Pražská šunka s okurkou
Prague ham with gherkins.
Ruská vejce
Hard boiled egg with mayonnaise, potato salad and sometimes a slice of salami.
Sýrový nářez
A serve of two or three cheeses.
Tlačenka s octem a cibulí
Seasoned jellied meat loaf with vinegar and fresh onion.
Uherský salám s okurkou
Hungarian salami with gherkin.
Vuřt/Buřt
Thick sausage.
Zavináče
Rollmops – herring fillets rolled around onion and/or gherkin, and pickled.

Soups

beef	*Hovězí*
beef chunks with spices	*Gulašová*
broth with egg	*Bujón*
mushroom	*Houbová*
pea	*Hrachová*
potato	*Bramborová*
tomato with a little rice	*Rajská*
tripe and spices	*Drštková*
vegetable	*Zeleninová*

Main Meals

Dušená roštěnka
  Braised slices of beef in sauce.

Hovězí guláš
  Beef chunks in a brown sauce.

Hovězí karbanátky
  A type of beef hamburger with bread crumbs, egg and onion.

Meruňkové knedlíky
  Apricots wrapped in pastry and topped with cottage cheese, melted butter and sugar.

Okurkový salát
  Cucumber salad.

Pečená husa/kachna/kuře
  Roast goose/duck/chicken.

Plněné papriky
  Capsicum stuffed with a mixture of minced meat and rice, served with tomato sauce.

Přírodní řízek
  Pork or veal schnitzel without the breadcrumbs.

Řízek (telecí nebo vepřový)
  Veal or pork schnitzel.

Segedínský guláš
  A goulash with three types of meat and saurkraut in sauce.

Sekaná pečeně
  Roast minced meat.

Svíčková
  Roasted beef served with a sour cream sauce and spices.

Švestkové knedlíky
  Plums wrapped in pastry and topped with crushed poppy seeds, melted butter and sugar.

Telecí pečeně
  Roast veal.
Vepřová pečeně
  Roasted pork with caraway seed.
Zajíc na smetaně
  Hare in a cream sauce.
Znojemská pečeně
  Slices of roast beef in a gherkin sauce.

Desserts

pineapple	*Ananas*
blueberries	*Borůvky*
pears	*Hrušky*
apple strudel	*Jablkový závin*
strawberries	*Jahody*
preserved and canned fruit	*Kompot*
raspberries	*Maliny*
apricots	*Meruňky*
plums	*Švestky*
cherries/sour cherries	*Třešně/višně*
poppy-seed cake	*Makový koláč*
fruit slices	*Ovocné koláče*
pancakes with canned fruit/ ice cream	*Palačinky s kompotem/ zmrzlinou*
meringue with whipped cream	*Rakvičky*
ice cream	*Zmrzlina*
chocolate	*Čokoládová*
coffee	*Kávová*
fruit punch	*Punčová*

nut	*Oříšková*
vanilla	*Vanilková*

Drinks – Nonalcoholic

coffee	*Káva*
black coffee	*Černá káva*
espresso	*Espreso*
Vienna coffee with whipped cream	*Vídeňská káva*
white coffee	*Bílá káva*
fruit juice	*Ovocná šťáva/Džus*
hot chocolate	*Kakao*
ice	*Led*
lemonade, but it quite often refers to all soft drinks.	*Limonáda*
mineral water	*Minerálka*
milk	*Mléko*
sugar	*Cukr*
tea (with sugar/milk)	*Čaj (s cukrem/mlékem)*
water	*Voda*

Drinks – Alcoholic

beer	*Pivo*
spirits	*Lihoviny*
wine	*Víno*

Shopping

How much is it?
   ko-lik-to sto-yee?   Kolik to stojí?

bookshop	*knyih-ku-pets-tvee*	knihkupectví
camera shop	*fo-to po-trzheh-bi*	foto potřeby
clothing store	*o-dyeh-vi*	oděvy
delicatessen	*lah-hoot-ki*	lahůdky
general store, shop	*smee-sheh-nair*	smíšené zboží/
	zbo-zhee/po-trah-vi-ni, o-pkhod	potraviny, obchod
laundry	*praa-dehl-nah*	prádelna
market	*trh*	trh
newsagency	*no-vi-no-vee*	novinový stánek/
	staa-nehk/tah-baak	tabák
pharmacy	*lair-kaar-nah*	lékárna
shoeshop	*o-buv*	obuv
souvenir shop	*su-veh-nee-ri*	suvenýry
stationers	*pah-peer-nyits-tvee*	papírnictví
supermarket	*sah-mo-op-slu-hah*	samoobsluha
vegetable shop	*zeh-leh-nyi-nah*	zelenina a ovoce
	ah o-vo-tseh	

I would like to buy ...
    *raad **bikh**-si koh-pil ...* (m)   Rád bych si koupil ...
    *raa-dah **bikh**-si koh-pi-lah ...*(f)   Ráda bych si koupila ...
Do you have other ...?
    maa-teh yi-nair ...?   Máte jiné ...?
I don't like it.
    *to-seh mi **neh**-lee-bee*   To se mi nelíbí.
Can I look at it?
    *mo-hu-seh **nah**-to po-dyee-vaht?*   Mohu se na to podívat?

I'm just looking.
   yehn-seh dyee-vaam   Jen se dívám.
Can you write down the
price?
   moo-zheh-teh-mi
   nah-psaht tseh-nu?   Můžete mi napsat cenu?
Do you accept credit
cards?
   przhi-yee-maa-teh
   oo-vyeh-ro-vair kahr-ti?   Přijímáte úvěrové karty?
Could you lower the price?
   neh-moo-zheh-teh-
   mi nyeh-tso sleh-vit?   Nemůžete mi něco slevit?
I don't have much money.
   neh-maam mots
   peh-nyehs   Nemám moc peněz.

Can I help you?
   tso-si przheh-yeh-teh?   Co si přejete?
Will that be all?
   bu-deh-to fsheh?   Bude to vše?
Would you like it wrapped?
   przheh-yeh-teh si-to
   zah-bah-lit?   Přejete si to zabalit?
Sorry, this is the only one.
   pro-miny-teh to-hleh yeh Promiňte, tohle je
   po-sleh-dnyee kus   poslední kus.
How much/many do you
want?
   ko-lik ku-soo si
   prveh-yeh-teh?   Kolik kusů si přejete?

Souvenirs

earrings	**naa**-u-shnyi-tseh	náušnice
handicraft	**li**-do-vair **u**-myeh-nyee	lidové umění
necklace	**naa**-hr-dehl-nyeek	náhrdelník
pottery	**keh**-rah-mi-kah	keramika
ring	**pr**-stehn	prsten
rug	**ko**-beh-rehts	koberec

Clothing

clothing	**o**-dyehv	oděv
coat	**kah**-baat	kabát
dress	**shah**-ti	šaty
jacket	**sah**-ko	sako
jumper (sweater)	**sveh**-tr	svetr
shirt	**ko**-shi-leh	košile
shoes	**bo**-ti	boty
skirt	**su**-knyeh	sukně
trousers	**kahl**-ho-ti	kalhoty

It is too ...

ysoh mi mots ...		Jsou mi moc ...
big	**veh**-li-kair	veliké
small	**mah**-lair	malé
short	**kraat**-kair	krátké
long	**dloh**-hair	dlouhé
tight	**tyehs**-nair	těsné
loose	**vol**-nair	volné

It doesn't fit.
neh-seh-*dyee mi to*   Nesedí mi to.

Materials

cotton	*bah*-vl-nah	bavlna
handmade	*ru*-chnyeh *vi*-ro-beh-nair	ručně vyrobené
leather	*koo*-zheh	kůže
brass	*mo*-sahz	mosaz
gold	*zlah*-to	zlato
silver	*strzhree*-bro	stříbro
pure alpaca	*chis*-taa *ahl*-pah-ko-vaa *vl*-nah	čistá alpaková vln
silk	*hehd*-vaa-bee	hedvábí
wool	*vl*-nah	vlna

Colours

black	*chehr*-nee	černý
blue	*mo*-dree	modrý
brown	*hnyeh*-dee	hnědý
green	*zeh*-leh-nee	zelený
orange	*o*-rahn-zho-vee	oranžový
pink	*roo*-zho-vee	růžový
red	*chehr*-veh-nee	červený
white	*bee*-lee	bílý
yellow	*zhlu*-tee	žlutý

Toiletries

comb	*hrzheh*-behn	hřeben
condoms	*preh*-zehr-vah-ti-vi	prezervativy

deodorant	*deh-o-do-rant*	deodorant
hairbrush	*kahr-taach nah-vlah-si*	kartáč na vlasy
moisturising cream	*pleh-tyo-vee krairm*	pleťový krém
razor	*brzhi-tvah*	břitva
sanitary napkins	*vlozh-ki*	vložky
shampoo	*shahm-pawn*	šampón
shaving cream	*ho-li-tsee krairm*	holicí krém
soap	*mee-dlo*	mýdlo
sunblock cream	*krairm nah o-pah-lo-vua-nyee*	krém na opalování
tampons	*tahm-paw-ni*	tampóny
tissues	*pah-pee-ro-vair kah-pehs-nyee-ki*	papírové kapesníky
toilet paper	*to-ah-leh-tnyee pah-peer*	toaletní papír
toothbrush	*kahr-taa-chehk nah zu-bi*	kartáček na zuby
toothpaste	*pahs-tah nah zu-bi*	pasta na zuby

Stationery & Publications

map	*mah-pah*	mapa
newspaper	*no-vi-ni*	noviny
newspaper in English	*no-vi-ni fahn-glich-tyi-nye*	noviny v angličtině
novels in English	*knyi-hi fahn-gli-chtyi-nyeh*	knihy v angličtině
paper	*pah-peer*	papír
pen (ballpoint)	*pro-pi-so-vach-ka*	propisovačka
scissors	*noozh-ki*	nůžky

Photography

How much is it to process
this film?
    ko-lik sto-yee   Kolik stojí vyvolání filmu?
    vi-vo-laa-nyee fil-mu?
When will it be ready?
    gdi bu-deh ho-to-vee?   Kdy bude hotový?
I'd like a film for this camera.
    maa-teh film do to-ho-to   Máte film do tohoto
    fo-to-ah-pah-raa-tu?   fotoaparátu?

B&W (film)	*chehr-no-bee-lee*	černobílý
camera	*fo-to-ah-pah-raat*	fotoaparát
colour (film)	*bah-reh-vnee*	barevný
film	*film*	film
flash	*blehsk*	blesk
lens	*ob-yehk-tif*	objektiv
light meter	*ehks-po-zi-meh-tr*	expozimeter

Smoking

A packet of cigarettes, please.
    pro-sil bikh kra-bich-ku   Prosil bych krabičku cigaret.
    tsi-gah-reht (m)
    pro-si-lah bikh kra-bich-   Prosila bych krabičku cigaret.
    ku tsi-gah-reht (f)

Are these cigarettes strong/
mild?

ysoh-ti **tsi**-gah-reh-ti   Jsou ty cigarety příliš silné/
przhee-lish **sil**-nair/   jemné?
yehm-nair?

Do you have a light?

maa-teh **zaa**-pahl-ki/   Máte zápalky/zapalovač?
zah-pah-lo-vahch?

cigarette papers	**tsi**-gah-reh-to-vair **pah**-peer-ki	cigaretové papírky
cigarettes	**tsi**-gah-reh-ti	cigarety
filtered	**sfil**-trehm	s filtrem
lighter	**zah**-pah-lo-vahch	zapalovač
matches	**zaa**-pahl-ki/**sir**-ki	zápalky/sirky
menthol	**mehn**-tol-ki	mentolky
pipe	**deem**-kah	dýmka
tobacco (pipe)	**tah**-baak (pro **deem**-ku)	tabák (pro dýmku)

Sizes & Comparisons

small	**mah**-lair	malé
big	**veh**-li-kair	veliké
heavy	**tyezh**-kair	těžké
light	**leh**-kair	lehké
more	**vee**-tseh	více
less	**mair**-nyeh	méně
too much/many	**przhee**-lish **ho**-dnyeh/**mno**-ho	Příliš hodně/mnoho
many	**mno** ho	mnoho

enough	*dost*	dost
also	**tah**-*kair*	také
a little bit	*tro*-*khu*	trochu

Health

Where is the ...?
   gde-*yeh* ...?   Kde je ...?

chemist	*lair*-*kaar-nah*	lékárna
dentist	***zub**-nyee **lair**-kahrzh/**zu**-bahrzh*	zubní lékař/zubař
doctor	**dok**-*tor*	doktor
hospital	*neh*-*mo-tsnyi-tseh*	nemocnice

I am sick.
   ysehm **neh**-*mo-tsnee* (m)   Jsem nemocný.
   ysehm **neh**-*mo-tsnaa* (f)   Jsem nemocná.
My friend is sick.
   mooy **przhee**-*tehl yeh*   Můj přítel je nemocný.
   neh-*mo-tsnee* (m)
   mo-yeh **przhee**-*tehl-ki-*   Moje přítelkyně je nemocná.
   nyeh yeh **neh**-*mots-naa* (f)
Could I see a female
doctor?
   przhaa-*la bikh-si* **nahf**-*shtyee-vit* **dok**-*tor-ku*?   Přála bych si navštívit doktorku?
What's the matter?
   tso-yeh vaam?   Co je vám?
Where does it hurt?
   gdeh **vaas**-*to bo-lee*?   Kde vás to bolí?

It hurts here.
    bo-lee-myeh zdeh   Bolí mě zde.
My ... hurts.
    bo-lee-myeh ...   Bolí mě ...

Parts of the Body

ankle	*kot-nyeek*	kotník
arm	*pah-zheh*	paže
back	*zaa-dah*	záda
chest	*nah pr-soh*	na prsou
ear	*u-kho*	ucho
eye	*o-ko*	oko
finger	*prst*	prst
foot	*kho-dyi-dlo*	chodidlo
hand	*ru-kah*	ruka
head	*hlah-vah*	hlava
heart	*u srd-tseh*	u srdce
leg	*no-hah*	noha
mouth	*foo-stehkh*	v ústech
nose	*nos*	nos
skin	*koo-zheh*	kůže
spine	*paa-tehrzh*	páteř
stomach	*zhah-lu-dehk*	žaludek
teeth	*zu-bi*	zuby
throat	*hr-dlo*	hrdlo

Ailments

I have ...
    maam ...   Mám ...
constipation   *zaats-pu*   zácpu

CZECH

a cough	*kah*-shehl	kašel
diarrhoea	*proo*-yehm	průjem
fever	*ho*-rehch-ku	horečku
hepatitis	*zhloh*-tehn-ku	žloutenku
an infection	*in*-fehk-tsi	infekci
influenza	*khrzhip*-ku	chřipku
lice	*fshi*	vši
low/high blood	*nyeez-kee/vi*-so-kee	nízký/vysoký
pressure	*kreh*-vnyee tlak	krevní tlak
sprain	*pod*-vr-tnu-tyee	podvrtnutí
sunburn	*oo*-zheh	úžeh
a venereal	*po*-hlah-vnyee	pohlavní nemoc
disease	*neh*-mots	
worms	*chehr*-vi	červy

I have ...
ysehm ...   Jsem ...
anaemia.	*khu*-do-kreh-vnee	chudokrevný
a burn	*po-paa*-leh-nee	popálený
a cold	*nah*-khlah-zeh-nee	nachlazený

I have ...
bo-lee-myeh ...   Bolí mě ...
a headache	*hlah*-vah	hlava
a sore throat	*fkr*-ku	v krku
a stomachache	*brzhi*-kho	břicho

Some Useful Words & Phrases

I'm ...
    maam ...   Mám ...

diabetic	*tsu-krof-ku*	cukrovku
epileptic	*eh-pi-leh-psi-i*	epilepsii
asthmatic	*ahst-mah*	astma

I'm allergic to antibiotics/
penicillin
    ysehm ah-lehr-gits-kee   Jsem alergický
    nah ahn-ti-bio-ti-kah/   na antibiotika/
    peh-ni-tsi-lin   penicilin.

I'm pregnant.
    ysehm tyeh-ho-tnaa   Jsem těhotná.

I'm on the pill.
    u-zhee-vaam ahn-ti-   Užívám antikoncepční prášky
    kon-tsehp-chnyee
    praash-ki

I haven't had my period
for ... months.
    neh-mehn-stru-o-vah-   Nemenstruovala jsem
    lah ysehm uzh ...   už ... měsíce.
    myeh-see-tseh

I have been vaccinated.
    bil ysehm o-chko-   Byl jsem očkovaný.
    vah-nee (m)
    bi-lah ysehm o-chko-   Byla jsem očkovaná.
    vah-naa (f)

I have my own syringe.
    maam svo-yee i-nyeh-   Mám svoji injekční stříkačku.
    kchnyee strzhee-kahch-ku

I feel better/worse.
    *tsee-tyeem-seh **lair**-peh/*   Cítím se lépe/hůře.
    ***hoo**-rzheh*

accident	***neh**-ho-dah*	nehoda
addiction	***nahr**-ko-mah-nieh*	narkomanie
antibiotics	***ahn**-ti-bio-ti-kah*	antibiotika
antiseptic	***ahn**-ti-sehp-tits-kee/*	antiseptický/
	***deh**-zin-fehk-chnyee*	dezinfekční
aspirin	***ahs**-pi-rin*	aspirin
bandage	***ob**-vahz*	obvaz
blood pressure	***kreh**-vnyee tlahk*	krevní tlak
blood test	***kreh**-vnyee **skoh**-*	krevní zkouška
	shkah	
contraceptives	***ahn**ti-kon-tsehp-*	antikoncepční
	*chnyee **pro**-strzhed-ki*	prostředky
injection	*i-**nyehk**-tseh*	injekce
injury	***zrah**-nyeh-nyee*	zranění
medicine	***lair**-kahrzh-stvee*	lékařství
menstruation	***mehn**-stru-ah-tseh*	menstruace
nausea	***zveh**-daa-nyee*	zvedání žaludku
	***zhah**-lud-ku*	
oxygen	***ki**-sleek*	kyslík
vitamins	***vi**-tah-mee-ni*	vitamíny
wound	***raa**-nah*	rána

At the Chemist
I need medication for ...
    *po-**trzheh**-bu-yi **lair**-ki ...*   Potřebuji léky ...

I have a prescription.
    *maam **przhehd**-pis*   Mám předpis.

At the Dentist

I have a toothache.
    ***bo**-lee-myeh zub*   Bolí mě zub.
I've lost a filling.
    ***vi**-pah-dlah-mi **plom**-bah*   Vypadla mi plomba.
I've broken a tooth.
    *maam **zlo**-meh-nee zub*   Mám zlomený zub.
My gums hurt.
    ***bo**-lee-myeh **daa**-snyeh*   Bolí mě dásně.
I don't want it extracted.
    ***neh**-tr-hehy-teh-mi*   Netrhejte mi tento zub.
    ***tehn**-to zub*
Please give me an
anaesthetic.
    ***pro**-seem, **umr**-tvyeh-teh* Prosím, umrtvěte mi to.
    ***mi**-to*

Time & Dates

Telling the time in Czech is difficult to explain in the short space
of this chapter. Ask for specific times to be written down.

What time is it?
    ***ko**-lik-yeh **ho**-dyin?*   Kolik je hodin?
What date is it today?
    ***ko**-li-kaa-tair-ho yeh*   Kolikátého je dnes?
    dnehs?

Could you write that down?
nah-pi-shteh mi-to,   Napište mi to, prosím!
pro-seem!

in the morning	*raa-no*	ráno
in the afternoon	*ot-po-leh-dneh*	odpoledne
in the evening	*veh-chehr*	večer

Days of the Week

Monday	*pon-dyeh-lee*	Pondělí
Tuesday	*oo-teh-ree*	Úterý
Wednesday	*strzheh-dah*	Středa
Thursday	*chtvr-tehk*	Čtvrtek
Friday	*paa-tehk*	Pátek
Saturday	*so-bo-tah*	Sobota
Sunday	*neh-dyeh-leh*	Neděle

Months

January	*leh-dehn*	Leden
February	*oo-nor*	Únor
March	*brzheh-zehn*	Březen
April	*du-behn*	Duben
May	*kvyeh-tehn*	Květen
June	*chehr-vehn*	Červen
July	*chehr-veh-nehts*	Červenec
August	*sr-pehn*	Srpen
September	*zaa-rzhee*	Září
October	*rzhee-yehn*	Říjen
November	*lis-to-pahd*	Listopad
December	*pro-si-nehtz*	Prosinec

Seasons

summer	*lair-to*	léto
autumn	*pod-zim*	podzim
winter	*zi-mah*	zima
spring	*yah-ro*	jaro

Present

today	*dnehs*	dnes
this morning	*dnehs raa-no*	dnes ráno
tonight	*dnehs veh-chehr/*	dnes večer/
	dnehs vno-tsi	dnes v noci
this week	*tehn-to tee-dehn*	tento týden
this year	*leh-tos/vleh-tosh-*	letos/v letoš-
	nyeem ro-tseh	ním roce
now	*tehdy*	teď

Past

yesterday	*fcheh-rah*	včera
day before yesterday	*przheh-dehf-chee-rehm*	předevčirem
last night	*fcheh-rah veh-chehr*	včera večer
last week/year	*mi-nu-lee tee-dehn/ rok*	minulý týden/rok

Future

tomorrow	*zee-trah*	zítra
day after tomorrow	*po-zee-trzhee*	pozítří
tomorrow afternoon	*zee-trah ot-po-leh-dneh/veh-chehr*	zítra odpoledne/ večer

CZECH

| next week | *przheesh*-tyee *tee*-dehn | příští týden |
| next year | *przheesh*-tyee rok | příští rok |

During the Day

afternoon	*ot*-po-leh-dneh	odpoledne
dawn, very early morning	*svee*-taa-nyee/ *vehl*-mi *br*-zo *raa*-no	svítání/ velmy brzo ráno
day	dehn	den
early	*br*-zo	brzo
midnight	*pool*-nots	půlnoc
morning (between 9 am and midday)	*raa*-no/ *do*-po-leh-dneh	ráno/ dopoledne
night	nots	noc
noon	*po*-leh-dneh	poledne
sundown	*zaa*-pahd *slun*-tseh	západ slunce
sunrise	*vee*-khod *slun*-tseh	východ slunce

Numbers & Amounts

0	*nu*-lah	nula
1	*yeh*-dnah	jedna
2	dvah	dva
3	trzhi	tři
4	*chti*-rzhi	čtyři
5	pyeht	pět
6	shehst	šest
7	*seh*-dum	sedm
8	*o*-sum	osm

9	*deh*-vyeht	devět
10	*deh*-seht	deset
11	*yeh*-deh-naatst	jedenáct
12	*dvah*-naatst	dvanáct
13	*trzhi*-naatst	třináct
14	*chtr*-naatst	čtrnáct
15	*pah*-tnaatst	patnáct
16	*shehst*-naatst	šestnáct
17	*seh*-dum-naatst	sedmnáct
18	*o*-sum-naatst	osmnáct
19	*deh*-vah-teh-naatst	devatenáct
20	*dvah*-tseht	dvacet
21	*dva*-tseht *yeh*-dnah/	dvacet jedna/
	yeh-dna-dvah-tseht	jednadvacet
30	*trzhi*-tseht	třicet
40	*chti*-rzhi-tseht	čtyřicet
50	*pah*-deh-saat	padesát
60	*sheh*-deh-saat	šedesát
70	*seh*-dum-deh-saat	sedmdesát
80	*o*-sum-deh-saat	osmdesát
90	*deh*-vah-deh-saat	devadesát
100	*sto*	sto
1000	*tyi*-seets	tisíc
one million	*mi*-li-yawn	milión
1st	*pr*-vnyee	první
2nd	*dru*-hee	druhý
3rd	*trzheh*-tyee	třetí
¼	*chtvr*-tyi-nah	čtvrtina
⅓	*trzheh*-tyi-nah	třetina

CZECH

80 Czech

| ½ | *po-lo-vi-nah* | polovina |
| ¾ | *trzhi-chtvr-tyi-nah* | třičtvrtina |

Some Useful Words

a little (amount)	*tro-khu*	trochu
double	*dvoh-yi-tee*	dvojitý
a dozen	*tu-tseht*	tucet
Enough!	*dost!*	Dost!
few	*nyeh-ko-lik*	několik
less	*mair-nyeh*	méně
many	*mno-ho*	mnoho
more	*vee-tseh*	více
once	*yeh-dnoh*	jednou
a pair	*paar*	pár
percent	*pro-tsehn-to*	procento
some	*nyeh-kteh-ree*	některý
too much	*przhee-lish*	příliš hodně
	ho-dnyeh	
twice	*dvah-kraat*	dvakrát

Abbreviations

AMU	Academy of Performing Arts
ATS	Austrian schilling
cm/m/km	cm/m/km
č./čís.	number/s
ČAD	Czech Coachline
ČČK	Czech Red Cross
ČD	Czech Railway
ČEDOK	Czech Travel Agency
ČR	Czech Republic

ČSA	Czech & Slovak Airlines
ČSFR	Czech & Slovak Federal Republic
ČTK	Czech Press Agency
DEM	Deutschmark
EU	EU
atd.	etc
FRF	French franc
GBP	British pound
h or hod	hour, or halíř (h), small unit of currency
hl. m.	capital city
JZD	State Farming Cooperative
Kč	Czech crown
KU or UK	Charles University – Prague
nám	town square
OSN	United Nations
p/pí/sl	Mr/Mrs/Ms
SBČ	Czech State Bank
ul	street
USD	American dollar

FRENCH

French

Introduction

French, like Italian, Spanish, Romanian and Portuguese, is one of the Romance languages – those descended from Latin. It began to emerge as a distinct language in the 9th century AD. The earliest surviving text in French is that of the *Strasbourg Oaths* (842 AD), an agreement uniting two of Charlemagne's grandsons against the third in a quarrel over the division of the empire. It was not until the 11th century, however, that a vernacular literature really established itself in France, with the development of verse epics called *chansons de gestes*.

During the 13th and 14th centuries, the emergence of France as a centralised state favoured the spread of the dialect of the Parisian region (Francien), to the detriment of regional dialects and the Provençal language in the south.

The edict of Villers-Cotterets, issued by François I in 1539, made the use of French compulsory for official documents. During the French Rennaissance, in the 16th century, efforts were made to enrich and dignify the national tongue, to make it a worthy vehicle for serious literature. This involved coining words from Greek and Latin roots, and the adoption of etymological spellings, which later reformers have not been able to rationalise. During the 17th century there was a reaction to this trend. The poet Malherbe and the grammarian Vaugelas, a founding member of the French Academy, *Académie française*, were influential in a movement to 'purify' the language and codify its usage, establishing norms which have, to a large extent, remained in force.

The Academy, established in 1635, has preserved its purist stand, opposing, in recent years, the introduction of English words such as 'look' or 'background'. The widespread use of such 'franglais', though it may pose a threat to the integrity of the French language, does not make communication significantly easier for the Anglophone in France.

There are about 122 million Francophones throughout the world, of whom about 58 million live in France. French is one of the official languages in Belgium, Switzerland and Luxembourg, which have around four million, 1.2 million and 300,000 Francophones respectively. French is also spoken by about 150,000 inhabitants of the Val d'Aosta in north-western Italy, and it has a million speakers in Monaco. Major areas outside Europe where you'll find French spoken are Africa, Indochina, the Pacific, Canada (Quebec), and the USA (especially Maine and Louisiana).

French grammar is broadly similar to that of the other Romance languages. An important distinction is made in French, as in Italian and Spanish, between the two forms of 'you' (singular), which in French are *tu* and *vous*. *Tu* is only used in addressing people you know well, children, and animals. When addressing an adult who is not a personal friend, *vous* should be used unless the person invites you to use *tu* (*Tu peux me tutoyer*). In general, younger people insist less on this distinction, and they may use *tu* right from the beginning of an acquaintance.

All nouns in French are either masculine or feminine, or both, and adjectives reflect the gender. The feminine form of both nouns and adjectives is indicated by a silent 'e' added to the masculine form: student, *étudiant* (m)/*étudiante* (f). In the feminine form, the final consonant (in this case the *t*) is pronounced.

As in the example here, throughout this chapter the feminine

FRENCH

word or variant follows the masculine. The gender of a noun i often indicated by a preceding article 'the/a/some': *le/un/du* (m) *la/une/de la* (f); or possessive adjective 'my/your/his/her' *mon/ton/son* (m), *ma/ta/sa* (f). The possessive adjectives agree in number and gender with the thing possessed: his/her mother *sa mère*.

There are three ways of asking questions in French. For example, to ask the time in French you can invert the subject and the verb *(Avez-vous l'heure?)*; or you can begin with *est-ce que* and keep the normal word order *(Est-ce que vous avez l'heure?)*; or you can rely on intonation to indicate that you are asking a question *(Vous avez l'heure?)*. The first way of asking questions is rather formal. The second two ways are more common in spoken French, and so will be used for most of the questions in this section.

Pronunciation

Stress in French is much weaker than in English – all it really does is lengthen the final syllable of the word – so it is important for the Anglophone to make an effort to pronounce each syllable with approximately equal stress.

French has a number of sounds which are notoriously difficult to produce. The main causes of trouble are:

1) The distinction between **ü** (as in *tu*) and **oo** (as in *tout*). For both sounds, the lips are rounded and projected forward, but for **ü**, the tongue is towards the front of the mouth, its tip against the lower front teeth, while for **oo** the tongue is towards the back of the mouth, its tip behind the gums of the lower front teeth.

2) The nasal vowels. During the production of nasal vowels the

breath escapes partly through the nose and partly through the mouth. There are no nasal vowels in English; in French there are three, indicated in the text as õ, †, ã, as in *bon vin blanc*, 'good white wine'. These sounds occur where a syllable ends in a single **n** or **m**: the **n** or **m** in this case is not pronounced, but indicates the nasalisation of the preceding vowel.

ã   as for the 'ah' sound in 'father', but with a slightly smaller opening between the lips, and the breath escaping partly through the nose. The usual spellings are **an**, **am**, **en**, and **em**.

õ   as for the 'o' in 'pot', but with the lips closer and rounded, and the breath escaping partly through the nose. The usual spelling is **on**, **om**. It is important to distinguish this sound from ã.

ẽ   as for the 'eh' sound in 'bet', but with a slightly larger opening between the lips, and the breath escaping partly through the nose. The usual spellings are **in**, **im**, **yn**, **ym**, **ain**, **aim**, **ein**, **eim**, **en** preceded by **i** or **é**, **un** or **um**.

Remember that for õ, the jaws are closer together and the lips rounded. Practice distinguishing pairs of words such as *tonton*, tõtõ, 'uncle', and *tentant*, tãtã, 'tempting.'

3) **l** and **r**. The **l** is always pronounced with the tip of the tongue touching the back of the upper incisors, and the surface of the tongue higher than for an English 'l'. Be especially careful to maintain this tongue position for **l**s at the ends of words, as in *il* or *elle*. The standard **r** of Parisian French is produced by moving the bulk of the tongue backwards to constrict the air flow in the pharynx, while the tip of the tongue rests behind the lower front teeth. It is quite similar to the noise made by some people before

FRENCH

spitting, but with much less friction. For those who know
Spanish, it also like the *jota*, except that it is 'softer' and voiced
(involves vibration of the vocal cords).

In general, try not to diphthongise vowels – keep the tongue
in the same position during their entire production, and project
the lips forward and round them well to produce the rounded
vowels **o**, **ü**, **er** and **oo**.

Greetings & Civilities
Top Useful Phrases

Hello.
  bō-zhoor   Bonjour.
Goodbye.
  oh rer-vwahr   Au revoir.
Yes./No.
  wee/nō   Oui./Non.
Excuse me.
  ehk-skü-zei mwah   Excusez-moi.
May I? Do you mind?
  voo pehr-meh-tei? sah ner   Vous permettez? Ça ne vous
  voo fei ryẽ?   fait rien?
Sorry. (excuse me, forgive me)
  pahr-dõ   Pardon.
Please.
  seel voo plei   S'il vous plaît.
Thank you.
  mehr-see   Merci.
Many thanks.
  mehr-see boh-koo   Merci beaucoup.
That's fine. You're welcome.
  trei byẽ. zher voo zã pree   Très bien. Je vous en prie.

FRENCH

Greetings

Good morning.
bō-zhoor — Bonjour.

Good afternoon.
bō-zhoor — Bonjour.

Good evening/night.
bō-swahr — Bonsoir.

How are you?
ko-mã tah-lei voo? — Comment-allez vous?

Well, thanks.
byē mehr-see. — Bien, merci.

Forms of Address

Madam/Mrs	*mah-dahm*	Madame
Sir/Mr	*mer-syer*	Monsieur
Miss	*mahd-mwah-zehl*	Mademoiselle
companion, friend	*ah-mee*	ami (m)/amie (f)

Small Talk
Meeting People

What is your name?
ko-mã voo zah-plei voo? — Comment vous appelez-vouz?

My name is ...
zher mah-pehl ... — Je m'appelle ...

I'd like to introduce you to ...
zhem-rei voo prei-zã-tei ... — J'aimerais vous présenter ...

I'm pleased to meet you.
ã-shã-tei — Enchanté/-ée.

FRENCH

Nationalities

Where are you from?
voo ver-ne doo?   Vous venez d'où?

I am …
zher vyē …   Je viens …

from Australia	*do-strah-lee*	d'Australie
from Canada	*dü kah-nah-dah*	du Canada
from England	*dā-gler-tehr*	d'Angleterre
from France	*der frãs*	de France
from New Zealand	*der noo-vehl zei-lãd*	de Nouvelle Zélande
from Scotland	*dei-kos*	d'Écosse
from Switzerland	*der swees*	de Suisse
from the USA	*dei zei-tah zü-nee*	des États-Unis
from Wales	*dü pei-ee der gahl*	du Pays de Galles

Age

How old are you?
kehl ahzh ah-vei voo?   Quel âge avez-vous?
I am … years old.
zhei … ã   J'ai … ans.

Occupations

What (work) do you do?
kehl ei votr metyer?   Quel est votre métier?

I am (a/an) …
zher swee …   Je suis …

artist	*ahr-teest*	artiste
business person	*om/fahm dah-fehr*	homme (m)/ femme (f) d'affaire.

FRENCH

doctor	*mehd-sē*	médecin
engineer	*ē-zhen-yerr*	ingénieur
farmer	*ah-gree-kül-terr*	agriculteur
journalist	*zhoor-nah-leest*	journaliste
lawyer	*ah-vo-kah*	avocat
mechanic	*mei-kah-nee-syē*	mécanicien (m)
	mei-kah-nee-syehn	mécanicienne (f)
nurse	*ē-feer-myei*	infirmier (m)
	ē-feer-myehr	infirmière (f)
office worker	*ā-plwah-yei der*	employé/-ée de
	bü-roh	bureau
student	*ei-tü-dyā*	étudiant (m)
	ei-tü-dyāt	étudiante (f)
teacher	*pro-feh-serr*	professeur
waiter	*sehr-verr*	serveur (m)
	sehr-verz	serveuse (f)
writer	*ei-kreev-ē*	écrivain

Religion

What is your religion?
kehl ei votr rer-lee-zhyō?   Quelle est votre religion?

I am not religious.
zher ner swee pah   Je ne suis pas croyant.
krwah-yā

I am …
zher swee …   Je suis …

Buddhist	*boo-deest*	bouddhiste
Catholic	*kuh-to-leek*	catholique
Christian	*krei-tyē/kreit-yehn*	chrétien (m)
		chrétienne (f)

FRENCH

Hindu	ē-doo	hindou (m)
		hindoue (f)
Jewish	zhweef/zhweev	juif (m)/juive (f)
Muslim	mü-zül-mā	musulman (m)
	mü-zül-mahn	musulmane (f)

Family

Are you married?
voo zeht mah-ryei? Vous êtes marié/-ée?

I am single.
zher swee sei-lee-bah-tehr Je suis célibataire.

I am married.
zher swee mah-ryei Je suis marié/-ée.

How many children do you have?
voo zah-vei kō-byē dā-fā? Vous avez combien d'enfants?

I don't have any children.
zher nei pah dā-fā Je n'ai pas d'enfants.

I have a daughter/a son.
zhei ün feey/ē fees J'ai une fille/un fils.

How many brothers/sisters do
you have?
voo zah-vei kō-byē der Vous avez combien de
frehr/serr? frères/sœurs?

Is your husband/wife here?
eh-sker votr mahree/fahm Est-ce que votre mari/
ei lah? femme est là?

Do you have a boyfriend/
girlfriend?
eh-sker voo zah-vei ē Est-ce que vous avez un
per-tee tah-mee/ün per-teet petit ami/une petite amie?
ah-mee?

FRENCH

brother	*ler frehr*	le frère
children	*lei zãfã*	les enfants
daughter	*lah feey*	la fille
family	*lah fah-meey*	la famille
father	*ler pehr*	le père
grandfather	*ler grã-pehr*	le grand-père
grandmother	*lah grã-mehr*	la grand-mère
husband	*ler mah-ree*	le mari
mother	*lah mehr*	la mère
sister	*lah serr*	la sœur
son	*ler fees*	le fils
wife	*lah fahm*	la femme

Feelings

I (don't) like …
   … (ner) mer plei (pah)   … (ne) me plaît (pas).
I am sorry. (condolence)
   zher swee dei-zo-lei   Je suis désolé/-ée.
I am grateful.
   zher voo swee rer-ko-neh-sã/   Je vous suis reconnaissant (m)/
   rer-ko-neh-sãt   reconnaissante (f).

I am …
   zhei …   J'ai …

cold	*frwah*	froid
hot	*shoh*	chaud
hungry	*fẽ*	faim
right	*rei-zõ*	raison
sleepy	*so-meihy*	sommeil
thirsty	*swahf*	soif

FRENCH

I am …
   zher swee …   Je suis …

angry	*fah-shei*	fâché/-ée
happy	*er-rer*	heureux (m)
	er-rerz	heureuse (f)
in a hurry	*preh-sei*	pressé/-ée
sad	*treest*	triste
tired	*fah-tee-gei*	fatigué/-ée

I am well.   *zher vei byẽ*   Je vais bien.

Language Difficulties

Do you speak English? ·
   voo pahr-lei ã-glei?   Vous parlez anglais?
Does anyone speak English?
   ehs-keel-yah kehl-kẽ kee   Est-ce qu'il y a quelqu'un
   pahrl ã-glei?   qui parle anglais?
I speak a little …
   zher pahrl! ẽ per der …   Je parle un peu de …
I don't speak …
   zher ner pahrl pah   Je ne parle pas …
I (don't) understand.
   zher (ner) kõ-prã (pah)   Je (ne) comprends (pas).
Could you speak more slowly?
   eh-sker voo poo-ryei   Est-ce que vous pourriez
   pahr-lei plü lã-tmã?   parler plus lentement?
Could you repeat that?
   eh-sker voo poo-ryei   Est-ce que vous pourriez
   rei-pei-tei selah?   répéter cela?
How do you say …?
   ko-mã tehs-kõ dee …?   Comment est-ce qu'on dit …?

What does ... mean?
ker ver deer ...?   Que veut dire ...?

I speak ...
zher pahrl ...   Je parle ...
English   *ã-glei*   anglais
French   *frã-sei*   français
German   *ahl-mã*   allemand
Italian   *ee-tah-lyē*   italien
Spanish   *es-pa-nyol*   espagnol

Some Useful Phrases
Sure.
byē sür   Bien sûr.
Just a minute.
ah-tã-dei ün mee-nüt   Attendez une minute.
It's important.
sei tē-por-tã   C'est important.
It's not important.
ser nei pah zē-por-tã   Ce n'est pas important.
It's possible.
sei po-seebl   C'est possible.
It's not possible.
ser nei pah po-seebl   Ce n'est pas possible.
Good luck!
bon shãs!   Bonne chance!
Wait!
ah-tã-dei!   Attendez!

FRENCH

Signs

BAGGAGE COUNTER	CONSIGNE
CHECK-IN COUNTER	ENREGISTREMENT
CUSTOMS	DOUANE
EMERGENCY EXIT	ISSUE DE SECOURS
ENTRANCE	ENTRÉE
EXIT	SORTIE
FREE ADMISSION	ENTRÉE GRATUITE
HOT/COLD	CHAUD/FROID
INFORMATION	RENSEIGNEMENTS
NO ENTRY	ENTRÉE INTERDITE
NO SMOKING	DÉFENSE DE FUMER
OPEN/CLOSED	OUVERT/FERMÉ
PROHIBITED	INTERDIT
RESERVED	RÉSERVÉ
TELEPHONE	TÉLÉPHONE
TOILETS	TOILETTES

Emergencies

POLICE	POLICE
POLICE STATION	COMMISSARIAT DE POLICE

Help!
oh ser-coor!   Au secours!
It's an emergency!
sei tür-zhã!   C'est urgent!

There's been an accident!
   eel-yah ü ē nak-see-dā!

Il y a eu un accident!

Call a doctor!
   ah-plei ē meid-sē!

Appelez un médecin!

Call an ambulance!
   ah-plei ün ã-bü-lās!

Appelez une ambulance!

I've been raped.
   zhei ei-tei vyo-lei

J'ai été violée.

I've been robbed!
   zhei ei-tei volei!

J'ai été volé/-ée!

Call the police!
   ah-plei lah po-lees!

Appelez la police!

Where is the police station?
   oo ei ler ko-mee-sahr-yah der po-lees?

Où est le commissariat de police?

Go away!
   lei-sei mwah trã-keel!
   fee-shei mwah lah pei!

Laissez-moi tranquille!
Fichez-moi la paix!

Thief!
   oh vo-lerr!

Au voleur!

I am ill.
   zher swee mah-lahd

Je suis malade.

My friend is ill.
   mõ nah-mee ei mah-lahd

Mon ami/-e est malade.

I am lost.
   zher mer swee ei-gah-rei

Je me suis égaré/-ée.

Where are the toilets?
   oo sõ lei twah-leht?

Où sont les toilettes?

FRENCH

Could you help me please?
eh-sker voo poo-ryei
mei-dei seel voo plei?

Est-ce que vous pourriez
m'aider, s'il vous plaît?

Could I please use the
telephone?
eh-sker zher poo-rei
ü-tee-lee-zei ler tei-lei-fon?

Est-ce que je pourrais
utiliser le téléphone?

I'm sorry. I apologise.
zher swee dei-zo-lei
zher mehk-sküz

Je suis désolé/-ée.
Je m'excuse.

I didn't realise I was doing
anything wrong.
zher nei sah-vei pah ker
zhah-vei tor der ler fehr

Je ne savais pas que j'avais
tort de le faire.

I didn't do it.
ser nei pah mwah kee lah fei

Ce n'est pas moi qui l'a fait

I wish to contact my embassy/
consulate.
zher ver kõ-tahk-tei
lã-bah-sahd/ler kõ-sü-lah

Je veux contacter
l'ambassade/le consulat.

I speak English.
zher pahrl ã-glei

Je parle anglais.

I have medical insurance.
zhei der lah-sü-rãs
mah-lah-dee

J'ai de l'assurance maladie.

My possessions are insured.
mei byẽ sõ tah-sü-rei

Mes biens sont assurés.

FRENCH

... was stolen.		On m'a volé ...
õ mah vo-lei ...		
I've lost ...		J'ai perdu ...
zhei pehrdü ...		
my bags	*mei bah-gahzh*	mes bagages
my handbag	*mõ sahk ah mẽ*	mon sac à main
my money	*mõ nahr-zhã*	mon argent
my travellers'	*mei shehk der*	mes chèques de
cheques	*vwah-yahzh*	voyage
my passport	*mõ pahs-por*	mon passeport

Paperwork

name	*nõ ei prei-nõ*	nom et prénom
address	*ah-drehs*	adresse
date of birth	*daht der neh-sãs*	date de naissance
place of birth	*lyer der neh-sãs*	lieu de naissance
age	*ahzh*	âge
sex	*sehks*	sexe
nationality	*nah-syo-nah-lee-tei*	nationalité
religion	*kõ-feh-syõ*	confession
reason for travel	*rei-zõ dü vwah-yahzh*	raison du voyage
profession	*mei-tyei*	métier
marital status	*see-twah-syõ der*	situation de
	fah-meey	famille
passport	*pahs-por*	passeport
passport number	*nü-mer-oh der*	numéro de
	pahs-por	passeport
visa	*vee-zah*	visa
identification	*pyehs dee-dã-tee-tei*	pièce d'identité
birth certificate	*ehk-streh der*	extrait de
	neh-sãs	naissance

FRENCH

driver's licence	*pehr-mee der kõ-dweer*	permis de conduire
car owner's title	*teetr der pro-pree-yei-tei dün vwah-tür*	titre de propriété d'une voiture
car registration	*kahrt greez*	carte grise
customs	*dwahn*	douane
immigration	*ee-mee-grah-syõ*	immigration
border	*frõ-tyehr*	frontière

Getting Around

ARRIVALS	ARRIVÉES
BUS STATION	GARE ROUTIÈRE
BUS STOP	ARRÊT D'AUTOBUS
DEPARTURES	DÉPARTS
SUBWAY	MÉTRO
TICKET OFFICE	GUICHET
TIMETABLE	HORAIRE
TRAIN STATION	GARE

What time does ... leave/
arrive?
   ... pahr/ahreev ah kehl err?   ... part/arrive à quelle
                                           heure?

the (air)plane	*lah-vyõ*	l'avion
the boat	*ler bah-toh*	le bateau
the bus (city)	*l(o-to-)büs*	l'(auto)bus
the bus (intercity)	*l(o-to-)kahr*	l'(auto)car
the train	*ler trẽ*	le train
the tram	*ler trahm-wei*	le tramway

Directions

Where is …?
oo ei …?
Où est …?

How do I get to …?
ko-mã fehr poor ah-lei ah …?
Comment faire pour aller à …?

I want to go to …
zher ver ah-lei ah …
Je veux aller à …

Is it far from/near here?
sei lwē/prei dee-see?
C'est loin/près d'ici?

Can I walk there?
zher per ee ah-lei ah pyei?
Je peux y aller à pied?

Can you show me (on the map)?
eh-sker voo poo-vei mer ler mō-trei (sür lah kahrt)?
Est-ce que vous pouvez me le montrer (sur la carte)?

Are there other means of getting there?
ehs-keel-yah ē nohtr mwah-yē dee ah-lei?
Est-ce qu'il y a un autre moyen d'y aller?

Go straight ahead.
kō-teen-wei too drwah
Continuez tout droit.

It's two blocks down.
sei der rü plü lwah
C'est deux rues plus loin.

Turn left …
toor-nei ah gohsh …
Tournez à gauche …

Turn right …
toor-nei ah drwaht …
Tournez à droite …

at the next corner
  oh pro-shẽ kwẽ

au prochain coin

at the traffic lights
  oh fer

aux feux

behind	*deh-ryehr*	derrière
in front of	*der-vā*	devant
far	*lwẽ*	loin
near	*prosh*	proche
opposite	*ã fahs der*	en face de

Booking Tickets

Excuse me, where is the ticket office?
  ehk-skü-zei mwah oo ei ler gee-shei?

Excusez-moi, où est le guichet?

Where can I buy a ticket?
  oo ehs-ker zher per ahsh-tei ẽ bee-yei?

Où est-ce que je peux acheter un billet?

I want to go to ...
  zher ver ah-lei ah ...

Je veux aller à ...

Do I need to book?
  ehs-keel foh rei-zehr-vei ün plahs/lei plahs?

Est-ce qu'il faut réserver une place/les places?

You need to book.
  eel foh rei-zehr-vei ün plahs/lei plahs

Il faut réserver une place/les places.

I would like to book a seat to ...
  zher voo-drei re-zehr-vei ün plahs poor ...

Je voudrais réserver une place pour ...

It is full.
sei kō-plei

C'est complet.

Is it completely full?
eel nyah vreh-mā pah der plahs?

Il n'y a vraiment pas de place?

Can I get a stand-by ticket?
ehş-ker zher per ahsh-tei ē bee-yei sā gah-rā-tee?

Est-ce que je peux acheter un billet sans garantie?

I would like …
zher voo-drei …

Je voudrais …

a one-way ticket	*ē bee-yei ah-lei sēpl*	un billet aller simple
a return ticket	*ē bee-yei ah-lei ei rertoor*	un billet aller et retour
two tickets	*der bee-yei*	deux billets
tickets for all of us	*dei bee-yei poor noo toos*	des billets pour nous tous
a student's fare	*ē bee-yei ah tah-reef rei-dwee (zher swee zei-tü-dyā/ zei-tü-dyāt)*	un billet à tarif réduit (je suis étudiant (m)/ étudiante (f))
a child's/ pensioner's fare	*ē bee-yei ah tah-reef rei-dwee (sei poor ē ā-fā/zher swee rer-treh-tei)*	un billet à tarif réduit (c'est pour un enfant/je suis retraité/-ée)
1st class	*prer-myehr klahs*	première classe
2nd class	*ser-gōd/der-zyehm klahs*	seconde/deuxième classe

FRENCH

Air

CHECKING IN LUGGAGE PICKUP	ENREGISTREMENT LIVRAISON DE BAGAGES

Is there a flight to ...?
ehs-keel-yah ē vol poor ...?
Est-ce qu'il y a un vol pour ...?

When is the next flight to ...?
ah kehl err pahr ler pro-shē nah-vyō poor ...?
À quelle heure part le prochain avion pour ...?

How long does the flight take?
ler vol dür kō-byē der tā?
Le vol dure combien de temps?

What is the flight number?
kehl ei ler nü-mer-oh dü vol?
Quel est le numéro du vol?

You must check in at ...
voo der-ve voo prei-sā-tei ah lā-rei-zhee-strermā ...
Vous devez vous présenter l'enregistrement ...

| airport tax | *tahks dah-ei-ro-por* | taxes d'aéroport |
| boarding pass | *kahrt dā-bahr-ker-mā* | carte d'embarquement |

FRENCH

Bus

BUS/TRAM STOP	ARRÊT D'AUTOBUS/DE TRAMWAY

There is the bus/tram stop?
oo ei lah-rei do-to-büs/der trahm-wei?

Où est l'arrêt d'autobus/de tramway?

Which bus goes to …?
kehl büs vah ah …?

Quel bus va à …?

Does this bus go to …?
ehs-ker ser büs vah ah …?

Est-ce que ce bus va à …?

How often do buses pass by?
lei büs pahs ah kehl frei-kãs?

Les bus passent à quelle fréquence?

What time is the … bus?
ler … büs pahs ah kehl err?

Le … bus passe à quelle heure?

next	*pro-shẽ*	prochain (m)
	pro-shehn	prochaine (f)
first	*prer-myei*	premier (m)
	prer-myehr	première (f)
last	*dehr-nyei*	dernier (m)
	dehr-nyehr	dernière (f)

Could you let me know when we get to …?
ehs-ker voo poo-vei mer ler deer kã noo zah-ree-võ ah …?

Est-ce que vous pouvez me le dire quand nous arrivons à …?

FRENCH

I want to get off!
zher ver dehs-ādr!   Je veux descendre!

Train

DINING CAR	WAGON-RESTAURANT
EXPRESS	RAPIDE
PLATFORM	QUAI
SLEEPING CAR	WAGON-LIT

Is this the right platform
for …?
sei byē ler kei poor …?   C'est bien le quai pour …?

Passengers must …
lei vwah-yah-zherr   Les voyageurs doivent …
dwahv …
change trains   *shā-zhei der trē*   changer de train
change platforms *shā-zhei der kei*   changer de quai

The train leaves from
platform …
ler trē pahr dü kei …   Le train part du quai …

Metro

METRO/UNDERGROUND CHANGE (for coins) THIS WAY TO WAY OUT	MÉTRO DISTRIBUTEUR DE MONNAIE CORRESPONDANCE SORTIE

Which line takes me to …?
kehl leeny/rahm vah ah …?   Quelle ligne/rame va à …?

What is the next station?
kehl ei lah pro-shehn stah-syō?   Quelle est la prochaine station?

Taxi

Can you take me to …?
ehs-ker voo poo-vei mer kō-dweer ah …?   Est-ce que vous pouvez me conduire à …?

Please take me to …
kō-dwee-ze mwah ah …, seel voo plei   Conduisez-moi à …, s'il vous plaît.

How much does it cost to go to …?
kehl ei ler pree der lah koors zhüs-kah ?   Quel est le prix de la course jusqu'à …?

Instructions

Here is fine, thank you.
ee-see sah vah, mehr-see   Ici ça va, merci.

108 French

The next corner, please.
oh pro-shẽ kwẽ der rü, seel voo plei

Au prochain coin de rue, s'il vous plaît.

Continue!
kõ-tee-nwe!

Continuez!

The next street to the left/right.
lah pro-shehn rü ah gohsh/ drwaht

La prochaine rue à gauche/ droite.

Stop here!
ah-reh-tei voo ee-see!

Arrêtez-vous ici!

Please slow down.
roo-lei plü lãt-mã, seel voo plei

Roulez plus lentement, s'il vous plaît.

Please wait here.
ah-tã-de ee-see seel voo plei

Attendez ici, s'il vous plaît.

Some Useful Phrases

The train is delayed/cancelled.
ler trẽ ah dü rer-tahr/ah ei-tei ah-nü-lei

Le train a du retard/a été annulé.

How long will it be delayed?
eel yo-rah kõ-byẽ der tã der rer-tahr?

Il y aura combien de temps de retard?

There is a delay of … minutes/hours.
eel yo-rah ẽ rer-tahr der … mee-noot/err

Il y aura un retard de … minutes/heures.

Can I reserve a place?
ehs-ker zher per rei-zehr-vei ün plahs?

Est-ce que je peux réserver une place?

How long does the trip take?
*ler trah-zhei dü-rer-rah
kō-byē der tā?*

Le trajet durera combien de temps?

Is it a direct route?
sei tē trē dee-rehkt?

C'est un train direct?

Is that seat taken?
*ehs-ker seht plahs ei
to-kü-pei?*

Est-ce que cette place est occupée?

I want to get off at …
zher ver dehs-ādr ah …

Je veux descendre à …

Excuse me.
ehk-skü-ze mwah

Excusez-moi.

Where can I hire a bicycle?
*oo ehs-ker zher per lwei
ē vei-loh?*

Où est-ce que je peux louer un vélo?

Car

DETOUR	DÉVIATION
GARAGE	GARAGE/STATION SERVICE
GIVE WAY	CÉDEZ LA PRIORITÉ
MECHANIC	MÉCANICIEN
NO ENTRY	ENTRÉE INTERDITE
NO PARKING	STATIONNEMENT INTERDIT
ONE WAY	SENS UNIQUE
REPAIRS	RÉPARATIONS
SELF SERVICE	LIBRE-SERVICE
SUPER	SUPER
UNLEADED	SANS PLOMB

FRENCH

Where can I rent a car?
oo ehs-ker zher per lwei ün vwah-tür?

Où est-ce que je peux louer une voiture?

How much is it daily/weekly?
kehl ei ler tah-reet pahr zhoor/pahr ser-mehn?

Quel est le tarif par jour/par semaine?

Does that include insurance/mileage?
ehs-ker lah-sü-räs/ler kee-lo-mei-trahzh ei kõ-pree?

Est-ce que l'assurance/le kilométrage est compris?

Where's the next petrol station?
oo ei lah pro-shehn stah-syõ sehr-vees?

Où est la prochaine station service?

Please fill the tank.
ler plẽ seel voo plei

Le plein, s'il vous plaît.

I want … litres of petrol (gas).
do-ne mwah … leetr dehs-äs seel voo plei

Donnez-moi … litres d'essence, s'il vous plaît.

Please check the oil and water.
kõ-tro-lei lweel ei loh seel voo plei

Controllez l'huile et l'eau, s'il vous plaît.

How long can I park here?
poor kõ-byẽ der tã ehs-ker zher peux stah-syõ-nei ee-see?

Pour combien de temps est-ce que je peux stationner ici?

Does this road lead to?
ehs-ker seht root mehn ah …?

Est-ce que cette route mène à …?

FRENCH

air (for tyres)	*ler kō-prehs-err (poor gō-flei le pner)*	le compresseur (pour gonfler les pneus)
battery	*lah bah-tree*	la batterie
brakes	*le frĕ*	les freins
clutch	*lā-bre-yahzh*	l'embrayage
driver's licence	*ler pehr-mee der kō-dweer*	le permis de conduire
engine	*ler mo-terr*	le moteur
lights	*le fahr*	les phares
oil	*lweel*	l'huile
puncture	*lah krer-ve-zō*	la crevaison
radiator	*ler rah-dyah-ter*	le radiateur
road map	*lah kahrt roo-tyehr*	la carte routière
tyres	*le pner*	les pneus
windscreen	*ler pahr breez*	le pare-brise

Car Problems

I need a mechanic.
   zhei ber-zwĕ dē mei-kah-nee-syē   J'ai besoin d'un mécanicien.

What make is it?
   kehl ei lah mahrk?   Quelle est la marque?

The battery is flat.
   lah bah-tree ei tah plah   La batterie est à plat.

The radiator is leaking.
   ler rah-dyah-terr fwee   Le radiateur fuit.

I have a flat tyre.
   ler pner sei dei-gō-flei   Le pneu s'est dégonflé.

It's overheating.
   ler mo-terr shohf   Le moteur chauffe.

FRENCH

It's not working.
eel/ehl ner mahrsh pah   Il (m)/elle (f) ne marche pas.

Accommodation

CAMPING GROUND	CAMPING
GUEST HOUSE	PENSION DE FAMILLE
HOTEL	HÔTEL
MOTEL	MOTEL
YOUTH HOSTEL	AUBERGE DE JEUNESSE

I am looking for …
zher shehrsh …   Je cherche …
Where is …?
oo es-keel-yah …?   Où est-ce qu'il y a …?

a cheap hotel	*ē-noh-tehl bõ mahr-shei*	un hôtel bon marché
a good hotel	*ē-bõ-noh-tehl*	un bon hôtel
a nearby hotel	*ē-noh-tehl pah lwē dee-see*	un hôtel pas loin d'ici
a clean hotel	*ē-noh-tehl propr*	un hôtel propre

What is the address?
kehl ei lah-drehs?   Quelle est l'adresse?
Could you write the address, please?
ehs-ker voo poo-vei ei-kreer lah-drehs seel voo plei?   Est-ce vous pouvez écrire l'adresse, s'il vous plaît?

FRENCH

At the Hotel

Do you have any rooms
available?

*ehs-ker voo zah-vei de
shābr leebr?*

Est-ce que vous avez des
chambres libres?

I would like …
zher voo-drei … Je voudrais …

a single room	*ün shābr ah ē lee*	une chambre à un lit
a double room	*ün shābr doobl*	une chambre double
to share a dorm	*koo-shei dā zē dor-twahr*	coucher dans un dortoir
a bed	*ē lee*	un lit

I want a room with …
*zher ver ün shābr
ah-vehk …*

Je veux une chambre
avec …

a bathroom	*sahl der bē*	salle de bain
a shower	*doosh*	douche
a television	*tei-lei-vee-zyō*	télévision
a window	*ün fer-nehtr*	une fenêtre

I'm going to stay for …
zher rehs-ter-rei … · Je resterai …

one day	*ē zhoor*	un jour
two days	*der zhoor*	deux jours
one week	*ün ser-mehn*	une semaine

FRENCH

Do you have identification?
*ehs-ker voo zha-vei ün
pyehs dee-dã-tee-tei?*

Est-ce que vous avez une
pièce d'identité?

Your membership card, please.
*votr kahrt dah-dei-rã seel
voo plei*

Votre carte d'adhérent, s'il
vous plaît.

Sorry, we're full.
dei-zo-lei me sei kõ-plei

Désolé, mais c'est complet.

How long will you be staying?
*voo rehs-ter-re kõ-byē der
tã?*

Vous resterez combien de
temps?

How many nights?
kõ-byē der nwee?

Combien de nuits?

It's ... per day/per person.
*ler pree ei ... pahr zhoor/
pahr pehr-son*

Le prix est ... par jour/par
personne.

How much is it per night/per
person?
*kehl ei ler pree pahr
nwee/pahr pehr-son?*

Quel est le prix par nuit/par
personne?

Can I see it?
zher per lah vwahr?

Je peux la voir?

Are there any others?
eel yã-nah dohtr?

Il y en a d'autres?

Are there any cheaper rooms?
*voo nah-vei pah der
shãbr mwahn shehr?*

Vous n'avez pas de
chambres moins chères?

Can I see the bathroom?
*zher per vwahr lah sahl der
bē?*

Je peux voir la salle de bain`

Is there a reduction for
students/children?
> *ehs-ker voo zah-vei ē*
> *tah-reef rei-dwee poor lei*
> *zei-tü-dyā/le zā-fā?*

Est-ce que vous avez un
tarif réduit pour les
étudiants/les enfants?

Does it include breakfast?
> *ehs-ker ler per-tee*
> *dei-zher-nei ei kō-pree?*

Est-ce que le petit déjeuner
est compris?

It's fine, I'll take it.
> *sei byē zher lah prā*

C'est bien, je la prends.

I'm not sure how long I'm
staying.
> *zher ner sei pah ehg-zahk-*
> *ter-mā kō-byē der tā zher*
> *rehs-ter-rei*

Je ne sais pas exactement
combien de temps je
resterai.

Is there a lift (elevator)?
> *ehs-keel-yah ē nah-sā-serr?*

Est-ce qu'il y a un
ascenseur?

Where is the bathroom?
> *oo ei luh sahl der bē?*

Où est la salle de bain?

Is there hot water all day?
> *ehs-keel-yah der loh shohd*
> *pā-dā toot lah zhoor-nei?*

Est-ce qu'il y a de l'eau
chaude pendant toute la
journée?

Do you have a safe where I
can leave my valuables?
> *ehs-ker voo zah-vei ē kofr*
> *for poor dei-poh-zei mei*
> *zob-zhei der vah-lerr?*

Est-ce que vous avez un
coffre-fort pour déposer mes
objets de valeur?

FRENCH

Is there somewhere to wash clothes?

ehs-keel-yah ē ā-drwah oo ō per fehr lah lehs-eev?

Est-ce qu'il y a un endroit où on peut faire la lessive?

Can I use the kitchen?

ehs-ker zher per mer sehr-veer der lah kwee-zeen?

Est-ce que je peux me servir de la cuisine?

Can I use the telephone?

ehs-ker zher per ü-tee-lee-zei ler tei-lei-fon?

Est-ce que je peux utiliser le téléphone?

Requests & Complaints

Please wake me up at ...

rei-vei-yei mwah ah ..., seel voo plei

Réveillez-moi à ..., s'il vous plaît.

The room needs to be cleaned.

eel foh neh-twah-yei lah shābr

Il faut nettoyer la chambre.

Please change the sheets.

shā-zei lei drah, seel voo plei

Changez les draps, s'il vous plaît.

I can't open/close the window.

lah fer-nehtr ei blo-kei

La fenêtre est bloquée.

I've locked myself out of my room.

zher mer swee ā-fehr-mei der-or

Je me suis enfermé/-ée dehors.

The toilet won't flush.

lah shahs doh ner mahrsh pah

La chasse d'eau ne marche pas.

I don't like this room.
seht shãbr ner mer plei pah

Cette chambre ne me plaît pas.

It's too small.
ehl ei troh per-teet

Elle est trop petite.

It's noisy.
ehl ei brü-yãt

Elle est bruyante.

It's too dark.
ehl ei troh sõbr

Elle est trop sombre.

It's expensive.
sei shehr

C'est cher.

Some Useful Phrases

I am/We are leaving now.
zher pahr/noo pahr-tõ mē-tnã

Je pars/Nous partons maintenant.

I would like to pay the bill.
zher voo-dre rei-glei (lah not)

Je voudrais régler (la note).

name	*prei-nõ*	prénom
surname	*nõ*	nom
room number	*nü-mei-roh der shãbr*	numéro de chambre

Some Useful Words

address	*lah-drehs*	l'adresse
air-conditioned	*klee-mah-tee-zei*	climatisé
balcony	*ler bahl-kõ*	le balcon
bathroom	*lah sahl der bẽ*	la salle de bain

FRENCH

bed	*ler lee*	le lit
bill	*lah not*	la note
blanket	*lah koo-vehr-tür*	la couverture
candle	*lah boo-zhee*	la bougie
chair	*lah shehz*	la chaise
clean	*propr*	propre
cupboard	*ler plah-kahr*	le placard
dark	*sõbr*	sombre
dirty	*sahl*	sale
double bed	*grã lee*	grand lit
electricity	*lei-lehk-tree-see-tei*	l'électricité
excluded	*pah kõ-pree*	pas compris
fan	*ler vã-tee-lah-terr*	le ventilateur
included	*kõ-pree*	compris
key	*lah klei*	la clé
lift (elevator)	*lah-sã-serr*	l'ascenseur
light bulb	*lã-pool*	l'ampoule
lock (n)	*lah seh-rür*	la serrure
mattress	*ler maht-lah*	le matelas
mirror	*ler meer-wahr*	le miroir
padlock	*ler kahd-nah*	le cadenas
pillow	*lo-rei-yei*	l'oreiller
room (in hotel)	*lah shãbr*	la chambre
sheet	*ler drah*	le drap
shower	*lah doosh*	la douche
soap	*ler sah-võ*	le savon
suitcase	*lah vah-leez*	la valise
swimming pool	*lah pee-seen*	la piscine
table	*lah tahbl*	la table
toilet	*lah kü-veht*	la cuvette

FRENCH

toilet paper	*ler pah-pyei*	le papier
	ee-zhyei-neek	hygiénique
towel	*ün sehr-vyeht der bẽ*	une serviette de
		bain
water	*loh*	l'eau
cold water	*loh frwahd*	l'eau froide
hot water	*loh shohd*	l'eau chaude
window	*lah fer-nehtr*	la fenêtre

Around Town

I'm looking for ...
   zher shehrsh ...   Je cherche ...

the art gallery	*ler mü-zei dahr*	le musée d'art
a bank	*ün bãk*	une banque
the church	*lei-gleez*	l'église
the city centre	*ler sãtr veel*	le centre-ville
the ... embassy	*lã-bah-sahd der ...*	l'ambassade de ...
my hotel	*mõ noh-tehl*	mon hôtel
the market	*ler mahr-shei*	le marché
the museum	*ler mü-zei*	le musée
the police	*lah po-lees*	la police
the post office	*lah post*	la poste
a public toilet	*dei twah-leht*	des toilettes
the telephone centre	*lei kah-been tei-lei-fo-neek*	les cabines téléphoniques
the tourist information office	*lo-fees der too-reesm/ ler sẽ-dee-kah dee-nee-syah-teev*	l'office du tourisme/le syndicat d'initiative

FRENCH

What time does it open?
*kehl ei lerr der
loo-vehr-tür?*
Quelle est l'heure de
l'ouverture?

What time does it close?
*kehl ei lerr der
fehr-mer-tür?*
Quelle est l'heure de
fèrmeture?

What street/suburb is this?
sei kehl rü/kehl kahr-tye?
C'est quelle rue/quel quartier?

For directions, see the Getting Around section, pages 101-102.

At the Bank

I want to exchange some
money/traveller's cheques.
*zher ver shā-zhei der
lahr-zhā/dei shehk der
vwah-yahzh*
Je veux changer de l'argent/
des chèques de voyage.

What is the exchange rate?
kehl ei ler koor dü shāzh?
Quel est le cours du change?

How many francs per dollar?
kō-byē der frā ler dolahr?
Combien de francs le dollar?

Can I have money transferred
here from my bank?
*ehs-ker zher per fehr ee-see
ē veer-mā der mō kōt ā bāk?*
Est-ce que je peux faire ici
un virement de mon compte
en banque?

How long will it take to
arrive?
*kō-byē der tā ehs-keel
foh-drah ah-tādr?*
Combien de temps est-ce
qu'il faudra attendre?

Has my money arrived yet?
ehs-ker mõ nahr-zhã ei tah-ree-vei? Est-ce que mon argent est arrivé?

bank draft	*ün treht bā-kehr*	une traite bancaire
bank notes	*dei bee-yei der bāk*	des billets de banque
cashier	*ler kehs-yei*	le caissier (m)
	lah kehs-yehr	la caissière (f)
coins	*der lah mone/dei pyehs*	de la monnaie/des pièces
credit card	*ün kahrt der krei-dee*	une carte de crédit
exchange	*ler shāzh*	le change
loose change	*der lah mone*	de la monnaie
signature	*lah seen-yah-tür*	la signature

At the Post Office

I would like to send …
zher voo-drei ā-vwah-yei … Je voudrais envoyer …

a letter	*ün lehtr*	une lettre
a postcard	*ün kahrt pos-tahl*	une carte postale
a parcel	*ẽ ko-lee*	un colis
a telegram	*ẽ tei-lei-grahm*	un télégramme

I would like some stamps.
zher voo-drei dei tēbr Je voudrais des timbres.

How much does it cost to send this to …?
ah kõ-byẽ ehs-keel foh ah-frã-sheer sei-see poor …? À combien est-ce qu'il faut affranchir ceci pour …?

FRENCH

an aerogram	*ē-nah-ei-ro-grahm*	un aérogramme
air mail	*pahr ah-vyō*	par avion
envelope	*ün ãv-lop*	une enveloppe
mail box	*ün bwaht oh lehtr*	une boîte aux lettres
parcel	*ē ko-lee*	un colis
registered mail	*ã rer-ko-mã-dei*	en recommandé
surface mail	*pahr vwah der tehr/ pahr vwah mah-ree-teem*	par voie de terre/ par voie maritime

Telephone

I want to ring …
  zher voo-drei ah-plei …   Je voudrais appeler …
The number is …
  ler nü-mei-roh ei …   Le numéro est …
I want to speak for three minutes.
  zher ver pahr-lei poor trwah mee-nüt   Je veux parler pour trois minutes.
How much does a three-minute call cost?
  kehl ei ler pree dün ko-mü-nee-kah-syō der trwah mee-nüt?   Quel est le prix d'une communication de trois minutes?
How much does each extra minute cost?
  kehl ei ler pree der shahk mee-nüt sü-plei-mã-tehr?   Quel est le prix de chaque minute supplémentaire?

FRENCH

I would like to speak to Mr
Perez.
*zher voo-drei pahr-lei
ah-vehk mer-syer peh-rehs*
    Je voudrais parler avec
Monsieur Perez.
I want to make a reverse-
charges phone call.
*zher ver tei-lei-fo-nei ã
pei-sei-vei*
    Je veux téléphoner en PCV.
It's engaged.
la leeny ei to-kü-pei
    La ligne est occupée.
I've been cut off.
noo zah-võ ei-tei koo-pei
    Nous avons été coupés.

Sightseeing

Do you have a guidebook/
local map?
*ehs-ker voo zah-ve ẽ geed
too-ree-steek/ün kahrt der
lah rei-zhyõ?*
    Est-ce que vous avez un
guide touristique/une carte
de la région?
What are the main attractions?
*kehl sõ le zã-drwah le plü
zẽ-tei-rehs-ã?*
    Quels sont les endroits les
plus intéressants?
What is that?
kehs-ker sei (ker sah)?
    Qu'est-ce que c'est (que ça)?
How old is it?
eel/ehl ah kehl ahzh?
    Il (m)/Elle (f) a quel âge?
Can I take photographs?
*ehs-ker zher per prãdr
dei fo-toh?*
    Est-ce que je peux prendre
des photos?

124 French

FRENCH

What time does it open/close?
kehl ei lerr doo-vehr-tür/ der fehr-mer-tür?

Quelle est l'heure d'ouverture/de fermeture?

ancient	*ã-teek*	antique
archaeological	*ahr-kei-o-lo-zheek*	archéologique
beach	*lah plahzh*	la plage
building	*ler bah-tee-mã*	le batiment
castle	*ler shah-toh*	le château
cathedral	*lah kah-tei-drahl*	la cathédrale
church	*lei-gleez*	l'église
concert hall	*lah sahl der kõ-sehr*	la salle de concert
library	*lah bee-blyo-tehk*	la bibliothèque
main square	*lah plahs sã-trahl*	la place centrale
market	*ler mahr-shei*	le marché
monastery	*ler mo-nah-stehr*	le monastère
monument	*ler mo-nü-mã*	le monument
mosque	*lah mos-kei*	la mosquée
old city	*lah vyehy veel*	la vieille ville
palace	*lei pah-lei*	le palais
opera house	*(ler tei-ahtr der) lo-pei-rah*	(le théatre de) l'opéra
ruins	*lei rü-ween*	les ruines
stadium	*ler stahd*	le stade
statues	*lei stah-tü*	les statues
synagogue	*lah see-nah-gog*	la synagogue
temple	*ler tãpl*	le temple
university	*lü-nee-vehr-see-tei*	l'université

FRENCH

Entertainment

What's there to do in the evenings?
kehs-kō per fehr ler swahr?
Qu'est-ce qu'on peut faire le soir?

Are there any discos?
ehs-keel-yah dei dees-ko-tehk?
Est-ce qu'il y a des discothèques?

Are there places where you can hear local folk music?
ehs-keel-yah dei zē-drwah oo ō per ei-koo-tei der lah mü-seek folk-lo-reek lo-kahl?
Est-ce qu'il y a des endroits où on peut écouter de la musique folklorique locale?

How much does it cost to get in?
kehl ei ler pree der lā-trei?
Quel est le prix de l'entrée?

cinema	*ler see-nei-mah*	le cinéma
concert	*ler kō-sehr*	le concert
discotheque	*lah dees-ko-tehk*	la discothèque
theatre	*ler tei-ahtr*	le théatre

In the Country
Weather

What's the weather like?
kehl tã feh-teel?
Quel temps fait-il?

The weather is ... today.
eel fei ... oh-zhoor-dwee
Il fait ... aujourd'hui.

Will it be ... tomorrow?
ehs-keel fer-ra ... der-mē?
Est-ce qu'il fera ... demain

FRENCH

It is …
eel fei …		Il fait …
cold	*frwah*	froid
foggy	*dü broo-yahr*	du brouillard
hot	*shoh*	chaud
sunny	*boh*	beau
windy	*dü vã*	du vent

It's cloudy.	*ler tã ei koo-vehr*	Le temps est couvert.
It's frosty.	*eel zhehl*	Il gèle.
It's raining.	*eel pler*	Il pleut.
It's snowing.	*eel nehzh*	Il neige.

Camping

Am I allowed to camp here?
ehs-ker zher per kã-pei ee-see? — Est-ce que je peux camper ici?

Is there a campsite nearby?
ehs-keel-yah ē kã-peeng preh dee-see — Est-ce qu'il y a un camping près d'ici?

backpack	*ler sah-kah-doh*	le sac à dos
can opener	*loovr bwaht*	l'ouvre-boîte
compass	*lah boo-sol*	la boussole
crampons	*lei krã-põ*	les crampons
firewood	*ler bwah ah brü-lei*	le bois à brûler
gas cartridge	*lah kahr-toosh ah gahz*	la cartouche à gaz
hammock	*ler ah-mahk*	le hamac
ice axe	*ler pyo-lei*	le piolet

mattress	*ler maht-lah*	le matelas
penknife	*ler kah-neef*	le canif
rope	*lah kord*	la corde
tent	*lah tãt*	la tente
tent pegs	*lei pee-kei der tãt*	les piquets de tente
torch (flashlight)	*lah lãp der posh*	la lampe de poche
sleeping bag	*ler sahk der koo-shahzh*	le sac de couchage
stove	*ler rei-shoh*	le réchaud
water bottle	*lah goord*	la gourde

Food

breakfast	*ler per-tee dei-zher-nei*	le petit déjeuner
lunch	*ler dei-zher-nei*	le déjeuner
dinner	*ler dee-nei*	le dîner

Table for ..., please.
ün tahbl poor ... pehr-son, seel voo plei
Une table pour ... personnes, s'il vous plaît.

Can I see the menu please?
ehs-ker zher per vwahr lah kahrt?
Est-ce que je peux voir la carte?

I would like the set lunch, please.
zher prã ler mer-nü
Je prends le menu.

What does it include?
kehs-ker sah kõ-prã?
Qu'est-ce que ça comprend?

FRENCH

Is service included in the bill?
*ehs-ker ler sehr-vees ei
kõ-pree?*
Not too spicy please.
*pah troh ei-pee-sei
seel-voo plei*

Est-ce que le service est
compris?

Pas trop épicé s'il vous plaî

an ashtray	*ē sā-drye*	un cendrier
the bill	*lah-dee-syõ*	l'addition
a cup	*ün tahs*	une tasse
dessert	*ler de-sehr*	le dessert
a drink	*ün bwah-sõ*	une boisson
a fork	*ün foor-sheht*	une fourchette
fresh	*freh/frehsh*	frais (m)/fraîche (f)
a glass	*ē vehr*	un verre
a knife	*ē koo-toh*	un couteau
a plate	*ē plah*	un plat
spicy	*ei-pee-sei*	épicé
a spoon	*ün kwee-yehr*	une cuillère
stale	*pah freh/frehsh*	pas frais (m)/ fraîche (f)
sweet	*sü-krei*	sucré/-ée
teaspoon	*ün per-teet kwee-yehr*	une petite cuillère
toothpick	*ē kür dā*	un cure-dent

Vegetarian Meals

I am a vegetarian.
*zher swee vei-zhei-tahr-yē/
vei-zhei-tahr-yehn*

Je suis végétarien (m)/
végétarienne (f).

FRENCH

I don't eat meat.
zher ner mãzh pah der vyãd   Je ne mange pas de viande.
I don't eat ham.
zher ner mãzh pah der   Je ne mange pas de jambon.
zhã-bõ

Breakfast

breakfast cereal
a croissant
a hard-boiled egg
bread, butter, jam

Petit Dejeuner

de la céréale
un croissant
un œuf dur
du pain, du beurre, de la confiture

Snacks

Casse-croûtes

un cornet de frites
    A paper cone of chips.
une crêpe au sucre/au citron/au miel/à la confiture
    Thin pancake with sugar/with lemon/with honey/with jam.
un croque-madame
    Grilled cheese-and-ham sandwich with a fried egg.
un croque-monsieur
    Grilled cheese-and-ham sandwich.
marrons chauds
    Roast chestnuts.
un sandwich au fromage/jambon
    A cheese/ham sandwich.

In the Delicatessen

a carton of ...
a portion of ...
a slice

Á la Charcuterie

une barquette ... de
une part de ...
une tranche

bean salad	*des haricots en salade*
cheese	*du fromage*
gherkins	*des cornichons*
ham	*du jambon*
mayonnaise	*de la mayonnaise*
liver/rabbit/farmhouse pâté	*du pâté de foie/de lapin/de campagne*
potted meat (pork or goose)	*des rillettes*
Russian salad	*de la salade russe*

Starters — Hors d'Œuvres/ Entrées

anchovies	*anchois*
artichoke hearts	*cœurs d'artichaut*
clear soup	*consommé*
hard-boiled egg with mayonnaise	*œuf mayonnaise*
hearts of palm	*cœurs de palmier*
Marseillais fish soup	*bouillabaisse*
mussels with shallots in white-wine sauce	*moules marinières*
oysters	*huîtres*
raw vegetables with dressings	*crudités*
scallops	*coquilles Saint-Jacques*
shellfish soup	*bisque*
snails	*escargots*
thick soup, usually vegetable	*potage*

Meat & Poultry — Viandes et Volailles

chicken	*poulet*
duck	*canard*
mutton	*mouton*
bbit	*lapin*

FRENCH

ribsteak	*entrecôte*
sausage made of intestines	*andouille*
sirloin roast	*contrefilet*
sirloin steak	*faux filet*
spicy red sausage	*merguez*
thick slices of fillet	*tournedos*
tripe	*tripes*
turkey	*dinde*
veal	*veau*

Seafood — Fruits de Mer

bream	*brème*
clams	*palourdes*
eels	*anguilles*
fresh cod	*cabillaud*
herring	*hareng*
John Dory	*Saint-Pierre*
king prawns	*gambas*
lobster	*homard*
mackerel	*maquereau*
octopus	*poulpe*
prawns	*crevettes roses*
salmon	*saumon*
salt cod	*morue*
sea bream	*daurade*
shrimps	*crevettes grises*
squid	*calmar*
spiny lobster	*langouste*
trout	*truite*
tuna	*thon*

FRENCH

Vegetables	Légumes
asparagus	*asperges*
avocado	*avocat*
broad beans	*fèves*
cabbage	*chou*
cauliflower	*choufleur*
chickpeas	*pois chiches*
corn	*maïs*
cucumber	*concombre*
dwarf kidney beans	*flageolets*
french or string beans	*haricots verts*
garlic	*ail*
gherkin	*cornichon*
leek	*poireau*
lettuce	*laitue*
mushrooms	*champignons*
onion	*oignon*
peas	*petits pois*
potato	*pomme de terre*
pumpkin	*citrouille*
radish	*radis*
rice	*riz*
spinach	*épinards*
sweet pepper or capsicum	*poivron*
truffles	*truffes*

Typical Dishes   **Plats Typiques**

bœuf bourgignon
   Beef stew with burgundy, onions and mushrooms.
cassoulet
   Casserole of beans and meat (often goose).

FRENCH

choucroute
  Pickled cabbage with sausages, bacon and salami.
coq au vin
  Chicken cooked with wine, onions and mushrooms.
poulet roti
  Roast chicken.
ratatouille
  Eggplant, zucchini, tomato and garlic dish.
steak au poivre
  Steak with pepper sauce.
steak frites
  Steak with chips.
steak tartare
  Raw chopped beef, raw onion and egg yolk.

Sample Menu: One
An average menu from Toulouse: *Une entrée, une viande, une boisson* -- an entrée, a meat dish, and a drink.

Entrées
confit de canard
  Conserve of duck.
terrine de poisson
  Fish pâté.
salade multicolore au basilic
  Salad with peppers, tomatoes, radishes, cucumber, egg, corn and basil.
salade au bleu
  Salad with blue cheese and walnuts.
salade crudité
  Raw vegetable salad.

FRENCH

Meat Dishes

andouillette sauce au poivre
  Tripe sausage with pepper sauce.
brochette de cœurs
  Heart kebab.
entrecôte grillée, sauce au bleu ou au poivre
  Grilled rib steak with blue cheese or pepper sauce.
cotriade
  Fillet of fish with seafood and a saffron sauce.
brochette de volailles au citron
  Poultry kebab with lemon.
tagliatelles Bolognaise ou au bleu
  Tagliatelli with bolognese or blue cheese sauce.
¼ de vin compris
  A quarter of a litre of wine included.

Sample Menu: Two

A typical budget Parisian menu:

un kir
  Blackcurrant juice and white wine.
hors d'œuvres à volonté
  A choice of entrées.

plat au choix
  A choice of the following main courses:
    pavé grillé
      A thick steak, grilled.
    côte d'agneau
      Lamb cutlet.

truite aux amandes
  Trout with almonds.
brochettes mixtes
  Kebabs.

fromage ou dessert
  Cheese or dessert.
vin compris
  (Table) wine included.

Sample Menu: Three
A more expensive Parisian menu:

Entrées

concombre à la crème – ciboulette
  Cucumber with cream and chives.
salade de tomates – basilic, huile vierge
  Tomato salad with basil and virgin olive oil.
suchi de poisson cru – sur lit de soja croquant
  Raw fish sushi on a bed of crunchy soya bean sprouts.
fromage blanc battu aux fines herbes
  Cream cheese blended with sweet herbs.
méli-mélo de légumes vapeur
  Mixed steamed vegetables.
boudin antillais – feuille de chêne, pommes tièdes en robe
  West-Indian sausage with lettuce and hot potatoes in their
  jackets.

Main Courses

filets de rascasse grillés aux tagliatelles safranées
  Grilled fillets of scorpion fish with tagliatelli seasoned with
  saffron.

émincé de haddock fumé, pommes mousselines
Slivers of smoked haddock with mashed potatoes.
moelleux de porc au curry, riz sauvage
Tender pork curry with wild rice.
demi-cannette rotie, pommes château
Half a roast duckling with quartered potatoes sautéed in butter.
émincé de poulet mariné, aux grains de coriandre en salade
Slivers of marinated chicken with coriander seeds and salad

Fruit & Nuts

almonds	*amandes*
apple	*pomme*
cherries	*cerises*
chestnuts	*marrons*
grapefruit	*pamplemousse*
grapes	*raisins*
greegages (kind of plum)	*mirabelles*
hazlenuts	*noisettes*
peach	*pêche*
peanuts	*cacahouètes*
pear	*poire*
plum	*prune*
raspberries	*framboises*
strawberries	*fraises*
walnuts	*noix*
watermelon	*pastèque*

Desserts

charlotte
Custard and fruit in lining of almond fingers.

clafoutis
　Fruit tart, usually with berries.
fromage blanc
　Cream cheese.
glace
　Ice cream.
île flottante, crème vanille
　Soft meringues floating on custard with vanilla cream.
mousse au chocolat, crème anglaise
　Chocolate mousse with custard.
parfait
　Frozen mousse.
poires Belle Hélène
　Pears and ice-cream in a chocolate sauce.
sorbet aux choix
　A choice of sorbets.
tarte aux pommes fines
　Apple tart.

Drinks – Nonalcoholic

a short black coffee	*un café*
a large/small milk coffee	*un grand/petit crème*
a grapefruit juice	*un jus de pamplemousee*
an orange juice	*un jus d'orange*
a cup of tea	*un thé*
lemon/white tea	*thé au citron/au lait*

Drinks – Alcoholic
Pre-dinner Drinks

	Apéritifs
blackcurrant juice and white wine	*kir*

FRENCH

blackcurrant juice and champagne	*kir royale*
aniseed liqueur, served with water	*pastis*
beer mixed with a sweet liqueur	*picon bière*
cognac and grape juice	*pineau*
fermented gentian	*suze*

Wines / Vins

English	Vins
dry	*sec*
mature and sparkling	*méthode champenoise*
red	*rouge*
sparkling	*mousseux*
sweet	*demi-sec*
table wine	*vin de table/vin ordinaire*
very dry	*brut*
very sweet	*doux*
white	*blanc*

Shopping

How much is it?
  sei kō-byē?   C'est combien ?

bookshop	*ün lee-breh-ree*	une librairie
camera shop	*ün boo-teek der fo-to-grahf*	une boutique de photographe
clothing store	*ē mah-gah-zē der kō-fehk-syō*	un magasin de confection
delicatessen	*ün shahr-kü-tree*	une charcuterie

FRENCH

general store, shop	*ẽ mah-gah-zẽ dah-lee-mã-tah-syõ zhei-nei-rahl*	un magasin d'alimentation générale
laundry	*ün blã-shees-ree*	une blanchisserie
market	*ẽ mahr-shei*	un marché
newsagency/ stationers	*ün pah-pei-tree*	une papeterie
pharmacy	*ün fahr-mah-see*	une pharmacie
shoeshop	*ẽ mah-gah-zẽ der shoh-sür*	un magasin de chaussures
souvenir shop	*ẽ mah-gah-zẽ der soov-neer*	un magasin de souvenirs
supermarket	*ẽ sü-pehr-mahr-shei*	un supermarché
vegetable shop	*ẽ mahr-shã der lei-güm*	un marchand de légumes

I would like to buy ...
zher voo-drei ...   Je voudrais ...

Do you have others?
ehs-ker voo zã nah-vei dohtr?   Est-ce que vous en avez d'autres?

I don't like it.
ser-lah ner mer plei pah   Cela ne ma plaît pas.

Can I look at it?
ehs-ker zher per ler/lah vwahr?   Est-ce que je peux le/la voir?

I'm just looking.
zher ner fei ker rer-gahr-dei   Je ne fais que regarder.

Can you write down the price?
ehs-ker voo poo-vei ei-kreer ler pree?   Est-ce que vous pouvez écrire le prix?

FRENCH

Do you accept credit cards?
ehs-ker zher per peh-yei
ah-vehk mah kahrt der
krei-dee?
Est-ce je peux payer avec
ma carte de crédit?

Could you lower the price?
voo ner poo-vei pah bei-sei
ler pree?
Vous ne pouvez pas baisser
le prix?

I don't have much money.
zher nei pah boh-koo
dahr-zhā
Je n'ai pas beaucoup
d'argent.

Can I help you?
zher per voo zei-dei?
Je peux vous aider?

Will that be all?
voo voo-lei ohtr shohz?
sei too?
Vous voulez autre chose?
C'est tout?

Would you like it wrapped?
zher voo lāv-lop?
Je vous l'enveloppe?

Sorry, this is the only one.
dei-zo-lei eel-nyah ker
ser-lwee see/sehl see
Désolé/-ée, il n'y a que
celui-ci (m)/celle-ci (f).

How much/many do you
want?
voo dei-zee-rei kō-byē?
Vous désirez combien?

Souvenirs

earrings	*dei bookl do-rehy*	des boucles d'oreilles
handicraft	*dei zob-zhei ahr-teez-ah-noh*	des objets artisanaux

FRENCH

jewellery	der lah bee-zhoo-tree	de la bijouterie
lace	der lah dā-tehl	de la dentelle
miniature statue	ün stah-tweht	une statuette
necklace	ẽ ko-lyei	un collier
poster	ẽ pos-tehr/oon ah-feesh	un poster/une affiche
pottery	dei po-tree	des poteries
ring	ün bahg	une bague
rug	ẽ per-tee tah-pee/ün kahr-peht	un petit tapis/une carpette

Clothing — Vêtements

coat	ẽ mã-toh	un manteau
dress	ün rob	une robe
jacket	ün vehst	une veste
jumper (sweater)	ẽ pü-lo-verr	un pullover
shirt	ün sher-meez	une chemise
shoes	de shoh-sür	des chaussures
skirt	ün zhüp	une jupe
trousers	ẽ pã-tah-lõ	un pantalon

It doesn't fit.
  ser nei pah lah bon tahy   Ce n'est pas la bonne taille.

It is too …
  sei troh …   C'est trop …

big	grã	grand
small	per-tee	petit
long	lõ	long
short	koor	court

FRENCH

| tight | *ei-trwah* | étroit |
| loose | *lahrzh* | large |

Materials

cotton	*ã ko-tõ*	en coton
handmade	*fei ah lah mẽ*	fait à la main
leather	*ã kweer*	en cuir
of brass	*ã kweevr*	en cuivre
of gold	*ã nor*	en or
of silver	*ã nahr-zhã*	en argent
silk	*ã swah*	en soie
wool	*ã lehn*	en laine

Toiletries

comb	*ẽ pehny*	un peigne
condoms	*dei prei-zehr-vah-teef*	des préservatifs
deodorant	*ẽ dei-o-do-rã*	un déodorant
hairbrush	*ün bros ah sher-ver*	une brosse à cheveux
moisturising cream	*der lah krehm ee-drah-tãt*	de la crème hydratante
razor	*ẽ rahz-wahr*	un rasoir
sanitary napkins	*dei sehr-vyeht ee-zhyei-neek*	des serviettes hygiéniques
shampoo	*dü shãp-wẽ*	du shampooing
shaving cream	*der lah moos ah rah-zei*	de la mousse à raser
soap	*dü sah-võ*	du savon
sunblock cream	*der la krehm oht pro-tehk-syõ*	de la crème haute protection

tampons	*dei tāpō ee-zhyei-neek*	des tampons hygiéniques
tissues	*dei moo-shwahr ã pah-pyei*	des mouchoirs en papier
toilet paper	*dü pah-pyei ee-zhyei-neek*	du papier hygiénique
toothbrush	*ün bros ah dã*	une brosse à dents
toothpaste	*dü dã-tee-frees*	du dentifrice

Stationery & Publications

map (of town)	*ĕ plahn*	un plan
map (of region)	*ün kahrt*	une carte
newspaper	*ē zhoor-nahl*	un journal
newspaper in English	*ē zhoor-nahl ã nã-glei*	un journal en anglais
novels in English	*dei ro-mã ã nã-glei*	des romans en anglais
paper	*dü pah-pyei*	du papier
pen (ballpoint)	*ē stee-loh (ah) beey*	un stylo (à) bille
scissors	*dei see-zoh*	des ciseaux

Photography

How much is it to process this film?

kō-byē koo-trah ler deiv-lop-mã der ser feelm? — Combien coûtera le développement de ce film?

When will it be ready?

kã teh-sker ser ser-rah preh? — Quand est-ce que ce sera prêt?

I'd like a film for this camera.

zher voo-drei ē feelm poor seht ah-pah-rehy der fo-toh — Je voudrais un film pour cet appareil de photo.

B&W (film)	*nwahr ei blã*	noir et blanc
camera	*ẽ nah-pah-rehy der fo-toh*	un appareil de photo
colour (film)	*koo-lerr*	couleurs
film	*ẽ feelm*	un film
flash	*ẽ flahsh*	un flash
lens	*ẽ nob-zhehk-teef*	un objectif
light meter	*ẽ pohz-mehtr*	un posemètre

Smoking

A packet of cigarettes, please.

ẽ pah-ket der see-gah-reht seel voo plei

Un paquet de cigarettes, s'il vous plaît.

Are these cigarettes strong/mild?

ehs-ker sei see-gah-reht sõ fort/lei-zhehr?

Est-ce que ces cigarettes sont fortes/légères?

Do you have a light?

voo zah-ve dü fer?

Vous avez du feu?

cigarette papers	*dei pah-pyei ah see-gah-reht*	des papiers à cigarettes
cigarettes	*dei see-gah-reht*	des cigarettes
filtered	*a-vehk feeltr*	avec filtre
lighter	*ẽ bree-kei*	un briquet
matches	*dei zah-lü-meht*	des allumettes
menthol	*mã-to-lei*	mentholées
pipe	*ün peep*	une pipe
tobacco (pipe)	*dü tah-bah (poor lah peep)*	du tabac (pour la pipe)

FRENCH

Colours

black	*nwahr*	noir/-e
blue	*bler*	bleu/-e
brown	*brẽ/brün*	brun (m)/brune (f)
green	*vehr/vehrt*	vert (m)/verte (f)
pink	*rohz*	rose
red	*roozh*	rouge
white	*blã*	blanc (m)
	bläsh	blanche (f)
yellow	*zhohn*	jaune

Sizes & Comparisons

small	*per-tee/per-teet*	petit/-e
big	*grã/grãd*	grand/-e
heavy	*loor/loord*	lourd/-e
light	*lei-zhei/lei-zhehr*	léger (m)/légère (f)
more	*plü*	plus
less	*mwẽ*	moins
too much/many	*troh*	trop
many	*boh-koo*	beaucoup
enough	*ah-se*	assez
also	*oh-see*	aussi
a little bit	*ẽ per*	un peu

Health

Where is …?		
oo ei …?		Où est …?
the doctor	*ler meid-sẽ*	le médecin
the hospital	*lo-pee tahl*	l'hôpital
the chemist	*ler fahr-mah-syẽ*	le pharmacien
the dentist	*ler dã-teest*	le dentiste

FRENCH

I am sick
zher swee mah-lahd
Je suis malade.

My friend is sick.
mõ nah-mee ei mah-lahd
Mon ami/-e est malade.

Could I see a female doctor?
ehs-ker zher per vwahr ün meid-sē fahm?
Est-ce que je peux voir une médecin femme?

What's the matter?
kehs-kee ner vah pah?
Qu'est-ce qui ne va pas?

Where does it hurt?
oo ehs-ker voo zah-vei mahl?
Où est-ce que vous avez mal?

It hurts here.
zhei ün doo-lerr ee-see
J'ai une douleur ici.

My ... hurts.
mõ/mah ... mer fei mahl
Mon (m)/ma (f) ... me fait mal.

Parts of the Body

ankle	*sher-veey*	cheville
arm	*brah*	bras
back	*doh*	dos
chest	*pwah-treen*	poitrine
ear	*o-rehy*	oreille
eye	*er-y*	œil
finger	*dwah*	doigt
foot	*pyei*	pied
hand	*mē*	main
head	*teht*	tête
heart	*kerr*	cœur
leg	*zhãb*	jambe

FRENCH

mouth	*boosh*	bouche
nose	*nei*	nez
ribs	*kot*	côtes
skin	*poh*	peau
spine	*ei-sheen*	échine
stomach	*ehs-to-mah*	estomac
teeth	*dā*	dents
throat	*gorzh*	gorge

Ailments

I have …		
zhei …		J'ai …
an allergy	*ün ah-lehr-zhee*	une allergie
a blister	*ün ā-pool*	une ampoule
a burn	*ün brü-lür*	une brûlure
a cough	*ün too*	une toux
diarrhoea	*lah dyah-rei*	la diarrhée
fever	*der lah fyehvr*	de la fièvre
glandular fever	*la mo-no-nü-klei-ohz ē-fehk-syerz*	la mononucléose infectieuse
a headache	*mahl ah lah teht*	mal à la tête
hepatitis	*lei-pah-teet*	l'hépatite
indigestion	*ün ē-dee-zhehs-tyõ*	une indigestion
an infection	*ün ē-fehk-syõ*	une infection
influenza	*lah greep*	la grippe
lice	*dei poo*	des poux
a pain	*ün doo-lerr*	une douleur
sore throat	*mahl ah lah gorzh*	mal à la gorge
a stomachache	*mahl oh vātr*	mal au ventre

FRENCH

a venereal	ün mah-lah-dee	une maladie
disease	vei-nei-ryehn	vénérienne
worms	dei vehr	des vers

I have a cold.
zher swee ã-rü-mei Je suis enrhumé/-ée.
I have constipation.
zher swee kõ-stee-pei Je suis constipé/-ée.
I have low/high blood
pressure.
zher fei der lee-pehr-tã-syõ/ Je fais de l'hypertension/
lee-poh-tã-syõ l'hypotension.
I have a sprain.
zher mer swee do nei ün Je me suis donné une
ã-tors entorse.
I have sunburn.
zhei pree ẽ koo der so-lehy J'ai pris un coup de soleil.

Some Useful Words & Phrases
I'm ...
zher swee ... Je suis ...
diabetic	dyah-bei-teek	diabétique
epileptic	ei-pee-lehp-teek	épileptique
asthmatic	ah-smah-teek	ashtmatique
anaemic	ah-nei-meek	anémique

I'm allergic to antibiotics/
penicillin
zher swee ah-lehr-zheek oh Je suis allergique aux anti-
zã-tee-byo-teek/ah lah biotiques/à la pénicilline.
pei-nee-see-leen

I'm pregnant.
zher swee ā-sēt — Je suis enceinte.

I'm on the pill.
zher prã lah pee-lül — Je prends la pilule.

I haven't had my period for ... months.
zher nei pah ü mei rehgl der-pwee ... mwah — Je n'ai pas eu mes règles depuis ... mois.

I have been vaccinated.
zher mer swee fei vahk-see-nei — Je me suis fait vacciner.

I have my own syringe.
zhei mah propr serrēg — J'ai ma propre seringue.

I feel better/worse.
zher mer sã myer/plü mahl — Je me sens mieux/plus mal.

accident	*ē nahk-see-dā*	un accident
addiction	*lah dei-pā-dās/lah tok-see-ko-mah-nee*	la dépendance/la toxicomanie
antibiotics	*dei zā-tee-byo-teek*	des antibiotiques
antiseptic	*der lā-tee-sehp-teek*	de l'antiseptique
aspirin	*der lah-spee-reen*	de l'aspirine
bandage	*ē pās-mā*	un pansement
bite	*ün mor-sür*	une morsure
blood pressure	*lah tā-syō (ahr-te-ryehl)*	la tension (artérielle)
blood test	*ü-nah-nah-leez der sā*	une analyse de sang
contraceptive	*ē kõ-trah-sehp-teef*	un contraceptif
injection	*ün nē-zhehk-syõ/ün pee-kür*	une injection/une piqûre

injury	*ün blehs-ür*	une blessure
menstruation	*lei rehgl*	les règles
nausea	*lah noh-zei*	la nausée
oxygen	*lok-see-zhehn*	l'oxygène
vitamins	*dei vee-tah-meen*	des vitamines

At the Chemist

I need medication for …
   zhei ber-zwē dē
   mei-dee-kah-mā poor …
I have a prescription.
   zhei ün or-do-nās

J'ai besoin d'un
médicament pour …

J'ai une ordonnance

At the Dentist

I have a toothache.
   zhei mahl oh dā
I've lost a filling.
   zhei pehr-dü ē plō-bahzh
I've broken a tooth.
   zher mer swee kah-sei ün dā
My gums hurt.
   me zhā-seev mer fō mahl
I don't want it extracted.
   *zher ner ver pah ker voo
lah-rah-shye*
Please give me an anaesthetic.
   *ah-vehk ah-nehs-tei-zee seel
voo plei*

J'ai mal aux dents.

J'ai perdu un plombage.

Je me suis cassé une dent.

Mes gencives me font mal.

Je ne veux pas que vous
l'arrachiez.

Avec anesthésie, s'il vous
plaît.

Time & Dates

Note that the French normally use the 24-hour clock.

What time is it?
kehl err ei teel?   Quelle heure est-il?

It is …
eel ei … err   Il est … heures.
in the morning   *dü mah-tē*   du matin
in the afternoon   *der lah-preh mee-dee*   de l'après-midi
in the evening   *dü swahr*   du soir

What date is it today?
noo som kehl zhoor   Nous sommes quel jour
oh-zhoor-dwee?   aujourd'hui?

Days of the Week
Monday	*lē-dee*	lundi
Tuesday	*mahr-dee*	mardi
Wednesday	*mehr-krer-dee*	mercredi
Thursday	*zher-dee*	jeudi
Friday	*vā-drer-dee*	vendredi
Saturday	*sahm-dee*	samedi
Sunday	*dee-māsh*	dimanche

Months
January	*zhā-vye*	janvier
February	*feiv-rye*	février
March	*mahrs*	mars
April	*ah-vreel*	avril
May	*meh*	mai
June	*zhwē*	juin
July	*zhwee-yeh*	juillet
August	*oo(t)*	août
September	*sehp-tābr*	septembre

FRENCH

October	*ok-tobr*	octobre
November	*no-vãbr*	novembre
December	*dei-sãbr*	décembre

Seasons

summer	*lei-tei*	l'été
autumn	*lo-ton*	l'automne
winter	*lee-vehr*	l'hiver
spring	*ler prẽ-tã*	le printemps

Present

today	*oh-zhoor-dwee*	aujourd'hui
this morning	*ser mah-tẽ*	ce matin
tonight	*ser swahr*	ce soir
this week/year	*seht ser-mehn/ah-nei*	cette semaine/année
now	*mẽt-nã*	maintenant

Past

yesterday	*yehr*	hier
day before yesterday	*ah-vã tyehr*	avant-hier
yesterday morning	*yehr mah-tẽ*	hier matin
last night	*yehr swahr*	hier soir
last week/year	*lah-nei/lah ser-mehn dehr-nyehr*	l'année/la semaine dernière

Future

tomorrow	*der-mẽ*	demain
day after tomorrow	*ah-preh der-mẽ*	après-demain
tomorrow morning	*der-mẽ mah-tẽ*	demain matin

tomorrow afternoon/evening	*der-mē ah-preh mee-dee/swahr*	demain après-midi/soir
next week	*lah ser-mehn proshehn*	la semaine prochaine
next year	*lah-nei pro-shehn*	l'année prochaine

During the Day

afternoon	*lah-preh mee-dee*	l'après-midi
dawn, very early morning	*lohb*	l'aube
day	*ler zhoor*	le jour
early	*toh*	tôt
midnight	*meen-wee*	minuit
morning	*ler mah-tē*	le matin
night	*lah nwee*	la nuit
noon	*mee-dee*	midi
sunset	*ler koo-shei dü so-lehy*	le coucher du soleil
sunrise	*ler ler-vei dü so-lehy*	le lever du soleil

Numbers & Amounts

0	*zeiroh*	zéro
1	*ē*	un
2	*der*	deux
3	*trwah*	trois
4	*kahtr*	quatre
5	*sēk*	cinq
6	*sees*	six
7	*seht*	sept
8	*weet*	huit
9	*nerf*	neuf

10	*dees*	dix
11	*õz*	onze
12	*dooz*	douze
13	*trehz*	treize
14	*kah-torz*	quatorze
15	*kẽz*	quinze
16	*sehz*	seize
17	*dee-seht*	dix-sept
18	*dee-zweet*	dix-huit
19	*deez-nerf*	dix-neuf
20	*vẽ*	vingt
21	*vẽ tei ẽ*	vingt et un
22	*vẽ der*	vingt-deux
30	*trãt*	trente
40	*kah-rãt*	quarante
50	*sẽ-kãt*	cinquante
60	*swah-sãt*	soixante
70	*swah-sãt dees*	soixante-dix
80	*kahtr vẽ*	quatre-vingts
90	*kahtr vẽ dees*	quatre-vingt-dix
100	*sã*	cent
1000	*meel*	mille
one million	*ẽ mee-lyõ*	un million
1st	*prer-myei*	premier (m) (1er)
	prer-myehr	première (f) (1ère)
2nd	*ser-gõ/ser-gõd*	second/-e (2e)
	der-zyehm	deuxième
3rd	*trwah-zyehm*	troisième (3e)
¼	*ẽ kahr*	un quart

FRENCH

⅓	*ē tyehr*	un tiers
½	*ē der-mee*	un demi
¾	*trwah kahr*	trois quarts

Some Useful Words

a little (amount)	*ē per*	un peu
double	*doobl*	double
a dozen	*ün doo-zehn*	une douzaine
Enough!	*ah-se!*	Assez!
few	*per der/kehl-ker*	peu de/quelques
less	*mwē*	moins
many	*boh-koo der*	beaucoup de
more	*plü*	plus
once	*ün fwah*	une fois
a pair	*ün pehr*	une paire
percent	*poor sã*	pour cent
some	*dü/der lah/de*	du/de la/des
too much	*troh*	trop
twice	*der fwah*	deux fois

Abbreviations

ap. J.-C./av. J.-C.	AD/BC
BCBG	'Sloane Ranger', from a 'good' family
la UE	EU
la CGT	association of French trade unions
HLM	public housing flats
M/Mme/Mlle	Mr/Mrs/Ms
l'ONU	UN
le PC	the Communist Party
le PS	the Socialist Party
PTT	on post boxes and post offices

FRENCH

RER	system of trains serving the outer suburbs of Paris
le RPR	right-wing political party
Rte/Av	Rd/Av
le SIDA	AIDS
TTC	all-inclusive
l'UDF	right-wing political party

German

Introduction

It might be a surprise to know that German is, in fact, a clo
relative of English. English, German and Dutch are all know
as West Germanic languages. It means that you know lots c
German words already – *Arm*, *Finger*, *Gold* – and you'll be ab
to figure out many others – *Mutter* (mother), *trinken* (drink), *g*
(good). A primary reason why English and German have grow
apart is that the Normans, on invading England in 1066, broug
with them a large number of non-Germanic words. It's mea
that English has lots of synonyms, with the more basic wor
being Germanic, and the more literary or specialised one comir
from French; for instance, 'start' and 'green' as opposed
'commence' and 'verdant'.

German grammar is often described as difficult – it is ofte
cited that there are many different ways to say 'the', and th
words have 'lots of endings'. However, most of these concep
that seem so alien actually have remnants in English. Germa
also has the advantage of being comparatively easy to pr
nounce. It is beyond the scope of this book to outline how to p
your own sentences together from scratch, but there are mar
examples of model sentences where you can choose the ke
word you want: for instance 'It is too … (big/small/ short/long'

German is spoken throughout Germany and Austria, and
most of Switzerland. It is also extremely useful in other cou
tries of the region, especially with older people. Although yo
may hear different dialects, there is a strong tradition of
prescribed official language, used in this book, which wi

always be understood. In some tourist centres English is so widely spoken that you may not have a chance to use German, even if you want to! However, as soon as you try to meet ordinary people or move out of the big cities, especially in what was East Germany, the situation is totally different. Your efforts to speak the local language will be very much appreciated and will make your trip much more enjoyable and fulfilling. *Gute Reise!*

GERMAN

Pronunciation

German is a relatively 'phonetic' language; that is, its spelling isn't as weird as English! You can almost always tell how a word is pronounced by the way it's spelt. Some letters can be pronounced several ways, but you can normally tell which way to use from the context.

Unlike English or French, German does not have silent letters: you pronounce the **k** at the start of the word *Knie*, 'knee', the **p** at the start of *Psychologie*, 'psychology', and the **e** at the end of *ich habe*, 'I have'.

One distinctive feature of German is that all nouns are written with a capital letter. The language has a fairly complicated grammar involving gender, whereby words are given masculine, feminine or neuter forms. In this chapter, the feminine form is given first, the masculine second.

Vowels

As in English, vowels can be pronounced long (like the 'o' in 'pope') or short (like the 'o' in 'pop'). As a rule, German vowels are long before one consonant and short before two consonants: the **o** is long in the word *Dom*, 'cathedral', but short in the word *doch*, 'after all'.

Letter/s	Pronunciation Guide	Sounds
a	*ah*	short, as the 'u' sound in 'cut'
	aa	long, as in 'father'
au	*ow*	as in 'vow'
ä	*a*	short, as in 'act'
	air	long, as in 'hair'
äu	*oy*	as in 'boy'
	eh	short, as the 'e' in 'bet'
e	*eh*	short, as in 'bet'
	ay	long, as in 'day'
ei	*ai*	as the 'ai' in 'aisle'
	oy	as in 'boy'
eu	*oy*	as in 'boy'
i	*ec*	long, as in 'see'
i	*i*	short, as in 'in'
ie	*ee*	as in 'see'
o	*oh*	long, as in 'note'
	o	short, as in 'pot'
ö	*er*	as the 'er' in 'fern'
u	*u*	as the 'u' in 'pull'
ü	*ü*	like the 'u' in 'pull' but with stretched lips

GERMAN

Consonants

Most German consonants sound similar to their English counterparts. One important difference is that **b, d** and **g** sound like 'p', 't' and 'k', respectively, at the end of a word.

Letter/s	Pronunciation Guide	Sounds
b	*b/p*	normally the English 'b', but 'p' at end of a word
ch	*kh*	the *ch* in Scottish *loch*
d	*d/t*	normally as the English 'd', but 't' at end of a word
g	*gh/k/kh*	normally as the hard English 'g', but 'k' at the end of a word, and *ch*, as in the Scottish *loch,* at the end of a word, after **i**
j	*y*	as the 'y' in 'yet'
qu	*kv*	'k' plus 'v'
r	*r*	as the English 'r', but rolled at the back of the mouth
s	*s/z*	normally as the 's' in 'sun'; when followed by a vowel, as the 'z' in 'zoo'
sch	*sh*	as the 'sh' in 'ship'
sp, st	*shp/sht*	at the start of a word, 's' sounds like the 'sh' in 'ship'
tion	*tsiohn*	the **t** sounds like the 'ts' in 'hits'
ß	*s*	as in 'sun' (in some books, written as **ss**)
v	*f*	as the 'f' in 'fan'
w	*v*	as the 'v' in 'van'
z	*ts*	as the 'ts' in 'hits'

GERMAN

Stress

Stressed syllables are highlighted in bold in the pronunciation guide. However, stress in German is very straightforward; the overwhelming majority of German words are stressed on the first syllable. Some prefixes are not stressed (such as *besetzt* is stressed on the **setzt**); and certain foreign words, especiall from French, are stressed on the last syllable (*Organisatio Appe**tit**).

Greetings & Civilities
Top Useful Phrases

Hello. (Good day)
  *ghu-tehn **taak***   Guten Tag.
Goodbye.
  *owf **vee**-dehr-zayn*   Auf Wiedersehen.
Yes./No.
  yaa/nain   Ja./Nein.
Excuse me.
  *ehnt-**shul**-di-ghung*   Entschuldigung.
May I? Do you mind?
  dahrf ikh?/makht ehs   Darf ich? Macht es Ihnen
  *ee-nehn **eht**-vahs ows?*   etwas aus?
Sorry. (excuse me, forgive me)
  *ehnt-**shul**-di-ghung*   Entschuldigung.
Please.
  ***bi**-teh*   Bitte.
Thank you.
  ***dahng**-keh*   Danke.
Many thanks.
  ***fee**-lehn dahngk*   Vielen Dank.
That's fine. You're welcome.
  ***bi**-teh zayr*   Bitte sehr.

Greetings

Good morning.
  *ghu-tehn **mor**-ghehn*   Guten Morgen.

Good afternoon.
   ghu-tehn taak — Guten Tag.

Good evening/night.
   *ghu-tehn **aa**-behnt/* — Guten Abend./Gute Nacht.
   ghu-teh nahkht

How are you?
   *vee ghayt ehs **ee**-nehn?* — Wie geht es Ihnen?

Well, thanks.
   ***dahng**-keh, ghut* — Danke, gut.

GERMAN

Forms of Address

Madam/Mrs	***ghnair**-di-gheh froh/frow*	Gnädige Frau/ Frau
Sir/Mr	*main hehr/hehr*	Mein Herr/Herr
Miss	*froy-lain*	Fräulein
companion, friend	***froyn**-din* *froynt*	Freundin (f) Freund (m)

As there is yet no equivalent of Ms, *Frau* is regarded as a respectful address for older women whether they are married or not.

Small Talk
Meeting People

What is your name?
   *vee **hai**-sehn zee?* — Wie heißen Sie?

My name is …
   *ikh **hai**-seh …* — Ich heiße …

I'd like to introduce you to …
   *kahn ikh **ee**-nehn* — Kann ich Ihnen …
   *for-**shtih** lehn?* — vorstellen?

I'm pleased to meet you.
   ahn-gheh-naym   Angenehm.

Nationalities

Where are you from?
   *voh-**hayr** ko-mehn zee?*   Woher kommen Sie?

I am from …
   *ikh **ko-meh** ows …*   Ich komme aus …

Australia	*ow-**straa**-li-yehn*	Australien
Canada	***kah**-nah-dah*	Kanada
England	***ehng**-lahnt*	England
Germany	***doych**-lahnt*	Deutschland
Ireland	***ir**-lahnt*	Irland
New Zealand	*noy-**zay**-lahnt*	Neuseeland
Scotland	***shot**-lahnt*	Schottland
Switzerland	*dayr shvaits*	der Schweiz
the USA	*dayn fay-**rai**-nikh-tehn **shtaa**-tehn*	den Vereinigten Staaten
Wales	*wailz*	Wales

Age

How old are you?
   vee ahlt zint zee?   Wie alt sind Sie?
I am … years old.
   *ikh bin … **yaa**-reh ahlt*   Ich bin … Jahre alt.

Occupations

What (work) do you do?
   *ahls vahs **ahr**-bai-tehn zee?*   Als was arbeiten Sie?
I am a/an …
   ikh bin …   Ich bin …

GERMAN

artist	*künst-lehr-in*	Künstlerin (f)
	künst-lehr	Künstler (m)
business person	*geh-**shafts**-frow*	Geschäftsfrau (f)
	*geh-**shafts**-mahn*	Geschäftsmann (m)
doctor	*arts-tin/ahrtst*	Ärztin (f)/Arzt (m)
engineer	*in-zheh-ni-**yer**-in*	Ingenieurin (f)
	*in-zhe-ni-**yer***	Ingenieur (m)
factory worker	*fah-**breek**-ahr-bai-tehr-in/fah-**breek**-ahr-bai-tehr*	Fabrikarbeiterin (f) Fabrikarbeiter (m)
farmer	*boy-yehr-in*	Bäuerin (f)
	bow-ehr	Bauer (m)
journalist	*zhur-nah-**list**-in*	Journalistin (f)
	*zhur-nah-**list***	Journalist (m)
lawyer	*rehkhts-ahn-vahlt-in*	Rechtsanwältin (f)
	rekhts-ahn-vahlt	Rechtsanwalt (m)
mechanic	*meh-**khah**-ni-kehr-in*	Mechanikerin (f)
	*meh-**khah**-ni-kehr*	Mechaniker (m)
nurse	*krahng-kehn-shveh-stehr*	Kranken-schwester (f)
	krahng-kehn-pflay-ghehr	Kranken-pfleger (m)
office worker	*bü-**roh**-ahn-gheh-shtehl-teh*	Büroangestellte (f)
	*bü-**roh**-ahn-gheh-shtehl-tehr*	Büroange-stellter (m)
scientist	*vi-sehn-shahft-lehr-in*	Wissenschaft-lerin (f)
	vi-sehn-shahft-lehr	Wissenschaftler (m)
student	*shtu-**dehnt**-in*	Studentin (f)
	*shtu-**dehnt***	Student (m)

GERMAN

GERMAN

teacher	*lay-rehr-in*	Lehrerin (f)
	lay-rehr	Lehrer (m)
waiter	*kehl-nehr-in*	Kellnerin (f)
	kehl-nehr	Kellner (m)
writer	*shrift-shtehl-ehr-in*	Schriftstellerin (f)
	shrift-shtehl-ehr	Schriftsteller (m)

Religion

What is your religion?
vahs ist i-reh reh-li-ghi-ohn? Was ist Ihre Religion?

I am not religious.
ikh bin nikht reh-li-gi-ers Ich bin nicht religiös.

I am …
ikh bin … Ich bin …

Buddhist	*bu-dist-in*	Buddhistin (f)
	bu-dist	Buddhist (m)
Catholic	*kah-to-leek-in*	Katholikin (f)
	kah-to-leek	Katholik (m)
Christian	*khrist-in*	Christin (f)
	khrist	Christ (m)
Hindu	*hin-du*	Hindu
Jewish	*yü-din*	Jüdin (f)
	yü-deh	Jude (m)
Muslim	*mos-lehm*	Moslem

Family

Are you married?
zint zee fehr-hai-rah-teht? Sind Sie verheiratet?

I am single.
ikh bin un-fehr-hai-rah-teht Ich bin unverheiratet.

I am married.
*ikh bin fehr-**hai**-rah-teht*   Ich bin verheiratet.

How many children do you have?
*vee-**fee**-leh **kin**-dehr **haa**-behn zee?*   Wieviele Kinder haben Sie?

I don't have any children.
*ikh **haa**-beh **kai**-neh **kin**-dehr*   Ich habe keine Kinder.

I have a daughter/a son.
*ikh **haa**-beh **ai**-neh **tokh**-tehr/**ai**-nehn zohn*   Ich habe eine Tochter/einen Sohn.

Do you have any brothers or sisters?
*haa-behn zee nokh gheh-**shvi**-stehr?*   Haben Sie noch Geschwister?

Is your husband/wife here?
*ist ihr mahn/**ih**-reh frow heer?*   Ist Ihr Mann/Ihre Frau hier?

Do you have a boyfriend/girlfriend?
*haa-behn zee **ai**-nehn froynt/**ai**-neh **froynd**-in?*   Haben Sie einen Freund/eine Freundin?

brother	*bru-dehr*	Bruder
children	*kin-dehr*	Kinder
daughter	*tokh-tehr*	Tochter
family	*fah-mi-li-eh*	Familie
father	*faa-tehr*	Vater
grandfather	*ghrohs-vaa-tehr*	Großvater
grandmother	*ghrohs-mu-tehr*	Großmutter

GERMAN

husband	*mahn*	Mann
mother	*mu-tehr*	Mutter
sister	**shveh**-*stehr*	Schwester
son	*zohn*	Sohn
wife	*frow*	Frau

Feelings

I (don't) like …
... *gheh-falt mir (nikht)*   ... gefällt mir (nicht).

I am angry.	*ikh bin **ber**-zeh*	Ich bin böse.
I am cold.	*mir ist kahlt*	Mir ist kalt.
I am grateful.	*ikh bin **dahngk**-bahr*	Ich bin dankbar.
I am happy.	*ikh bin **ghlük**-likh*	Ich bin glücklich
I am hot.	*mir ist hais*	Mir ist heiß.
I am hungry.	*ikh **haa**-beh **hung**-ehr*	Ich habe Hunger.
I am in a hurry.	*ikh **haa**-beh ehs **ai**-likh*	Ich habe es eilig.
I am right.	*ikh **haa**-beh rehkht*	Ich habe recht.
I am sad.	*ikh bin **trow**-rikh*	Ich bin traurig.
I am sleepy.	*ikh bin **mü**-deh*	Ich bin müde.
I am sorry.	*ehs tut mir lait*	Es tut mir leid.
I am thirsty.	*ikh **haa**-beh durst*	Ich habe Durst.
I am tired.	*ikh bin **mü**-deh*	Ich bin müde.
I am (un)well.	*ikh **fü**-leh mikh (nikht) vohl*	Ich fühle mich (nicht) wohl.
I am worried.	*ikh **mah**-kheh mir **zor**-ghehn*	Ich mache mir Sorgen.

Language Difficulties

Do you speak English?
shpreh-khehn zee ehng-lish?   Sprechen Sie Englisch?

Does anyone here speak
English?
*shprikht heer **yay**-mahnt
ehng-lish?*   Spricht hier jemand
Englisch?

I speak a little …
*ikh **shpreh**-kheh ain
bis-khehn …*   Ich spreche ein bißchen …

I don't speak …
*ikh **shpreh**-kheh kain …*   Ich spreche kein …

I (don't) understand.
*ikh fehr-**shtay**-eh (nikht)*   Ich verstehe (nicht).

Could you speak more slowly
please?
*kern-tehn zee **bi**-teh **lahng**-zahm-ehr **shpreh**-khehn?*   Könnten Sie bitte langsamer
sprechen?

Sorry? (I didn't hear.)
bi-teh?   Bitte?

Could you repeat that?
*kern-tehn zee dahs
vee-dehr-**hoh**-lehn?*   Könnten Sie das
wiederholen?

How do you say …?
vahs haist … owf doych?   Was heißt … auf deutsch?

What does … mean?
*vahs beh-**doy**-teht …?*   Was bedeutet …?

I speak …
*ikh **shpreh**-kheh …*   Ich spreche …
English   **ehng**-lish   Englisch

GERMAN

French	*frahn-**tser**-zish*	Französisch
German	*doych*	Deutsch
Italian	*i-tah-li-**ay**-nish*	Italienisch
Japanese	*yah-**paa**-nish*	Japanisch

Some Useful Phrases

Sure.
   klahr! — Klar!
Just a minute.
   *ain moh-**mehnt**!* — Ein Moment!
It's (not) important.
   *ehs ist (nikht) **vikh**-tikh* — Es ist (nicht) wichtig.
It's (not) possible.
   *ehs ist (nikht) **mergh**-likh* — Es ist (nicht) möglich.
Wait!
   ***vahr**-tehn zee maal!* — Warten Sie mal!
Good luck!
   feel ghlük! — Viel Glück!

Signs

LEFT LUGGAGE	GEPÄCKAUF-BEWAHRUNG
CHECK-IN COUNTER	ABFERTIGUNG
CUSTOMS	ZOLL
EMERGENCY EXIT	NOTAUSGANG
ENTRANCE	EINGANG
EXIT	AUSGANG
FREE ADMISSION	EINTRITT FREI
HOT/COLD	HEIß/KALT
INFORMATION	AUSKUNFT

GERMAN

NO ENTRY	KEIN ZUTRITT
NO SMOKING	RAUCHEN VERBOTEN
OPEN/CLOSED	OFFEN/GESCHLOSSEN
PROHIBITED	VERBOTEN
RESERVED	RESERVIERT
TELEPHONE	TELEFON
TOILETS	TOILETTEN (WC)

GERMAN

Emergencies

POLICE	POLIZEI
POLICE STATION	POLIZEIWACHE

Help!
hil-feh! — Hilfe!

It's an emergency!
*ehs ist ain **noht**-fahl!* — Es ist ein Notfall!

There's been an accident!
*ehs haht **ai**-nehn un-fahl
gheh-**ghay**-behn!* — Es hat einen Unfall gegeben!

Call a doctor!
*hoh-lehn zee **ai**-nehn ahrtst!* — Holen Sie einen Arzt!

Call an ambulance!
*ru-fehn zee **ai**-nehn
krahng-kehn-vaa-ghehn!* — Rufen Sie einen Krankenwagen!

I've been raped.
*ikh bin fehr **vahl**-tikht
vor-dehn* — Ich bin verwaltigt worden.

I've been robbed!
*ikh bin beh-**shtoh**-lehn **vor**-dehn!*
Ich bin bestohlen worden!

Call the police!
***ru**-fehn zee dee po-li-**tsai**!*
Rufen Sie die Polizei!

Where is the police station?
*voh ist dee poh-li-**tsai**-vah-kheh?*
Wo ist die Polizeiwache?

Go away!
***ghay**-ehn zee vehk!*
Gehen Sie weg!

I'll call the police!
*ikh **ru**-feh ai-nehn po-li-**tsist**-ehn!*
Ich rufe einen Polizisten!

Thief!
deep!
Dieb!

I am ill.
ikh bin krahngk
Ich bin krank.

My friend is ill.
***mai**-neh **froynd**-in (f)/ froynt (m) ist krahngk*
Meine Freundin (f)/Mein Freund (m) ist krank.

I am lost.
*ikh **haa**-beh mikh fehr-**irt***
Ich habe mich verirrt.

Where are the toilets?
*voh ist dee toh-ah-**leh**-teh?*
Wo ist die Toilette?

Could you help me please?
***ker**-nehn zee mir **bi**-teh **hehl**-fehn?*
Könnten Sie mir bitte helfen?

Could I please use the telephone?
***kern**-teh ikh **bi**-teh dahs teh-leh-**fohn** beh-**nu**-tsehn?*
Könnte ich bitte das Telefon benutzen?

I'm sorry. I apologise.
  ehs tut mir lait   Es tut mir leid.
  ehnt-shul-di-ghehn zee Entschuldigen Sie bitte.
  bi-teh

I didn't realise I was doing anything wrong.
  ikh vahr mir nikht beh-vust, Ich war mir nicht bewußt,
  eht-vahs un-rehkht-ehs   etwas Unrechtes getan zu
  gheh-tahn tsu haa-behn   haben.

I didn't do it.
  dahs haa-beh ikh nikht Das habe ich nicht getan.
  gheh-tahn

I wish to contact my embassy/consulate.
  ikh merkh-teh mikh mit Ich möchte mich mit meiner
  mai-nehr boht-shahft/   Botschaft/meinem Konsulat
  mai-nehm kon-zu-laat in in Verbindung setzen.
  fehr-bin-dung zeht-tsehn

I speak English.
  ikh shpreh-kheh   Ich spreche Englisch.
  ehng-lish

I have medical insurance.
  ikh bin in ai-nehr   Ich bin in einer
  krahng-kehn-kah-seh   Krankenkasse.

My possessions are insured.
  mai-neh zah-khehn zint Meine Sachen sind
  fehr-zi-khehrt   versichert.

GERMAN

I've lost …

*ikh **haa**-beh … vehr-**loh**-rehn*		Ich habe … verloren.
my bags	*mai-neh rai-zeh-tah-shehn*	meine Reisetaschen
my handbag	*mai-neh hahnt-tah-sheh*	meine Handtasche
my money	*main ghehlt*	mein Geld
my travellers' cheques	*mai-neh rai-zeh-shehks*	meine Reiseschecks
my passport	*main(-ehn) pahs*	mein(en) Paß (Use -en in Ich habe meinen Paß verloren)

Paperwork

name	*naa-meh*	Name
address	*ah-dreh-seh*	Adresse
date of birth	*gheh-burts-daa-tum*	Geburtsdatum
place of birth	*gheh-burts-ort*	Geburtsort
age	*ahl-tehr*	Alter
sex	*gheh-shlehkht*	Geschlecht
nationality	*nah-tsi-o-nah-li-tayt*	Nationalität
religion	*reh-li-ghi-ohn*	Religion
profession	*beh-ruf*	Beruf
marital status	*fah-mi-li-ehn-shtahnt*	Familienstand
passport	*(rai-zeh-)pahs*	(Reise)paß
passport number	*pahs-nu-mehr*	Paßnummer
visa	*vi-zum*	Visum
identification	*ows-vais-pah-pee-reh*	Ausweispapiere

birth certificate	*gheh-**burts**-ur-kun-deh*	Geburtsurkunde
driver's licence	*fü-rehr-shain*	Führerschein
car owner's title/ registration	*(krahft-)**faar**-tsoyk-breef*	(Kraft)fahrzeug-brief
customs	*tsol*	Zoll
immigration	***ain**-vahn-dehr-ung*	Einwanderung
border	***ghrehn**-tseh*	Grenze

Getting Around

ARRIVALS	ANKUNFT
BUS STOP	BUSHALTESTELLE
DEPARTURES	ABFAHRT
STATION	STATION
SUBWAY	U-BAHN (U)
TICKET OFFICE	FAHRKARTENSCHALTER
TIMETABLE	FAHRPLAN
TRAIN STATION	BAHNHOF (Bhf/Bf)

What time does ... leave?
vahn fairt ... ahp?   Wann fährt ... ab?
What time does ... arrive?
vahn komt ... ahn?   Wann kommt ... an?

the (air)plane	*dahs **fluk**-tsoyk*	das Flugzeug
the boat	*dahs bowt*	das Boot
the bus (city)	*dayr bus*	der Bus
the bus (intercity)	*dayr (ü-behr-lahnt-) bus*	der (Überland)bus

the train	*dayr tsuk*	der Zug
the tram	*dee **shtrah**-sehn-baan*	die Straßenbahn

Directions

Where is …?
voh ist …?

Wo ist …?

How do I get to …?
*vee **ko**-meh ikh nahkh …?*

Wie komme ich nach …?

Is it far from/near here?
*ist ehs vait/in dayr **na**-yeh?*

Ist es weit/in der Nähe?

Can I walk there?
*kahn ikh tsu fus **ghay**-ehn?*

Kann ich zu Fuß gehen?

Can you show me (on the map)?
***ker**-nehn zee mir (owf dayr **kahr**-teh) tsai-ghehn?*

Können Sie mir (auf der Karte) zeigen?

Are there other means of getting there?
*ghipt ehs **ahn**-deh-reh **mer**-ghlikh-kai-tehn, dort-**hin** tsu **faa**-rehn?*

Gibt es andere Möglichkeiten, dorthin zu fahren?

I'm looking for …
*ikh **zu**-kheh …*

Ich suche …

Go straight ahead.
***ghay**-ehn zee gheh-**raa**-deh-ows*

Gehen Sie geradeaus.

It's two streets down.
*ehs ist tsvai **shtrah**-sehn vai-tehr*

Es ist zwei Straßen weiter.

Turn left …
***bee**-ghehn zee … lingks ahp*

Biegen Sie … links ab.

Turn right ...
bee-ghehn zee ... rehkhts ahp
Biegen Sie ... rechts ab.

at the next corner
bai dayr nakh-stehn eh-keh
bei der nächsten Ecke

at the traffic lights
bai dayr ahm-pehl
bei der Ampel

behind	*hin-tehr*	hinter
in front of	*for*	vor
far	*vait*	weit
near	*naa-eh*	nahe
opposite	*ghay-ghehn-ü-behr*	gegenüber

GERMAN

Booking Tickets

Excuse me, where is the ticket office?
ehnt-shul-di-ghung, voh ist dayr faar-kahr-tehn-shahl-tehr?
Entschuldigung, wo ist der Fahrkartenschalter?

Where can I buy a ticket?
voh kahn ikh ai-neh faar-kahr-teh kow-fehn?
Wo kann ich eine Fahrkarte kaufen?

I want to go to ...
ikh merkh-teh nahkh ... fah-rehn
Ich möchte nach ... fahren.

Do I need to book?
mus muhn ai-nehn plahts reh-zehr-vee-rehn lah-sehn?
Muß man einen Platz reservieren lassen?

You need to book.
*mahn mus **ai**-nehn plahts reh-zehr-**vee**-rehn **lah**-sehn*

Man muß einen Platz reservieren lassen.

I'd like to book a seat to …
*ikh **merkh**-teh **ai**-nehn plahts nahkh … reh-zehr-**vee**-rehn **lah**-sehn*

Ich möchte einen Platz nach … reservieren lassen.

I would like …
*ikh **merkh**-teh …*

Ich möchte …

a one-way ticket	*ai-neh **ain**-tsehl-kahr-teh*	eine Einzelkarte
a return ticket	*ai-neh **rük**-fahr-kahr-teh*	eine Rückfahrkarte
two tickets	*tsvai **fahr**-kahr-tehn*	zwei Fahrkarten
tickets for all of us	***fahr**-kahr-tehn für uns **ah**-leh*	Fahrkarten für uns alle
student's concession	*mit fahr-prais-ehr-**mas**-i-ghung für shtu-**dehn**-tehn*	mit Fahrpreisermäßigung für Studenten
with child/ pensioner concession	*mit fahr-prais-ehr-**mas**-i-ghung für **kin**dehr/**rehnt**-nehr*	mit Fahrpreisermäßigung für Kinder/Rentner
1st class	***ehr**-steh **klah**-seh*	erste Klasse
2nd class	*tsvai-teh **klah**-seh*	zweite Klasse

It is full.
*ehr ist **ows**-gheh-bukht*

Er ist ausgebucht.

Is it completely full?
*ist ehr ghahnts **ows**-gheh-bukht?*

Ist er ganz ausgebucht?

Can I get a stand-by ticket?
*kahn ikh ain **stand**-bai ti-keht **kow**-fehn?*

Kann ich ein Standby-Ticket kaufen?

Air

CHECKING IN	ABFERTIGUNG
LUGGAGE PICKUP	GEPÄCKAUSGABE
REGISTRATION	GEPÄCKAUFGABE

Is there a flight to …?
*ghipt ehs **ai**-nehn fluk nahkh …?*

Gibt es einen Flug nach …?

When is the next flight to …?
*vahn ist dayr **nakh**-steh fluk nahkh …?*

Wann ist der nächste Flug nach …?

How long does the flight take?
*vee **lahng**-eh **dow**-ehrt dayr fluk?*

Wie lange dauert der Flug?

What is the flight number?
*vehl-kher **flug**-nu-mehr ist ehs?*

Welcher Flugnummer ist es?

You must check in at …
*zee **mü**-sehn um … **ain**-cheh-kehn*

Sie müssen um … einchecken.

airport tax	*fluk-hah-fehn-gheh-bür*	Flughafengebühr
boarding pass	*bort-kahr-teh*	Bordkarte
customs	*tsol*	Zoll

Bus

BUS/TRAM STOP	BUSHALTESTELLE/ STRAßENBAHNHALTE- STELLE

Where is the bus/tram stop?
*voh ist dee **bus**-hahl-teh-shteh-leh/**shtrah**-sehn-bahn-hahl-teh-shteh-leh?*
Wo ist die Bushaltestelle/ Straßenbahnhaltestelle?

Which bus goes to …?
***vehl**-khehr bus fairt nahkh …?*
Welcher Bus fährt nach …?

Does this bus go to …?
*fairt **dee**-zayr bus nahkh …?*
Fährt dieser Bus nach …?

How often do buses pass by?
*vee oft **faa**-rehn **bu**-seh for-**bai**?*
Wie oft fahren Busse vorbei?

Could you let me know when we get to …?
***kern**-tehn zee mir **bi**-teh **zaa**-ghehn, vehn vir in … **ahn**-ko-mehn?*
Könnten Sie mir bitte sagen, wenn wir in … ankommen?

I want to get off!
*ikh **merkh**-teh ows-shtai-ghehn!*
Ich möchte aussteigen!

What time is the … bus?
vahn fairt dayr … bus?
Wann fährt der … Bus?

next	**nakh**-steh bus	nächste
first	**ehr**-steh	erste
last	**lehts**-teh	letzte

Train

DINING CAR	SPEISEWAGEN
EXPRESS	SCHNELLZUG
PLATFORM NO	BAHNSTEIG
SLEEPING CAR	SCHLAFWAGEN

GERMAN

Passengers must ...
pah-sah-zhee-reh
mü-sehn ...   Passagiere müssen ...

change trains   *um-shtai-gehn*   umsteigen
change platforms   *owf ai-nehn ahn-*   auf einen anderen
                     deh-rehn baan-   Bahnsteig gehen
                     shtaik ghay-ehn

Is this the right platform
for ...?
fairt dayr tsuk nahkh ... owf   Fährt der Zug nach ... auf
dee-zehm baan-shtaik ahp?   diesem Bahnsteig ab?
The train leaves from
platform ...
dayr tsuk fairt owf   Der Zug fährt auf Bahsteig
baan-shtaik ... ahp.   ... ab.

dining car	*shpai-zeh-vaa-ghehn*	Speisewagen
express	*shnehl-tsuk*	Schnellzug
local	*naa-vehr-kehrs-tsuk*	Nahverkehrszug
sleeping car	*shlaaf-vah ghehn*	Schlafwagen

GERMAN

Metro

METRO/UNDERGROUND	U-BAHN
CHANGE (for coins)	WECHSELGELD
THIS WAY TO	AUSGANG ZU
WAY OUT	AUSGANG

Which line takes me to …?
vel-kheh li-ni-yeh fairt nahkh …?

Welche Linie fährt nach …?

What is the next station?
vee haist dayr nakh-steh baan-hof?

Wie heißt der nächste Bahnhof?

Taxi

Can you take me to …?
kern-ehn zee mir tsu … bring-ehn?

Können Sie mich zu … bringen?

Please take me to …
bring-ehn zee mikh bi-teh tsu …

Bringen Sie mich bitte zu …

How much is it to go to …?
vahs ko-steht ehs bis …?

Was kostet es bis …?

Instructions

Here is fine, thank you.
hahl-tehn zee bi-teh heer

Halten Sie bitte hier.

The next corner, please.
ahn dayr nakh-stehn eh-keh, bi-teh

An der nächsten Ecke, bitte.

Continue!
vai-tehr!

Weiter!

The next street to the left/right.
bee-ghehn zee ahn dayr
nakh-stehn eh-keh lingks/
rehkhts ahp

Biegen Sie an der nächsten
Ecke links/rechts ab.

Stop here!
haal-tehn zee bi-teh heer!

Halten Sie hier!

Please slow down.
faa-rehn zee bi-teh
lahng-sahm-ehr

Fahren Sie bitte langsamer.

Please wait here.
bi-teh vahr-tehn zee heer

Bitte warten Sie hier.

Some Useful Phrases

The train is delayed/cancelled.
dayr tsuk haht fehr-shpair-
tung/falt ows

Der Zug hat Verspätung/
fällt aus.

How long will it be delayed?
vee-feel fehr-shpair-tung
virt ehr haa-behn?

Wieviel Verspätung wird er
haben?

There is a delay of ... hours.
ehr haht ... shtun-dehn
fehr-shpair-tung

Er hat ... Stunden
Verspätung.

Can I reserve a place?
kahn ikh ai-nehn plahts
reh-zehr-vee-rehn lah-sehn?

Kann ich einen Platz
reservieren lassen?

How long does the trip take?
vee lahng-eh dow-ehrt dee
rai-zeh?

Wie lange dauert die Reise?

Is it a direct route?
*ist ehs **ai**-neh di-**rehk**-teh fehr-**bin**-dung?*
Ist es eine direkte Verbindung?

Is that seat taken?
*ist **dee**-zayr plahts beh-**zehtst**?*
Ist dieser Platz besetzt?

I want to get off at …
*ikh **merkh**-teh in … **ows**-shtai-ghehn*
Ich möchte in … aussteigen.

Excuse me.
*ehnt-**shul**-di-ghung*
Entschuldigung.

Where can I hire a bicycle?
*voh kahn ikh ain **faar**-raht **mee**-tehn?*
Wo kann ich ein Fahrrad mieten?

Car

DETOUR	UMLEITUNG
FREEWAY	AUTOBAHN
GARAGE	TANKSTELLE
GIVE WAY	VORFAHRT GEWÄHREN
MECHANIC	MECHANIKER
NO ENTRY	KEIN EINGANG
NO PARKING	PARKEN VERBOTEN
ONE WAY	EINBAHNSTRAßE
REPAIRS	REPARATUREN
SELF SERVICE	SELBSTBEDIENUNG
STOP	HALT
SUPER	SUPER
UNLEADED	BLEIFREI

Where can I hire a car?
voh kahn ikh ain ow-toh
mee-*tehn?*

Wo kann ich ein Auto
mieten?

How much is it daily/weekly?
vee-feel ko-steht ehs proh
taak/proh voh-kheh?

Wieviel kostet es pro
Tag/pro Woche?

Does that include insurance/
mileage?
ist dee fehr-zi-khehr-ung/
dahs ki-lo-may-tehr-ghehlt
in-beh-ghri-fehn?

Ist die Versicherung/das
Kilometergeld inbegriffen?

Where's the next petrol
station?
voh ist dee nakh-steh
tahngk-shteh-leh?

Wo ist die nächste
Tankstelle?

Please fill the tank.
fol-tahng-kehn, bi-teh

Volltanken, bitte.

I want ... litres of petrol (gas).
ghay-behn zee mir ...
li-tehr behn-tsin

Geben Sie mir ... Liter
Benzin.

Please check the oil and water.
bi-teh zay-ehn zee nahkh
erl unt vah-sehr

Bitte sehen Sie nach Öl und
Wasser.

How long can I park here?
vee lahg-eh kahn ikh heer
pahr-kehn?

Wie lange kann ich hier
parken?

Does this road lead to?
fürt dee-zeh shtrah-seh
nahkh ...?

Führt diese Straße nach ...?

air (for tyres)	*luft*	Luft
battery	*bah-teh-ree*	Batterie

brakes	*brehm-zehn*	Bremsen
clutch	*kup-lung*	Kupplung
driver's licence	*fü-rehr-shain*	Führerschein
engine	*moh-tor*	Motor
lights	*shain-vehr-fehr*	Scheinwerfer
oil	*erl*	Öl
puncture	*rai-fehn-pah-neh*	Reifenpanne
radiator	*kü-lehr*	Kühler
road map	*shtraa-sehn-kahr-teh*	Straßenkarte
tyres	*rai-fehn*	Reifen
windscreen	*vint-shuts-shai-beh*	Windschutzscheib

Car Problems

I need a mechanic.
    ikh brow-kheh ai-nehn   Ich brauche einen
    meh-khah-ni-kehr   Mechaniker.
What make is it?
    vehl-kheh mar-keh ist ehs?   Welche Marke ist es?
The battery is flat.
    dee bah-teh-ree ist layr   Die Batterie ist leer.
The radiator is leaking.
    dayr kü-lehr ist un-dikht   Der Kühler ist undicht.
I have a flat tyre.
    ikh hah-beh ai-neh pah-neh Ich habe eine Panne.
It's overheating.
    ehs loyft hais   Es läuft heiß.
It's not working.
    ehs fungk-tsi-o-neert nikht Es funktioniert nicht.

Accommodation

CAMPING GROUND	CAMPINGPLATZ
GUESTHOUSE	PENSION or GASTHAUS
HOTEL	HOTEL
MOTEL	MOTEL
YOUTH HOSTEL	JUGENDHERBERGE

I am looking for …
ikh zu-kheh … Ich suche …
Where is …?
voh ist …? Wo ist …?
a cheap hotel *ain bi-li-ghehs hoh-tehl* ein billiges Hotel
a good hotel *ain ghu-tehs hoh-tehl* ein gutes Hotel
a nearby hotel *ain hoh-tehl in dayr na-yeh* ein Hotel in der Nähe
a clean hotel *ain zow-beh-rehs hoh-tehl* ein sauberes Hotel

What is the address?
vahs ist dee ah-dreh-seh? Was ist die Adresse?
Could you write the address, please?
kern-tehn zee bi-teh dee ah-dreh-seh owf-shrai-behn? Könnten Sie bitte die Adresse aufschreiben?

GERMAN

At the Hotel

Do you have any rooms
available?

> *haa-behn zee nokh frai-yeh
> tsi-mehr?*

Haben Sie noch freie
Zimmer?

I would like …
> *ikh merkh-teh …*

Ich möchte …

a single room	*ain ain-tsehl-tsi-mehr*	ein Einzelzimmer
a double room	*ain do-pehl-tsi-mehr*	ein Doppelzimmer
a room with a bathroom	*ain tsi-mehr mit baat*	ein Zimmer mit Bad
to share a dorm	*ai-nehn shlaaf-zaal tai-lehn*	einen Schlafsaal teilen
a bed	*ain beht*	ein Bett

I want a room with a …
> *ikh merkh-teh ain tsi-mehr
> mit …*

Ich möchte ein Zimmer
mit …

bathroom	*baat*	Bad
shower	*du-sheh*	Dusche
television	*fehrn-say-ehn*	Fernsehen
view	*ows-zikht*	Aussicht

I'm going to stay for …
> *ikh blai-beh …*

Ich bleibe …

one day	*ai-neh nahkht*	eine Nacht
two days	*tsvai nakh-teh*	zwei Nächte
one week	*ai-neh vo-kheh*	eine Woche

Do you have identification?
*ker-nehn zee zikh
ows-vai-zehn?*

Können Sie sich ausweisen?

Your membership card, please.
mit-ghleets-ows-vais, bi-teh

Mitgliedsausweis, bitte.

Sorry, we're full.
*ehnt-shul-di-ghung, vir
haa-behn kai-neh tsi-mehr
frai*

Entschuldigung, wir haben
keine Zimmer frei.

How long will you be staying?
vee lahng-eh blai-behn zee?

Wie lange bleiben Sie?

How many nights?
vee-fee-leh nakh-teh?

Wieviele Nächte?

It's ... per day/per person.
*ehs kos-teht ... proh
nahkht/proh pehr-zohn*

Es kostet ... pro Nacht/pro
Person.

How much is it per night/per
person?
*vee-feel kos-teht ehs proh
nahkht/proh pehr-zohn?*

Wieviel kostet es pro
Nacht/pro Person?

Can I see it?
kahn ikh ehs zay-ehn?

Kann ich es sehen?

Are there any others?
*haa-behn zee nokh
ahn-deh-reh?*

Haben Sie noch andere?

Is there anything cheaper?
*ghipt ehs eht-vahs
bi-li-ghehr-ehs?*

Gibt es etwas Billigeres?

Can I see the bathroom?
kahn ikh dahs baat zay-ehn?

Kann ich das Bad sehen?

Is there a reduction for
students/children?
 *ghipt ehs ehr-**ma**-si-ghung
 für shtu-**dehn**-tehn/**kin**-
 dehr?*

Gibt es Ermäßigung für
Studenten/Kinder?

Does it include breakfast?
 *ist **frü**-shtük in-beh-ghri-
 fehn?*

Ist Frühstück inbegriffen?

It's fine, I'll take it.
 *ehs ist ghut, ikh **nay**-meh
 ehs*

Es ist gut, ich nehme es.

I'm not sure how long I'm
staying.
 *ikh vais nikht, vee **lahng**-eh
 ikh **blai**-beh*

Ich weiß nicht, wie lange
ich bleibe.

Is there a lift?
 *ghipt ehs **ai**-nehn lift?*

Gibt es einen Lift?

Where is the bathroom?
 voh ist dahs baat?

Wo ist das Bad?

Is there hot water all day?
 *ghipt ehs dayn **ghahn**-tsehn
 taak **vahrm**-ehs vah-sehr?*

Gibt es den ganzen Tag
warmes Wasser?

Do you have a safe where I
can leave my valuables?
 *haa-behn zee **ai**-nehn sayf,
 in daym ikh **mai**-neh vehrt-
 zah-khehn **lah**-sehn kahn?*

Haben Sie einen Safe, in
dem ich meine Wertsachen
lassen kann?

Is there somewhere to wash
clothes?
 *kahn mahn **ir**-ghehnt-voh
 va-sheh **vah**-shehn?*

Kann man irgendwo
Wäsche waschen?

Can I use the kitchen?
*kahn ikh dee **kü**-kheh beh-**nu**-tsehn?*

Kann ich die Küche benutzen?

Can I use the telephone?
*kahn ikh dahs teh-leh-**fohn** beh-**nu**-tsehn?*

Kann ich das Telefon benutzen?

Requests & Complaints

Please wake me up at …
*bi-teh **veh**-kehn zee mikh um …*

Bitte wecken Sie mich um …

The room needs to be cleaned.
*main **tsi**-mehr ist nikht gheh-**mahkht***

Mein Zimmer ist nicht gemacht.

Please change the sheets.
*vekh-zehln zee bi-teh dee **beht**-va-sheh*

Wechseln Sie bitte die Bettwäsche.

I can't open/close the window.
*ikh kahn dahs **fehn**-stehr nikht owf-mah-khehn/**tsu**-mah-khehn*

Ich kann das Fenster nicht aufmachen/zumachen.

I've locked myself out of my room.
*ikh **haa**-beh mikh ows **mai**-nehm **tsi**-mehr ows-gheh-shpehrt*

Ich habe mich aus meinem Zimmer ausgesperrt.

The toilet won't flush.
*dee **shpü**-lung in dayr to-ah-**leh**-teh fungk-tsi-o-**neert** nikht*

Die Spülung in der Toilette funktioniert nicht.

GERMAN

I don't like this room.
*dahs **tsi**-mehr gheh-**falt** mir nikht* Das Zimmer gefällt mir nicht.

It's too …
ehs ist tsu … Es ist zu …

small	*klain*	klein
noisy	*lowt*	laut
dark	***dung**-kehl*	dunkel
expensive	***toy**-ehr*	teuer

Some Useful Phrases

I am/We are leaving now.
*ikh **rai**-zeh/vir **rai**-zehn yehtst* Ich reise/Wir reisen jetzt.

I would like to pay the bill.
*kahn ikh **bi**-teh dee **rehkh**-nung **haa**-behn?* Kann ich bitte die Rechnung haben?

name	***naa**-meh*	Name
surname	***nahkh**-naa-meh*	Nachname
room number	***tsi**-mehr-nu-mehr*	Zimmernummer

Some Useful Words

address	*ah-**dreh**-seh*	Adresse
air-conditioned	*mit **kli**-mah-ahn-laa-gheh*	mit Klimaanlage
balcony	*bahl-**kon***	Balkon
bath	*baat*	Bad
bed	*beht*	Bett
bill	***rehkh**-nung*	Rechnung

blanket	*vol-deh-keh*	Wolldecke
candle	*kehr-tseh*	Kerze
chair	*shtul*	Stuhl
clean	*zow-behr*	sauber
cupboard	*shrahngk*	Schrank
dark	*dung-kehl*	dunkel
dirty	*shmut-tsikh*	schmutzig
double bed	*do-pehl-beht*	Doppelbett
electricity	*eh-lehk-trits-i-tairt*	Elektrizität
excluding …	*ow-sehr/ows-ghehn-no-mehn* …	außer/ausgenommen …
fan	*vehn-ti-laa-tor*	Ventilator
… included	… *in-beh-ghri-fehn*	… inbegriffen
key	*shlü-sehl*	Schlüssel
lift (elevator)	*lift*	Lift
light bulb	*glü-bir-neh*	Glühbirne
lock (n)	*shlos*	Schloß
mattress	*mah-trah-tseh*	Matratze
mirror	*shpee-ghehl*	Spiegel
padlock	*for-hang-eh-shlos*	Vorhängeschloß
pillow	*ki-sehn*	Kissen
quiet	*ru-ikh*	ruhig
room (in hotel)	*tsi-mehr*	Zimmer
sheet	*beht-laa-kehn*	Bettlaken
shower	*du-sheh*	Dusche
soap	*zai-feh*	Seife
suitcase	*ko-fehr*	Koffer
swimming pool	*shvim-baat*	Schwimmbad
table	*tish*	Tisch
toilet	*to-ah-leh-teh*	Toilette

GERMAN

toilet paper	*to-ah-**leh**-tehn-pah-peer*	Toilettenpapier
towel	***hahnt**-tukh*	Handtuch
water	***vah**-sehr*	Wasser
cold water	*kahl-tehs **vah**-sehr*	kaltes Wasser
hot water	*vahrm-ehs **vah**-sehr*	warmes Wasser
window	***fehn**-stehr*	Fenster

Around Town

I'm looking for ...
*ikh **zu**-kheh ...* Ich suche ...

the art gallery	*dee **kunst**-ghah-leh-ree*	die Kunstgallerie
a bank	*ai-neh bahngk*	eine Bank
the church	*dee **kir**-kheh*	die Kirche
the city centre	*dee **i**-nehn-shtaht*	die Innenstadt
the ... embassy	*dee ... **boht**-shahft*	die ... Botschaft
my hotel	*main hoh-**tehl***	mein Hotel
the market	*dayn mahrkt*	den Markt
the museum	*dahs mu-**zay**-um*	das Museum
the police	*dee po-li-**tsai***	die Polizei
the post office	*dahs **post**-ahmt*	das Postamt
a public toilet	*ai-neh **er**-fehnt-likh-eh to-ah-**leh**-teh*	eine öffentliche Toilette
the telephone centre	*dee teh-leh-**fohn**-tsehn-trah-leh*	die Telefonzen-trale
the tourist infor-mation office	*dahs frehm-dehn-fehr-**kehrz**-bü-roh*	das Fremdenver-kehrsbüro

What time does it open?
*um vee-**feel** ur mahkht ehs owf?* Um wieviel Uhr macht es auf?

What time does it close?
*um vee-**feel** ur mahkht ehs tsu?*
Um wieviel Uhr macht es zu?

What is the name of …?
vee haist …?
Wie heißt …?

his street   *dee-zeh **shtrah**-seh*   diese Straße
his suburb   *dee-zehr **for**-ort*   dieser Vorort

For directions, see the Getting Around section, page 176.

For directions, see the Getting Around section, page 176.

GERMAN

At the Bank

I want to exchange some money.
*ikh **merkh**-teh ghehlt **um**-tow-shehn*
Ich möchte Geld umtauschen.

I want to change some traveller's cheques.
*ikh **merkh**-teh **rai**-zeh-sheks **ain**-ler-zehn*
Ich möchte Reiseschecks einlösen.

What is the exchange rate?
*vee ist dayr **vehkh**-sehl-kurs?*
Wie ist der Wechselkurs?

How many marks per dollar?
*vee-**fee**-leh mahrk für **ai**-nehn do-lahr?*
Wieviele Mark für einen Dollar?

Can I have money transferred here from my bank?
*kahn ikh ghehlt ows **mai**-nehr bahngk ü-behr-vai-zehn **lah**-sehn?*
Kann ich Geld aus meiner Bank überweisen lassen?

When will it arrive?
*vahn virt ehs **ahn**-koh-mehn?*   Wann wird es ankommen?

Has my money arrived yet?
*ist main ghehlt shon **ahn**-ghe-ko-mehn?*   Ist mein Geld schon angekommen?

bank draft	*trah-teh*	Tratte
bank notes	***bahngk**-noh-tehn*	Banknoten
cashier	*kah-**seer**-ehr-in*	Kassiererin (f)
	*kah-**seer**-ehr*	Kassierer (m)
coins	***mün**-tsehn*	Münzen
commission	*gheh-**bür***	Gebühr
credit card	*kreh-**deet**-kahr-teh*	Kreditkarte
exchange office	***vehkh**-sehl-shtu-beh*	Wechselstube
loose change	***klain**-ghehlt*	Kleingeld
signature	***un**-tehr-shrift*	Unterschrift

At the Post Office

I would like to send …
*ikh **merkh**-teh … **zehn**-dehn*   Ich möchte … senden.

a letter	***ai**-nehn breef*	einen Brief
a postcard	***ai**-neh **pohst**-kahr-teh*	eine Postkarte
a parcel	*ain pah-**kayt***	ein Paket
a telegram	*ain teh-leh-**ghrahm***	ein Telegramm

I would like some stamps.
*ikh **merkh**-teh **breef**-mahr-kehn **kow**-fehn*   Ich möchte Briefmarken kaufen.

How much is the postage?
*vee-**feel** **kos**-teht dahs **por**-to?*

Wieviel kostet das Porto?

How much does it cost to send this to …?
*vee-**feel** **kos**-teht ehs, dahs nahkh … tsu **zehn**-dehn?*

Wieviel kostet es, das nach … zu senden?

an aerogram	*ai-nehn **luft**-post-laikht-breef*	einen Luftpost-leichtbrief
air mail	*pehr **luft**-post*	per Luftpost
envelope	***um**-shlaak*	Umschlag
mailbox	***breef**-kahs-tehn*	Briefkasten
parcel	*pah-**kayt***	Paket
registered mail	*payr **ain**-shrai-behn*	per Einschreiben
surface mail	*gheh-**vern**-likh-eh pohst*	gewöhnliche Post

GERMAN

Telephone

I want to make a long-distance call to …
*bi-teh ain **fehrn**-gheh-shprakh nahkh …*

Bitte ein Ferngespräch nach …

The number is …
*dee **nu**-mehr ist …*

Die Nummer ist …

I want to speak for three minutes.
*ikh **merkh**-teh drai mi-**nu**-tehn lahng **shpreh**-khen*

Ich möchte drei Minuten lang sprechen.

How much does a three-minute call cost?

*vee-**feel** kos-teht ain drai mi-**nu**-tehn gheh-**shprakh**?*

Wieviel kostet ein drei Minuten Gespräch?

How much does each extra minute cost?

*vee-**feel** kos-stet **yay**-deh tsu-**zats**-likh-eh mi-**nu**-teh?*

Wieviel kostet jede zusätzliche Minute?

I would like to speak to Mrs Schmidt.

*ikh **merkh**-teh frow shmit **shpreh**-khen*

Ich möchte Frau Schmidt sprechen.

I want to make a reverse-charges phone call.

*ikh **merkh**-teh ain **air**-gheh-shprakh*

Ich möchte ein R-Gespräch.

It's engaged.

*ehs ist beh-**zetst***

Es ist besetzt.

I've been cut off.

*ikh bin un-tehr-**bro**-khen **vor**-dehn*

Ich bin unterbrochen worden.

Sightseeing

Do you have a guidebook/street map?

haa-behn zee ai-nehn rai-zeh-fü-rehr/shtaht-plahn?

Haben Sie einen Reiseführer/Stadtplan?

What are the main attractions?

*vahs zint dee **howpt**-zay-ehns-vür-dikh-kai-tehn?*

Was sind die Hauptsehenswürdigkeiten?

What is that?
vahs ist dahs?   Was ist das?

How old is it?
vee ahlt ist dahs?   Wie alt ist das?

Can I take photographs?
dahrf ikh foh-to-ghrah-fee-rehn?   Darf ich fotografieren?

What time does it open/close?
vahn mahkht ehs owf/tsu?   Wann macht es auf/zu?

ancient	*ahlt*	alt
archaeological	*ahr-kha-o-loh-ghish*	archäologisch
beach	*shtrahnt*	Strand
building	*gheh-boy-deh*	Gebäude
castle	*shlos*	Schloß
cathedral	*dohm*	Dom
church	*kir-kheh*	Kirche
concert hall	*kon-tsehrt-ha-leh*	Konzerthalle
library	*bi-bli-oh-tehk*	Bibliothek
main square	*howpt-plahts*	Hauptplatz
market	*mahrkt*	Markt
monastery	*klo-stehr*	Kloster
monument	*dehngk-mahl*	Denkmal
mosque	*mo-shay*	Moschee
old city	*ahlt-shtaht*	Altstadt
opera house	*oh-pehrn-hows*	Opernhaus
palace	*pah-lahst*	Palast
ruins	*ru-ee-nehn*	Ruinen
stadium	*shtaa-di-on*	Stadion
statues	*shtaa-tu-ehn*	Statuen
synagogue	*si-nah-ghoh-gheh*	Sinagoge

| temple | *tehm*-pehl | Tempel |
| university | *u-ni-vehr-si-**tairt*** | Universität |

Entertainment

What's there to do in the evenings?
*vahs kahn mahn aa-behnts un-tehr-**nay**-mehn?* — Was kann man abends unternehmen?

Are there any discos?
ghipt ehs heer dis-kohs? — Gibt es hier Discos?

Are there places where you can hear local folk music?
*kahn mahn heer ir-**ghehnt**-voh ert-li-kheh **folks**-mu-zeek **her**-rehn?* — Kann man hier irgendwo örtliche Volksmusik hören

How much does it cost to get in?
*vee-**feel ko**-steht dayr ain-trit?* — Wieviel kostet der Eintritt?

cinema	*kee*-noh	Kino
concert	kon-*tsehrt*	Konzert
discotheque	*dis*-koh	Disco
theatre	tay-*aa*-tehr	Theater

In the Country
Weather

What's the weather like?
*vee ist dahs **veh**-tehr?* — Wie ist das Wetter?

Will it rain?
*virt ehs **raygh**-nehn?* — Wird es regnen?

Will it snow?

*virt ehs **shnai**-yehn?* Wird es schneien?

The weather is … today.

*dahs **veh**-tehr ist **hoy**-teh …* Das Wetter ist heute …

Will it be … tomorrow?

*virt ehs **mor**-ghehn … zain?* Wird es morgen … sein?

cloudy	*vol-kikh*	wolkig
cold	*kahlt*	kalt
fine	*shern*	schön
foggy	*nay-blikh*	neblig
frosty	*fro-stikh*	frostig
hot	*hais*	heiß
windy	*vin-dikh*	windig

GERMAN

Camping

Am I allowed to camp here?

*kahn ikh heer **tsehl**-tehn?* Kann ich hier zelten?

Is there a campsite nearby?

*ghipt ehs in dayr **nay**-yeh* Gibt es in der Nähe einen
*ai-nehn **kehm**-ping-plahts?* Campingplatz?

backpack	*ruk-zahk*	Rucksack
can opener	*doh-zehn-erf-nehr*	Dosenöffner
compass	*kom-pahs*	Kompaß
crampons	*shtaig-ai-zehn*	Steigeisen
firewood	*brehn-holts*	Brennholz
gas cartridge	*ghaas-flah-sheh*	Gasflasche
hammock	*hang-eh-mah-teh*	Hängematte
ice axe	*ais-pi-kehl*	Eispickel
mattress	*mah-trah-tseh*	Matratze

penknife	*tah-shehn-meh-sehr*	Taschenmesser
rope	*zail*	Seil
tent	*tsehlt*	Zelt
tent pegs	*tsehlt-hay-ring-eh*	Zeltheringe
torch (flashlight)	*tah-shehn-lahm-peh*	Taschenlampe
sleeping bag	*shlaaf-zahk*	Schlafsack
stove	*hayrt*	Herd
water bottle	*fehlt-flah-sheh*	Feldflasche

Food

Germans love a big breakfast. Wherever you stay in all Germa speaking areas, breakfast will almost always be included as p of the price. Even at cheap hotels you may get ham, sausa herrings, boiled eggs, bread rolls, and fresh fruit, as well coffee, milk and fruit juice. Some Germans have a 'seco breakfast' *(zweites Frühstück)* mid-morning, which can be l a smaller version of the earlier breakfast, only sometimes w beer; or it may be just a morning tea with cakes and coffee.

Traditionally lunch is the biggest meal of all, with din often being like a small breakfast – some eating places, in fa have a main menu for lunch and a smaller one for the eveni However, at most restaurants (called a *Restaurant* or *Gaststä* you can get a large dinner if you want.

Ethnic German food tends to be filling – lots of meat, es cially pork and chicken. Offal is quite common. Pickles (l sauerkraut-pickled cabbage), rather than fresh vegetables, very popular. And of course sausage – you'll see lots of sna bars (called an *Imbiß* or *Schnellimbiß*) basically just selling a ra of sausages. Now there are also all sorts of Asian and Turk restaurants and takeaways; and, of course, the international fa food chains.

Some areas, especially southern Germany and Austria, are renowned for their cakes and pastries – you are probably already familiar with apple strudel *(Apfelstrudel)* and Black Forest cake *(Schwarzwälder Kirschtorte)*. Vienna has been called the caffé capital of the world, with an unbelievable array of elegant establishments to visit for coffee and cake.

Pubs (a *Bierstube*) are popular and similar to those in England or Australia. They generally sell snacks and light food.

Restaurants normally have a menu displayed outside, so you can figure out what it all means first! Many offer a good-value set menu (a *Gedeck* or *Tagesmenü*). You do not usually wait to be seated when you enter, and it is common in less expensive restaurants for other people to sit at your table. The bill at the end of a meal always includes tax and service charge; however, you can leave a small tip – about 5% – if the service has been really good.

GERMAN

breakfast	*frü-shtük*	Frühstück
lunch	*mi-tahg-eh-sehn*	Mittagessen
dinner	*aa-behnt-eh-sehn*	Abendessen

Table for ..., please.
   ai-nehn tish für ..., bi-teh   Einen Tisch für ..., bitte.
Can I see the menu please?
   kahn ikh bi-teh dee shpai-   Kann ich bitte die
   zeh-kahr-teh haa-behn?   Speisekarte haben?
I would like the set lunch,
please.
   ikh ha-teh ghehrn dahs   Ich hätte gern das
   taa-ghehs-meh-nü bi-teh   Tagesmenü bitte.
What does it include?
   vahs ehnt-halt dahs?   Was enthält das?

Is service included in the bill?
*ist dee beh-**dee**-nung* Ist die Bedienung
***in**-beh-ghri-fehn?* inbegriffen?
Not too spicy please.
***bi**-teh nikht zayr **vür**-tsikh* Bitte nicht sehr würzig.

an ashtray	*ain **ah**-shehn-beh-khehr*	ein Aschenbecher
the bill	*dee **rehkh**-nung*	die Rechnung
a cup	*ai-neh **tah**-seh*	eine Tasse
dessert	***nahkh**-shpai-zeh*	Nachspeise
a drink	*ain geh-**trangk***	ein Getränk
a fork	*ai-neh **ghaa**-behl*	eine Gabel
fresh	*frish*	frisch
a glass	*ain ghlaas*	ein Glas
a knife	*ain **meh**-sehr*	ein Messer
a plate	*ain **teh**-lehr*	ein Teller
spicy	***vür**-tsikh*	würzig
a spoon	*ain **ler**-fehl*	ein Löffel
stale	*ahlt*	alt
sweet	*züs*	süß
teaspoon	***tay**-ler-fehl*	Teelöffel
toothpick	***tsaan**-shto-khehr*	Zahnstocher

Vegetarian Meals

I am a vegetarian.
*ikh bin veh-gheh-**taa**-ri-ehr-in* Ich bin Vegetarierin. (f)
*ikh bin veh-gheh-**taa**-ri-ehr* Ich bin Vegetarier. (m)
I don't eat meat.
*ikh **eh**-seh kain flaish* Ich esse kein Fleisch.

I don't eat chicken, or fish, or ham.

*ikh **eh**-seh kain **hün**-khehn, **kai**-nehn fish, unt **kai**-nehn shing-kehn*

Ich esse kein Hühnchen, keinen Fisch, und keinen Schinken.

Breakfast

fried egg	*Spiegelei*
ham	*Schinken*
honey	*Honig*
jam	*Marmelade*
sausage	*Wurst*
scrambled eggs	*Rühreier*

Staples & Condiments

bread	*Brot*
butter	*Butter*
cheese	*Käse*
mustard	*Senf*
noodles	*Nudeln*
pepper	*Pfeffer*
rice	*Reis*
rolls	*Brötchen*
salt	*Salz*
tomato sauce	*Tomatenketchup*

Appetisers & Snacks — Vorspeisen

Belegtes Brot	open sandwich
Kleine/Kalte Gerichte	small/cold dishes
Pfannkuchen	pancake
Pilze	mushrooms

GERMAN

Rollmops	pickled herrings
Russische Eier	eggs with mayonnaise
Schnitten	selection of cold meats and vegetables
Wurst	sausage
Blutwurst	blood sausage
Bockwurst	pork sausage
Bratwurst	fried pork sausage
Leberwurst	liver sausage
Weißwurst	veal sausage
Zwiebelwurst	liver-and-onion sausage

Soups

Bauernsuppe	'farmer's soup', cabbage and sausage
Erbsensuppe	pea soup
Fleischbrühe	consommé
Gemüsesuppe or *Frühlingssuppe*	vegetable soup
Graupensuppe	barley soup
Hühnersuppe	chicken soup
Tomatensuppe	tomato soup

Meat & Seafood

Fischgerichte	fish dishes
Fleischgerichte	meat dishes
Hauptgerichte	main courses
Backhähnchen	fried chicken
Beefsteak	hamburger
Brathuhn	roast chicken
Fisch	fish
Frikadellen	meatballs
Hackbraten	meatloaf

Hasenpfeffer	hare stew with mushrooms and onions
Holsteiner Schnitzel	veal with fried egg, accompanied by seafood
Kalbfleisch	veal
Kohlroulade	cabbage leaves stuffed with minced meat
Königsberger Klops	meatballs in a sour-cream-and-caper sauce
Kotelette	chops
Kutteln	tripe
Labskaus	thick meat-and-potato stew
Leber	liver
Ragout	stew
Rindfleisch	beef
Schlachtplatte	selection of pork and sausage
Schmorbraten	beef pot roast
Schweinebraten	roast pork
Schweinefleisch	pork
Wiener Schnitzel	crumbed veal
Zunge	tongue

GERMAN

Vegetables	**Gemüse**
beans	*Bohnen*
beetroot	*rote Beete*
cabbage	*Kohl*
carrots	*Karotten*
cauliflower	*Blumenkohl*
chips (French fries)	*Pommes frites*
cucumber, gherkins	*Gurken*
lettuce	*Salat*
onions	*Zwiebeln*
peas	*Erbsen*

potato salad	*Kartoffelsalat*
potatoes	*Kartoffeln*
mashed potatoes	*Kartoffelbrei*
fried potatoes	*Bratkartoffeln*
pumpkin	*Kürbis*
red cabbage	*Rotkohl*
salad	*grüner Salat*
tomatoes	*Tomaten*

Methods of Cooking

baked	*gebacken*
boiled	*gekocht*
cooked (fried, roasted, grilled or baked)	*gebraten*
in the (Vienna) style	*(Wiener) Art*
rare	*englisch*
smoked	*geräuchert*
stuffed	*gefüllt*
well-done	*gut durchgebraten*
with	*… mit …*

Dessert & Pastries — Nachspeisen und Kuchen

Apfelstrudel	apple strudel
Berliner Pfannkuchen	jam doughnut
Eis	ice cream
Königstorte	rum-flavoured fruit cake
Schwarzwälder Kirschtorte	Black Forest cake (chocolate layer cake filled with cream and cherries)
Spekulatius	almond biscuits
Torte	layer cake

Drinks – Nonalcoholic

apple juice	*Apfelsaft*
coffee	*Kaffee*
Vienna coffee (black, topped with whipped cream)	*Einspänner*
white coffee	*Milchkaffee*
fruit juice	*Fruchtsaft*
milkshake	*Milchshake*
mineral water (without bubbles)	*Mineralwasser (ohne Kohlensäure)*
peppermint tea	*Pfefferminztee*
tea	*Tee*
water	*Wasser*
with/without	*mit/ohne*
cream	*Sahne*
milk	*Milch*
sugar	*Zucker*

Drinks – Alcoholic

apple brandy	*Apfelschnaps*
apple cider	*Apfelwein*
beer	*Bier*
bitter	*Altbier*
malt beer, similar to stout	*Malzbier*
dark/strong	*Bock/Starkbier*
type of lager	*Pilsener*
made with wheat	*Weizenbier*
brandy	*Weinbrand*
champagne	*Sekt*
cherry brandy	*Kirschwasser*
spirit made from grain, often drunk after a meal	*Schnaps*

GERMAN

wine		*Wein*
chilled		*gekühlt*
dry		*trocken*
late harvest		*Spätlese*
mulled wine		*Glühwein*
red wine		*Rotwein*
sweet		*süß*
white wine		*Weißwein*
with ice		*mit Eis*

Shopping

How much is it?
*vee-**feel** **ko**-steht ehs?*   Wieviel kostet es?

bookshop	**bukh**-*hahnt-lung*	Buchhandlung
camera shop	**foh**-*to-gheh-shaft*	Fotogeschäft
clothing store	*beh-**klai**-dungs-gheh-shaft*	Bekleidungs-geschäft
delicatessen	*deh-li-kah-**teh**-sehn-gheh-shaft*	Delikatessen-geschäft
department store	**vaa**-*rehn-hows*	Warenhaus
laundry	**va**-*sheh-rai*	Wäscherei
market	*mahrkt*	Markt
newsagency/ stationer's	**tsai**-*tungs-hant-lehr/* **shraip**-*vah-rehn-gheh-shaft*	Zeitungshändler/ Schreibwaren-geschäft
pharmacy	*ah-po-**tay**-keh*	Apotheke
shoeshop	**shu**-*gheh-shaft*	Schuhgeschäft
souvenir shop	*zu-veh-**neer**-lah-dehn*	Souvenirladen

| supermarket | *zu-pehr-markt* | Supermarkt |
| vegetable shop | *gheh-mü-zeh-hahnt-lung* | Gemüsehandlung |

I would like to buy …
*ikh **merkh**-teh … **kow**-fehn*
Ich möchte … kaufen.

Do you have others?
***haa**-behn zee nokh **ahn**-deh-reh?*
Haben Sie noch andere?

I don't like it.
*ehs gheh **falt** mir nikht*
Es gefällt mir nicht.

Can I look at it?
***ker**-nehn zee ehs mir **tsai**-ghehn?*
Können Sie es mir zeigen?

I'm just looking.
*ikh **show**-eh mikh nur um*
Ich schaue mich nur um.

Can you write down the price?
***ker**-nehn zee dayn prais **owf**-shrai-behn?*
Können Sie den Preis aufschreiben?

Do you accept credit cards?
***nay**-mehn zee kreh-**deet**-kahr-tehn?*
Nehmen Sie Kreditkarten?

Could you lower the price?
***ker**-nehn zee dayn prais reh-du-**tsee**-rehn?*
Können Sie den Preis reduzieren?

I don't have much money.
*ikh **haa**-beh nur **vay**-nikh ghehlt*
Ich habe nur wenig Geld.

Can I help you?
*kahn ikh **ee**-nehn **hehl**-fehn?*
Kann ich Ihnen helfen?

GERMAN

Anything else?
*zonst nokh **eht**-vahs?*   Sonst noch etwas?

Would you like it wrapped?
*zoll ikh ehs **ee**-nehn*   Soll ich es Ihnen
***ain**-vi-kehln?*   einwickeln?

Sorry, this is the only one.
*ehnt-**shul**-di-ghung, dahs*   Entschuldigung, das ist das
*ist dahs **ain**-tsi-gheh*   einzige.

How much/many do you
want?
*vee-**feel**/vee-**fee**-leh*   Wieviel/Wieviele möchten
***merkh**-tehn zee?*   Sie?

Souvenirs

beer stein	***beer**-kruk*	Bierkrug
cuckoo clock	***ku**-kuks-ur*	Kuckucksuhr
earrings	***ohr**-ring-eh*	Ohrringe
embroidery	***shti**-keh-rai*	Stickerei
handicraft	*kunst-**hahnt**-vehrk*	Kunsthandwerk
necklace	***hahls**-keh-teh*	Halskette
porcelain	*por-tseh-**laan***	Porzellan
ring	*ring*	Ring

Clothing

clothing	***klai**-dung*	Kleidung
coat	***mahn**-tehl*	Mantel
dress	*klait*	Kleid
jacket	***yah**-keh*	Jacke
jumper (sweater)	*pul-**oh**-vehr*	Pullover
shirt	*hehmt*	Hemd
shoes	***shu**-eh*	Schuhe

| skirt | *rok* | Rock |
| trousers | **hoh**-*zeh* | Hose |

It doesn't fit.
ehs pahst nikht   Es paßt nicht.

It is too …
ehs ist tsu …   Es ist zu …

big/small	*ghrohs/klain*	groß/klein
short/long	*kurts/lahng*	kurz/lang
tight/loose	*ehng/vait*	eng/weit

GERMAN

Materials

brass, of	*ows **meh**-sing*	aus Messing
cotton	**bowm**-*vo-leh*	Baumwolle
gold, of	*ows gholt*	aus Gold
handmade	*hahnt-gheh-**ahr**-bai-teht*	handgearbeitet
leather	**lay**-*dehr*	Leder
silk	**zai**-*deh*	Seide
silver, of	*ows **zil**-behr*	aus Silber
wool	**vo**-*leh*	Wolle

Toiletries

comb	*kahm*	Kamm
condoms	*kon-**doh**-meh*	Kondome
deodorant	*day-oh-do-**rahnt***	Deodorant
hairbrush	**haar**-*bür-steh*	Haarbürste
moisturising cream	**foykh**-*tikh-kaits-kray-meh*	Feuchtigkeitscreme
razor	*rah-**zeer**-meh-sehr*	Rasiermesser
sanitary napkins	**daa**-*mehn-bin-dehn*	Damenbinden
shampoo	*shahm-**pu***	Shampoo

GERMAN

shaving cream	*rah-zeer-kray-meh*	Rasiercreme
soap	*zai-feh*	Seife
sunblock cream	*sahn-blok-kray-meh*	Sunblockcreme
tampons	*tahm-pons*	Tampons
tissues	*pah-peer-tü-khehr*	Papiertücher
toilet paper	*to-ah-leh-tehn-pah-peer*	Toilettenpapier
toothbrush	*tsahn-bür-steh*	Zahnbürste
toothpaste	*tsahn-pah-stah*	Zahnpasta

Stationery & Publications

map	*kahr-teh*	Karte
newspaper	*tsai-tung*	Zeitung
newspaper in English	*tsai-tung owf ehng-lish*	Zeitung auf Englisch
novels in English	*roh-maa-neh owf ehng-lish*	Romane auf Englisch
paper	*pah-peer*	Papier
pen (ballpoint)	*ku-ghehl-shrai-behr*	Kugelschreiber
scissors	*shay-reh*	Schere

Photography

When will the photos be ready?

| *vahn wehr-dehn dee foh-tohs fehr-tikh zain?* | Wann werden die Fotos fertig sein? |

I'd like a film for this camera.

| *ikh merkh-teh ai-nehn film für dee-zeh kah-meh-rah* | Ich möchte einen Film für diese Kamera. |

B&W (film)	*shvahrts*-vais	schwarzweiß
camera	*kah*-meh-rah	Kamera
colour (film)	*fahrp*-film	Farbfilm
film	*film*	Film
flash	*blits*	Blitz
lens	*lin*-zeh	Linse
light meter	beh-*likh*-tungs-meh-seh	Belichtungsmesse

GERMAN

Smoking

A packet of cigarettes, please.
ai-neh **shahkh**-tehl
tsi-ghah-**reh**-tehn *bi*-teh

Eine Schachtel Zigaretten bitte.

Are these cigarettes strong/mild?
zint **dee**-zeh tsi-ghah-**reh**-tehn shtahrk/milt?

Sind diese Zigaretten stark/mild?

Do you have a light?
haa-behn zee **foy**-ehr?

Haben Sie Feuer?

cigarette papers	tsi-ghah-**reh**-tehn-pah-pee-reh	Zigarettenpapiere
cigarettes	tsi-ghah-**reh**-tehn	Zigaretten
filtered	mit **fil**-tehr	mit Filter
lighter	**foy**-ehr-tsoyk	Feuerzeug
matches	**shtraikh**-herl-tsehr	Streichhölzer
menthol	**mehn**-tol	Menthol
pipe	**pfai**-feh	Pfeife
tobacco (pipe)	**taa**-bahk (**pfai**-fehn-taa-bahk)	Tabak (Pfeifentabak)

GERMAN

Colours

black	*shvahrts*	schwarz
blue	*blow*	blau
brown	*brown*	braun
green	*ghrün*	grün
orange	*o-r-zheh*	orange
pink	**roh**-*zah*	rosa
purple	**lee**-*lah*	lila
red	*roht*	rot
white	*vais*	weiß
yellow	*ghelp*	gelb

Sizes & Comparisons

small	*klain*	klein
big	*ghrohs*	groß
heavy	*shvehr*	schwer
light	*laikht*	leicht
more	*mayr*	mehr
less (not as much/ not as many)	*nikht zoh feel/nikht zoh **fee**-leh*	nicht so viel/nicht so viele
too much/many	*tsu feel/tsu **fee**-leh*	zu viel/zu viele
many	***fee**-leh*	viele
enough	*gheh-**nuk***	genug
also	*owkh*	auch
a little bit	*ain **bis**-khehn*	ein bißchen

Health

Where is …?		
voh ist …?		Wo ist …?
the doctor	*dayr ahrtst*	der Arzt
the hospital	*dahs **krahng**-kehn-hows*	das Krankenhaus

| the chemist | *dee ah-po-tay-keh* | die Apotheke |
| the dentist | *dayr tsaan-ahrtst* | der Zahnarzt |

I am sick.
  ikh bin krahngk   Ich bin krank.
My friend is sick.
  mai-neh froyn-din/main   Meine Freundin (f)/Mein
  froynt ist krahngk   Freund (m) ist krank.
Could I see a female doctor?
  kahn ikh ai-neh arts-tin   Kann ich eine Ärztin
  shpreh-khehn?   sprechen?
What's the matter?
  voh faylt ehs?   Wo fehlt es?
Where does it hurt?
  voh haa-behn zee   Wo haben Sie Schmerzen?
  shmehr-tsehn?
It hurts here.
  ehs tut mir heer vay   Es tut hier weh.
My … hurts.
  mir tut … vay   Mir tut … weh.

GERMAN

Parts of the Body

arm	*dayr ahrm*	der Arm
back	*dayr rü-kehn*	der Rücken
chest	*dayr brust-korp*	der Brustkorb
ear	*dahs korp*	das Ohr
eye	*dahs ow-gheh*	das Auge
finger	*dayr fing-ehr*	der Finger
foot	*dayr fus*	der Fuß
hand	*dee hahnt*	die Hand
head	*dayr kopf*	der Kopf
heart	*dahs hehrts*	das Herz

GERMAN

knee	*dahs knee*	das Knie
leg	*dahs bain*	das Bein
liver	*dee **lay**-behr*	die Leber
nose	*dee **naa**-zeh*	die Nase
skin	*dee howt*	die Haut
teeth	*dee **tsair**-neh*	die Zähne

Ailments

I have …		
*ikh **haa**-beh …*		Ich habe …
an allergy	*ai-neh' ah-lehr-**ghee***	eine Allergie
anaemia	*ah-na-**mee***	Anämie
a blister	*ai-neh **blaa**-zeh*	eine Blase
a cold	*ai-neh ehr-**kal**-tung*	eine Erkältung
constipation	*fehr-**shtop**-fung*	Verstopfung
a cough	*hu-stehn*	Husten
diarrhoea	*durkh-fahl*	Durchfall
fever	*fee-behr*	Fieber
a headache	*kopf-shmehr-tsehn*	Kopfschmerzen
indigestion	*ai-neh maa-ghehn-fehr-shti-mung*	eine Magenver-stimmung
an infection	*ai-neh in-fek-tsi-**ohn***	eine Infektion
influenza	*dee **ghri**-peh*	die Grippe
lice	*loy-zeh*	Läuse
low/high blood pressure	*nee-dri-ghehn/**how**-ehn blut-druk*	niedrigen/hohen Blutdruck
a pain	*shmehr-tsehn*	Schmerzen
sore throat	*hahls-shmehr-tsehn*	Halsschmerzen
sprain	*ai-neh mus-kehl-tseh-rung*	eine Muskel-zerrung
sunburn	*zo-nehn-brahnt*	Sonnenbrand

| venereal disease | *ai*-neh gheh-**shlehkhts**-krahngk-hait | eine Geschlechts-krankheit |
| worms | *vür*-mehr | Würmer |

Some Useful Words & Phrases

I'm ...		Ich bin ...
ikh bin ...		
diabetic	di-ah-**bay**-ti-kehr-in	Diabetikerin (f)
	di-ah-**bay**-tik	Diabetiker (m)
epileptic	eh-pi-**lehp**-ti-keh-rin	Epileptikerin (f)
	eh-pi-**lehp**-ti-kehr	Epileptiker (m)
asthmatic	ahst-**maa**-ti-keh-rin	Asthmatikerin (f)
	ahst-**maa**-ti-kehr	Asthmatiker (m)

GERMAN

I'm allergic to antibiotics/penicillin.
*ikh bin **ghay**-ghehn ahn-ti-bi-**oh**-ti-kah/peh-ni-**tsi**-lin ah-**lehr**-ghish*
Ich bin gegen Antibiotika/Penizillin allergisch.

I'm pregnant.
*ikh bin **shvahng**-ehr*
Ich bin schwanger.

I'm on the pill.
*ikh **nay**-meh dee **pi**-leh*
Ich nehme die Pille.

I haven't had my period for ... months.
*ikh **haa**-beh zait ... **moh**-nah-tehn **mai**-neh peh-ri-**oh**-deh nikht gheh-**hahbt***
Ich habe seit ... Monaten meine Periode nicht gehabt.

I have been vaccinated.
*ikh bin gheh-**impft***
Ich bin geimpft.

I feel better/worse.
*ikh **fü**-leh mikh **beh**-sehr/*   Ich fühle mich besser/
***shli**-mehr*   schlimmer.

accident	*un-fahl*	Unfall
addiction	*zukht*	Sucht
antibiotics	*ahn-ti-bi-oh-ti-kah*	Antibiotika
antiseptic	*ahn-ti-sehp-ti-kum*	Antiseptikum
bandage	*fehr-bahnt*	Verband
blood test	*blut-proh-beh*	Blutprobe
contraceptive	*fehr-hü-tungs-mi-tehl*	Verhütungsmittel
injury	*fehr-leh-tsung*	Verletzung
medicine	*meh-di-tseen*	Medizin
menstruation	*mehn-stru-ah-tsi-ohn*	Menstruation
nausea	*ü-behl-kait*	Übelkeit
vitamins	*vi-tah-mee-neh*	Vitamine

At the Chemist
I need medication for …
*ikh **brow**-kheh **eht**-vahs*   Ich brauche etwas gegen ..
***ghay**-ghehn* …
I have a prescription.
*ikh **haa**-beh ain reh-**tsehpt***   Ich habe ein Rezept.

At the Dentist
I have a toothache.
*ikh **haa**-beh **tsaan**-shmehr-*   Ich habe Zahnschmerzen.
tsehn
I've lost a filling.
*ikh **haa**-beh **ai**-ne **fü**-lung*   Ich habe eine Füllung
*fehr-**lo**-rehn*   verloren.

I've broken a tooth.
*mir ist ain tsaan **ahp**-gheh-bro-khehn*

Mir ist ein Zahn abgebrochen.

My gums hurt.
*dahs **tsaan**-flaish tut mir vay*

Das Zahnfleisch tut mir weh.

I don't want it extracted.
*ikh vil een nikht **tsee**-yehn **lah**-sehn*

Ich will ihn nicht ziehen lassen.

Please give me an anaesthetic.
***ghay**-behn zee mir **bi**-teh **ai**-neh **shpri**-tseh*

Geben Sie mir bitte eine Spritze.

GERMAN

Time & Dates

What date is it today?
*dayr vee-**feel**-teh ist **hoy**-teh?*

Der wievielte ist heute?

What time is it?
vee shpayt ist ehs?

Wie spät ist es?

It is … o'clock.
ehs ist … ur

Es ist … Uhr.

in the morning	***mor**-ghehns*	morgens
in the afternoon	***nahkh**-mi-tahks*	nachmittags
in the evening	***aa**-behnts*	abends

Days of the Week

Monday	***mohn**-taak*	Montag
Tuesday	***deens**-taak*	Dienstag
Wednesday	***mit**-vokh*	Mittwoch

Thursday	*do*-nehrs-taak	Donnerstag
Friday	*frai*-taak	Freitag
Saturday	*zahms*-taak	Samstag
Sunday	*zon*-taak	Sonntag

Months

January	*yah*-nu-aar	Januar
February	*feh*-bru-aar	Februar
March	*marts*	März
April	ah-*pril*	April
May	*mai*	Mai
June	*yu*-ni	Juni
July	*yu*-li	Juli
August	*ow*-ghust	August
September	zehp-*tehm*-behr	September
October	ok-*toh*-behr	Oktober
November	noh-*vehm*-behr	November
December	day-*tsehm*-behr	Dezember

Seasons

summer	*zo*-mehr	Sommer
autumn	*hehrpst*	Herbst
winter	*vin*-tehr	Winter
spring	*frü*-ling	Frühling

Present

today	*hoy*-teh	heute
this morning	*hoy*-teh *mor*-ghehn	heute morgen
tonight	*hoy*-teh *aa*-behnt	heute abend
this week	*dee*-zeh *vo*-kheh	diese Woche
year	*dee*-zehs yaar	dieses Jahr
now	*yehtst*	jetzt

Past

yesterday	**gheh**-*stehrn*	gestern
day before yesterday	**for**-*gheh-stehrn*	vorgestern
yesterday morning	**gheh**-*stehrn* **mor**-*ghehn*	gestern morgen
last night	**leht**-*steh nahkht*	letzte Nacht
last week	**leht**-*steh vo-kheh*	letzte Woche
last year	**leht**-*stehs yaar*	letztes Jahr

Future

tomorrow	**mor**-*ghehn*	morgen
day after tomorrow	**ü**-*behr-mor-ghehn*	übermorgen
tomorrow morning	**mor**-*ghehn frü*	morgen früh
tomorrow afternoon/evening	**mor**-*ghehn* **nahkh**-*mi-tahk/***aa**-*behnt*	morgen nachmittag/abend
next week	**nakh**-*steh vo-kheh*	nächste Woche
next year	**nakh**-*stehs yaar*	nächstes Jahr

During the Day

afternoon	**nahkh**-*mi-tahk*	Nachmittag
day	*taak*	Tag
early	*frü*	früh
midnight	**mi**-*tehr-nahkht*	Mitternacht
morning	**mor**-*ghehn*	Morgen
night	*nahkht*	Nacht
noon	**mi**-*tahk*	Mittag
sundown	**zo**-*nehn-un-tehr-ghahng*	Sonnenuntergang
sunrise	**zo**-*nehn-owf-ghahng*	Sonnenaufgang

GERMAN

Numbers & Amounts

0	*nul*	null
1	*ains*	eins
2	*tsvai (tsvoh)*	zwei (zwo on the telephone)
3	*drai*	drei
4	*feer*	vier
5	*fünf*	fünf
6	*zehkhs*	sechs
7	**zee**-*behn*	sieben
8	*ahkht*	acht
9	*noyn*	neun
10	*tsayn*	zehn
11	*ehlf*	elf
12	*tsverlf*	zwölf
13	**drai**-*tsayn*	dreizehn
14	**feer**-*tsayn*	vierzehn
15	**fünf**-*tsayn*	fünfzehn
16	**zehkh**-*tsayn*	sechzehn
17	**zeep**-*tsayn*	siebzehn
18	**ahkht**-*tsayn*	achtzehn
19	**noyn**-*tsayn*	neunzehn
20	**tsvahn**-*tsikh*	zwanzig
30	**drai**-*sikh*	dreißig
40	**feer**-*tsikh*	vierzig
50	**fünf**-*tsikh*	fünfzig
60	**zehkh**-*tsikh*	sechzig
70	**zeep**-*tsikh*	siebzig
80	**ahkht**-*tsikh*	achtzig
90	**noyn**-*tsikh*	neunzig
100	**hun**-*dehrt*	hundert

GERMAN

1000	*tow*-zehnt	tausend
one million	*ai*-neh mi-li-*ohn*	eine Million
1st	*ehr*-steh	erste
2nd	*tsvai*-teh	zweite
3rd	*dri*-teh	dritte
¼	ain *feer*-tehl	ein Viertel
⅓	ain *dri*-tehl	ein Drittel
½	*ai*-neh *half*-teh	eine Hälfte
¾	drai *feer*-tehl	drei Viertel

GERMAN

Some Useful Words

a little (amount)	ain *bis*-khehn	ein bißchen
double	nokh *ain*-mahl zoh	noch einmal so (literally: 'the same again')
a dozen	ain *du*-tsehnt	ein Dutzend
Enough!	gheh-*nuk!*	Genug!
a few	ain paar	ein paar
less	*vay*-ni-ghehr	weniger
a lot, much	feel	viel
many	*fee*-leh	viele
more	mayr	mehr
once	*ain*-mahl	einmal
a pair	ain paar	ein Paar
percent	proh-*tsehnt*	Prozent
some	*ai*-ni-gheh	einige
too much	tsu feel	zu viel
twice	*tsvai*-mahl	zweimal

Abbreviations

A.A.	AA
Ausw.	ID
Bhf	Station
BRD	Federal Republic of Germany (old)
DB	German Federal Railways
DDR	German Democratic Republic (old)
DJH	Youth Hostel (name of association)
DM	German Mark
EU	EU
GB	UK
HPA or HA	GPO (Main Post Office)
Hr./Fr.	Mr/Mrs
KW	Short Wave
n. Chr./v. Chr.	AD/BC
N/S	Nth/Sth
p. Adr.	c/o
Str.	St/Rd/etc
U	Underground (Railway)
usw.	etc
vorm./nachm.	am/pm
z.B.	eg

GERMAN

HUNGARIAN

Hungarian

Introduction

Hungarian, or Magyar as it is known to the Magyars (wh
constitute 95% of the population in Hungary), is a unique lar
guage in Europe. The roots of this Finno-Ugric tongue and i
people lie in the lands east of the Ural mountain chain, fror
where, in around 2000 BC, there was a major migration west. I
the process, the group split, some moving north to Finland an
Estonia, and the others, the Ugric people, moving through t
Hungary. The original language was also split along with th
two groups. In the two and a half millennia from 'departure' t
the conquest of Hungary in 896, when seven Magyar tribes oc
cupied the Danube basin and the foundations of modern Hur
gary were laid, the Ugric language evolved. While it picked u
certain Persian, Turkish and Bulgar words along the way, i
developed into modern Hungarian which is now only spoken i
Hungary. Finnish is the nearest European relative, bearing som
resemblances in form and structure, but the two languages ar
mutually incomprehensible.

There is a Hungarian-speaking population of 10.6 millio
in Hungary, and a sizable ethnic Hungarian-speaking commu
nity around the borders: nearly two million in Romania, mostl
in Transylvania (and making up one of the largest ethni
minorities in Europe), some 600,000 in the Slovak Republi
half a million in Vojvodina and Croatia, and 200,000 in Ukrain

However daunting it may appear at first sight, there i
certain regularity and code to the language which, once graspe
can help enormously. Word formation is agglutinative, meanir
that you start with a 'root' and build on it.

228

Here are a few basics. The suffix 't' is added in the accusative case. Verb conjugations have two forms, definite and indefinite, and the whole language rests on a complex set of vowel-harmony rules which dictate which ending to use. The definite article ('the' in English) has two forms in Hungarian: 'az' before a word starting with a vowel, and 'a' before a consonant.

There is a complicated set of rules governing prepositions, which in Hungarian are actually word endings. In order to simplify this Lonely Planet language guide we generally omitted the wide variety of endings that could be used, which depend on general vowel harmony rules combined with specific cases. Although this makes for some grammatically incorrect sentences, such as 'Which bus goes Buda?', there should be no problems in being understood. For your information, some of the common endings you may see or hear are: -ba, -be, -ra, -re, -hoz, -hez, -höz, -nal, -nál and -nél.

For beginners, good pronunciation will get you further than good grammar, and Hungarians are delighted to hear any of their tongue emerge from a non-Magyar.

HUNGARIAN

Pronunciation

The rules are simple, and the actual pronunciation just takes a little practice. In the vast majority of words there is a slight stress on the first syllable. Each syllable after the first is given equal weight, even in the longest words. There are no diphthongs – each vowel is pronounced. Most double consonants should be lengthened to the point where you can just distinguish the two letters.

Vowels

a	somewhere in between 'a' and 'o', nearly the 'o' in 'hot' or the 'a' in 'was'
á	a longer and more open sound, like the 'a' in 'father'
e	as in 'set'
é	somewhere between 'a' and 'e', as in 'make'
i	short as in 'pit'
í	like a long double 'e', as in 'fleet'
o	rounded and short as in 'solitude', 'orange'
ó	long as in 'door'
ö	short and rounded as in 'worse'
ő	a lengthened **ö** as in 'world'
u	short as in 'group'
ú	long, as in 'blue', 'two'
ü	like a simple **u** but more rounded, as in the French 'rue'. Similar to the 'u' sound in 'few' but shorter. (Rendered as *ü* in our pronunciation guide.)
ű	a lengthened **ü**, similar to 'feud' (Rendered as *üü* in our pronunciation guide.)

Consonants

Only those consonants which differ greatly from the English pronunciation have been listed here.

c	an English 'ts' as in 'hats'
cs	like the 'ch' in 'church'
gy	like a combination of 'd' and 'j' as in 'jury'
j	pronounced as the 'y' in 'yellow'
ly	traditionally used in some words instead of **j**

HUNGARIAN

ny	as in 'new'
r	as in 'red' but a pointed sound
s	'sh' as in 'shower'
sz	an English 's' as in 'see'
ty	like a combination of 't' and 'ch', as in 'statue'
zs	a buzzing sound, as in 'pleasure'

Greetings & Civilities
Top 10 Useful Phrases ·

Hello.
yoh nah-pot kee-vaa-nok! — Jó napot kívánok!

Goodbye.
vi-sont-laa-taash-rah! — Viszontlátásra! (formal, common use)

si-ah! — Szia! (informal only)

Yes./No.
i-ghen/nem — Igen./Nem.

Excuse me.
bo-chaa-naht — Bocsánat.

May I? Do you mind?
le-het? — Lehet?

Sorry. (excuse me, forgive me)
bo-chaa-naht — Bocsánat.

Please.
keh-rem — Kérem.

Thank you.
ker-ser-nerm — Köszönöm.

Many thanks.
nah-djon ker-ser-nerm — Nagyon köszönöm.

HUNGARIAN

That's fine. You're welcome.
   rend-ben see-ve-shen   Rendben. Szívesen.

Greetings
Good morning!
   yoh regh-ghelt!   Jó reggelt!
Good afternoon!
   yoh nah-pot!   Jó napot!
Good evening/night!
   yoh esh-teht/ehy-sah-kaat! Jó estét/éjszakát!

How are you?
   hodj vahn?   Hogy van?
Well, thanks.
   ker-ser-nerm, yohl   Köszönöm, jól.

Forms of Address

Madam/Mrs	*herldj/as-sony*	Hölgy/Asszony
Sir/Mr	*oor*	Úr
Miss	*kish-as-sony*	Kisasszony
companion	*taarsh*	társ
friend	*bah-raat*	barát

Note: Hungarian names start with the family name.

Small Talk
Meeting People
What is your name?
   hodj heev-yaak?   Hogy hívják?

My name is ...
ah ne-vem ...   A nevem ...

I'd like to introduce you to ...
se-ret-nehm ernt   Szeretném önt
be-mu-taht-ni ...   bemutatni ...

I'm pleased to meet you.
er-rü-lerk hodj   Örülök, hogy megismerhetem.
meg-ish-mer-he-tem

I like .../I don't like ...
ne-kem tet-sik .../   Nekem tetszik .../
ne-kem nem tet-sik ...   Nekem nem tetszik ...

Age

How old are you?
ern haany eh-vesh?   Ön hány éves?

I am ... years old.
... eh-vesh vah-djok   ... éves vagyok.

Nationalities

Where are you from?
ern hon-nahn yertt?   Ön honnan jött?

Australia	*ah-ust-raa-li-ah*	Ausztrália
Canada	*kah-nah-dah*	Kanada
England	*ahn-ghli-ah*	Anglia
Ireland	*eer-or-saagh*	Irország
New Zealand	*ooy zeh-lahnd*	Új-Zéland
Scotland	*shkoh-tsi-ah*	Skócia
the USA	*ahz edje-shült*	Az Egyesült
	aallahm-ok	Államok
Wales	*vels*	Wales

Occupations

What do you do?
mi ah fogh-lahl-ko-zaa-shah?   Mi a foglalkozása?

I am a/an ...
... *vah-djok*   ... vagyok

artist	*müü-vehs*	művész
business person	*üz-let-em-ber* (m)	üzletember
	üz-let-as-sony (f)	üzletasszony
doctor	*or-vosh*	orvos
engineer	*mehr-nerk*	mérnök
farmer	*ghahz-dah*	gazda
journalist	*ooy-shaagh-ee-roh*	újságíró
lawyer	*yo-ghaas*	jogász
manual worker	*fi-zi-kahi mun-kaash*	fizikai munkás
mechanic	*se-re-loer*	szerelő
nurse	*aa-po-loh* (m)	ápoló'
	aa-po-loh-noer (f)	ápolónő
office worker	*iro-dah-i dol-gho-zoh*	irodai dolgozó
scientist	*tu-dohsh*	tudós
student	*di-aak*	diák
teacher	*tah-naar* (m)	tanár
	tah-naar-noer (f)	tanárnő
waiter	*pin-tsehr* (m)	pincér
	pin-tsehr-noer (f)	pincérnő
writer	*ee-roh*	író

Religion

What is your religion?
  mi-yen vahl-laa-shoo?   Milyen vallású?
I am not religious.
  nem vah-djok   Nem vagyok vallásos.
  vahl-laa-shosh

I am ...
  ... vah-djok   ... vagyok

Buddhist	*bud-hish-tah*	buddhista
Catholic	*kah-to-li-kush*	katolikus
Christian	*ke-res-tehny*	keresztény
Hindu	*hin-du*	hindu
Jewish	*zhi-doh*	zsidó
Muslim	*mu-zul-maan*	muzulmán

Family

Are you married?
  fehry-nehl vahn ? (f)   Férjnél van?
  noers? (m)   Nős?
I am single.
  hah-yah-don vah-djok (f)   Hajadon vagyok.
  noert len vah-djok (m)   Nőtlen vagyok.
I am married.
  fehry-nehl vah-djok (f)   Férjnél vagyok
  noersh vah-djok (m)   Nős vagyok.
How many children do you
have?
  haany djer-me-ke vahn?   Hány gyermeke van?

HUNGARIAN

I don't have any children.
  ninch djer-me-kem   Nincs gyermekem.
I have a daughter/a son.
  edj laa-nyom/fi-ahm vahn   Egy lányom/fiam van.
How many brothers/sisters
 do you have?
  haany baaty-ya/   Hány bátyja/nővére van?
  noer-veh-re vahn?
Is your husband/wife here?
  itt vahn ah fehr-ye/   Itt van a férje/felesége?
  fe-le-sheh-ghe?
Do you have a boyfriend/
girlfriend?
  vahn bah-raat-yah/   Van barátja/barátnője?
  bah-raat-noer-ye?

brother	*fioo-tesht-vehr*	fiútestvér
children	*dje-re-kek*	gyerekek
daughter	*laany*	lány
family	*chah-laad*	család
father	*ah-pah*	apa
grandfather	*nahdj-pah-pah*	nagypapa
grandmother	*nahdj-mah-mah*	nagymama
husband	*fehry*	férj
mother	*ah-nyah*	anya
sister	*le-aany-tesht-vehr*	leánytestvér
son	*fioo*	fiú
wife	*fe-le-shehgh*	feleség

HUNGARIAN

Feelings

I am sorry. (condolence)
shahy-naa-lom Sajnálom.
I am grateful.
haa-laash vah-djok Hálás vagyok.

(I am ...)

angry	*mehr-ghesh vah-djok*	Mérges vagyok.
cold	*faa-zom*	Fázom.
hot	*me-le-ghem vahn*	Melegem van.
happy	*bol-dogh vah-djok*	Boldog vagyok.
hungry	*eh-hesh vah-djok*	Éhes vagyok.
thirsty	*som-yahsh vah-djok*	Szomjas vagyok.
in a hurry	*shi-e-tek*	Sietek.
right	*yohl vah-djok*	Jól vagyok.
sad	*so-mo-roo vah-djok*	Szomorú.
sleepy	*aal-mosh vah-djok*	Álmos vagyok.
tired	*faa-rahdt vah-djok*	Fáradt vagyok.
well	*yohl vah-djok*	Jól vagyok.
worried	*ahgh-ghoh-dom*	Aggódom.

HUNGARIAN

Language Difficulties

Do you speak English?
be-sehl ahn-gho-lul? Beszél angolul?
Does anyone speak English?
be-sehl vah-lah-ki Beszél valaki angolul?
ahn-gho-lul?
I speak a little ...
ehn be-seh-lek edj Én beszélek egy kicsit ... ul/ül.
ki-chit ... ul/ul

I don't speak ...
   nem be-seh-lek ... ul/ül   Nem beszélek ... ul/ül

I (don't) understand.
   (nem) ehr-tem   (Nem) Értem.

Could you speak more
slowly please?
   keh-rem tud-nah lahsh-   Kérem, tudna
   shahb-ban be-sehl-ni?   lassabban beszélni?

Could you repeat that?
   megh-ish-meh-tel-neh?   Megismételné?

How do you say ...?
   hodj kell mon-dah-ni ...?   Hogy kell mondani ...?

What does ... mean?
   mit ye-lent ...?   Mit jelent ...?

HUNGARIAN

Some Useful Phrases

Sure.
   per-se   Persze.

Just a minute.
   edj pil-lah-naht   Egy pillanat.

It's (not) important.
   (nem) fon-tosh   (Nem) Fontos.

It's (not) possible.
   (nem) le-het   (Nem) Lehet.

Wait!
   vaar-yon!   Várjon!

Good luck!
   shok se-ren-cheht!   Sok szerencsét!

Signs

BAGGAGE COUNTER	CSOMAG
CUSTOMS	VÁMKEZELÉS
EMERGENCY EXIT	VÉSZKIJÁRAT
ENTRANCE	BEJÁRAT
EXIT	KIJÁRAT
FREE ADMISSION	SZABAD BELÉPÉS
HOT/COLD	MELEG/HIDEG
INFORMATION	INFORMÁCIÓ
NO ENTRY	TILOS BELÉPNI
NO SMOKING	TILOS A DOHÁNYZÁS
OPEN/CLOSED	NYITVA/ZÁRVA
PROHIBITED	TILOS
RESERVED	FOGLALT
TELEPHONE	TELEFON
TOILETS	WC or TOALETT

HUNGARIAN

Emergencies

POLICE	RENDŐRSÉG
POLICE STATION	RENDŐRŐRSZOBA

Help!
   she-gheet-shehgh!   Segítség!
It's an emergency!
   shüür-ghoersh!   Sűrgős!

There's been an accident!
bah-le-shet ter-tehnt!   Baleset történt!

Call a doctor!
heev-yon edj or-vosht!   Hívjon egy orvost!

Call an ambulance!
heev-yah ah men-toer-ket! Hívja a mentőket!

I've been raped.
megh-eroer-sah-kol-tahk   Megerőszakoltak.

I've been robbed!
ki-rah-bol-tahk!   Kiraboltak!

Call the police!
*heev-yah ah ren-doer-   Hívja a rendőrséget!
sheh ghet!*

Where is the police station?
hol ah ren-doer-shehgh?   Hol a rendőrség?

Go away!
men-yen el!   Menjen el!

I'll call the police!
hee-vom ah ren-doert!   Hívom a rendőrt!

Thief!
tol-vahy!   Tolvaj!

I am ill.
be-tegh vah-djok   Beteg vagyok.

My friend is ill.
ah bah-raa-tom be-tegh   A barátom beteg.

I am lost.
el-teh-ved-tem   Eltévedtem.

Where are the toilets?
hol vahn ah veh-tseh?

Hol van a WC?

Could you help me please?
tud-nah she-ghee-te-ni keh-rem?

Tudna segíteni kérem?

Could I please use the telephone?
keh-rem hahs-naal-haht naam ah te-le-font?

Kérem, használhatnám a telefont?

I'm sorry. I apologise.
shahy-naa-lom el-neh-zehsht keh-rek

Sajnálom.
Elnézést kérek.

I didn't do it.
nem ehn chi-naal-tahm

Nem én csináltam.

I didn't realise I was doing anything wrong.
nem tud-tahm hodj vah-lah-mi ros-saht tet-tem

Nem tudtam, hogy valami rosszat tettem.

I wish to contact my embassy/consulate.
se-ret-nehk ah ker-vet-shehgh-ghel/kon-zu-laa-tush-shahl be-sehl-ni

Szeretnék a követséggel/konzulátussal beszélni.

I speak English.
be-seh-lek (ahn-gho-lul)

Beszélek (angolul).

I have medical insurance.
vahn be-tegh-biz-to-shee-taa-shom

Van betegbiztosításom.

HUNGARIAN

My possessions are insured.
vahn vah-djon-biz-to-shee-taa-shom   Van vagyonbiztosításom.

I've lost ...
el-ves-tet-tem ...   Elvesztettem ...
My ... was stolen.
el-lop-taak ah/ahz ... m   Ellopták a/az ... m.

my bags	*ah taash-kaa-i-maht*	a táskáimat
my handbag	*ah keh-zi-taash-kaa-maht*	a kézitáskámat
my money	*ah pehn-ze-met*	a pénzemet
my travellers' cheques	*ahz u-tah-zaa-shi chekk-ye-i-met*	az utazási csekkjeimet
my passport	*ahz oot-le-ve-le-met*	az útleve lemet

Paperwork

name	*nehv*	név
address	*tseem*	cím
date of birth	*sü-le-teh-shi daa-tum*	születési dátum
place of birth	*sü-le-teh-shi hey*	születési hely
age	*kor*	kor
sex	*nem*	nem
nationality	*nem-ze-ti-shehgh*	nemzetiség
next of kin	*ker-ze-li hoz-zaa-tahr-to-zoh*	közeli hozzátartoz
religion	*vahl-laash*	vallás
reason for travel	*ahz u-tah-zaash tsehl-yah*	az utazás célja

profession	fogh-lahl-ko-zaa-shah	foglalkozása
marital status	chah-laa-di aal-lah-pot	családi állapot
passport	oot-le-vehl	útlevél
passport number	oot-le-vehl-saam	útlevélszám
visa	vee-zum	vízum
tourist card	tu-rish-tah kaar-tyah	turista kártya
identification	se-mehy-ah-zo-nosh-shaagh	személyazonosság
birth certificate	sü-le-teh-shi ah nyah-kerny-vi ki-vo-naht	születésianyakonyvi kivonat
driver's licence	yo-gho-sheet-vaany	jogosítvány
car owner's title	for-ghahl-mi en-ghe-dehy	forgalmi engedély
car registration	gehp-ko-chi rend-saam	gépkocsi rendszám
customs	vaam	vám
immigration	be-vaan-dor-laash	bevándorlás
border	hah-taar	határ

Getting Around

ARRIVALS	ÉRKEZÉS
BUS STOP	AUTÓBUSZ MEGÁLLÓ
DEPARTURES	INDULÁS
STATION	ÁLLOMÁS

HUNGARIAN

SUBWAY	METRÓ
TICKET OFFICE	JEGYIRODA
TIMETABLE	MENETREND
TRAIN STATION	VASÚTÁLLOMÁS

What time does ... leave/
arrive?
   mi-kor in-dul/   Mikor indul/érkezik a ...?
   ehr-ke-zik ah ...?

aeroplane	*re-pü-loer-gehp*	repülőgép
boat	*hah-yoh*	hajó
bus (city)	*he-yi ahu-toh-bus*	helyi autóbusz
bus (intercity)	*taa-vol-shaa-ghi*	távolsági autóbusz
	ahu-toh-bus	
train	*vo-naht*	vonat
tram	*vil-lah-mosh*	villamos

Directions

Where is ...?
   hol vahn ah/ahz ...?   Hol van a/az ...?
How do I get to ...?
   hodj yu-tok ah/ahz ...?   Hogy jutok a/az ...?
Is it far from/near here?
   mes-se vahn in-nen/   Messze van innen/
   ker-zel vahn ide?   közel van ide?
Can I walk there?
   me-he-tek odah djah-   Mehetek oda gyalog?
   logh?

HUNGARIAN

Can you show me (on the map)?
megh tud-naa ne-kem mu-taht-ni (ah tehr-keh-pen)?
Meg tudná nekem mutatni (a térképen)?

Are there other means of getting there?
maash-kehp-pen ish el le-het odah yut-ni?
Másképpen is el lehet oda jutni?

I want to go to ...
se-ret-nehk ...men-ni
Szeretnék ... menni

Go straight ahead.
men-yen e-dje-ne-shen e-loere
Menjen egyenesen előre.

It's two blocks down.
keht haaz-termb-re vahn in-nen
Két háztömbre van innen.

Turn left ...
for-dul-yon bahl-rah ...
Forduljon balra ...

Turn right ...
for-dul-yon yobb-rah ...
Forduljon jobbra ...

at the next corner.
ah ker-vet-ke-zoer shah-rok-naal
a következő saroknál.

at the traffic lights.
ah kerz-le-ke-deh-shi laam-paa-naal
a közlekedési lámpánál.

| behind | mer-gert | mögött |
| in front of | e-loertt | előtt |

HUNGARIAN

far	*mes-se*	messze
near	*ker-zel*	közel
in front of	*e-loertt*	előtt
opposite	*sem-ben*	szemben

Booking Tickets

Excuse me, where is the ticket office?

el-neh-zehsht, hol vahn ah yedj-i-ro-dah? — Elnézést, hol van a jegyiroda

Where can I buy a ticket?

hol ve-he-tem megh ah ye-djet? — Hol vehetem meg a jegyet?

I want to go to ...

se-ret-nehk ... men-ni — Szeretnék ... menni.

Do I need to book?

sük-sheh-ghesh he-yet fog-lahl-nom? — Szükséges helyet foglalnom?

You need to book.

sük-sheh-ghesh he-yet fog-lahl-ni-ah — Szükséges helyet foglalnia.

I would like to book a seat to ...

se-ret-nehk edj he-yet fog-lahl-ni ... — Szeretnék egy helyet foglalni ...

I would like ...

se-ret-nehk ... — Szeretnék ...

a one-way ticket

edj ye-djet chahk odah — egy jegyet csak oda

a return ticket
  edj re-toor-ye-djet   egy retúrjegyet
two tickets
  keht ye-djet   két jegyet
tickets for all of us
  edj-edj ye-djet mind-   egy-egy jegyet
  ahny-nyi-unk-nahk   mindannyiunknak
a student's fare
  edj di-aak-ye-djet   egy diákjegyet
a child's/pensioner's fare
  edj dje-rek-ye-djet/   egy gyerekjegyet/
  nyugh-dee-yash-ye-djet   nyugdíjasjegyet

1st class
  el-shoer os-taay   első osztály
2nd class
  maa-shod-os-taay   másodosztály

It is full.
  te-le vahn   Tele van.
Is it completely full?
  tel-ye-shen te-le vahn?   Teljesen tele van?
Can I get a stand-by ticket?
  kahp-hah-tok edj stand-   Kaphatok egy stand-by jegyet?
  by ye-djet?

HUNGARIAN

Air

CHECKING IN	CHECK-IN
LUGGAGE PICKUP	CSOMAG ÁTVÉTEL
REGISTRATION	REGISZTRÁCIÓ

Is there a flight to ...?
vahn re-püloer-yaa-raht ...?
Van repülőjárat ...?

When is the next flight to ...?
mi-kor vahn ah ker-vet-ke-zoer re-püloer-yaa-raht ...?
Mikor van a következő repülőjárat ...?

How long does the flight take?
meny-nyi i-de-igh tahrt ah re-püloer-oot?
Mennyi ideig tart a repülőút?

What is the flight number?
meny-nyi ah yaa-raht-saam?
Mennyi a járatszám?

You must check in at ...
ah ... kell ye-lent-kez-ni-e
A ... kell jelentkeznie

airport tax	*re-pü-loer-teh-ri ah-doh*	repülőtéri adó
boarding pass	*be-saal-loh-kaar-tyah*	beszállókártya
customs	*vaam*	vám

Bus

BUS STOP	AUTÓBUSZ MEGÁLLÓ
TRAM STOP	VILLAMOS MEGÁLLÓ

Where is the bus/tram stop?
hol vahn ahz ahu-toh-bus/
ah vil-lah-mosh
megh-aal-loh?
Hol van az autóbusz/
a villamos megálló?

Which bus goes to ...?
me-yik ahu-toh-bus
medj ...?
Melyik autóbusz megy ... ?

Does this bus go to ...?
ez ahz ahu-toh-bus
medj ...?
Ez az autóbusz megy ...?

How often do buses pass by?
mi-yen djahk-rahn yaar-
nahk ahz ahu-toh-busok
Milyen gyakran járnak az
autóbuszok?

Could you let me know
when we get to ...?
sohl-nah keh-rem ah-mi-
kor megh-ehr-ke-zünk ...?
Szólna kérem, amikor
megérkezünk ...?

I want to get off!
se-ret-nehk le-saall-ni!
Szeretnék leszállni!

What time is the ... bus?
mi-kor in-dul ah/ahz ...
ahu-toh-bus?
Mikor indul a/az ... autóbusz?

next	*ker-vet-ke-zoer*	következő
first	*el-shoer*	első
last	*u-tol-shoh*	utolsó

HUNGARIAN

Metro

METRO/ UNDERGROUND	METRÓ/FÖLDALATTI
CHANGE (for coins)	VÁLTÁS
WAY OUT	KIJÁRAT

Which line takes me to ...?
  me-yik vo-nahl medj ...?   Melyik vonal megy...?
What is the next station?
  mi ah ker-vet-ke-zoer   Mi a következő állomás?
  aal-lo-maash?

Train

DINING CAR	ÉTKEZŐ KOCSI
EXPRESS	EXPRESSZ
PLATFORM	VÁGÁNY
SLEEPING CAR	HÁLÓKOCSI

Is this the right platform
for ...?
  er-roerl ah vaa-ghaany-   Erről a vágányról indul a
  rohl in-dul ah vo-naht ...?   vonat ...?
Passengers ...
  ahz u-tah-shok-nahk ...   Az utasoknak ...
must change trains
  aat kell saall-ni   át kell szállni

HUNGARIAN

must change platforms
maa-shik vaa-ghaany-
hoz kell men-ni

másik vágányhoz kell
menni

The train leaves from
platform ...
ah vo-naht ah ... saa-moo
vaa-ghaany-rohl in-dul

A vonat a ... számú vágány-ról
indul

dining car	*eht-ke-zoer ko-chi*	étkező kocsi
express	*ex-press*	expressz
local	*he-yi*	helyi
sleeping car	*haa-loh-ko-chi*	hálókocsi

Taxi

Can you take me to ...?
el tud-nah vin-ni ...? El tudna vinni ...?

Please take me to ...
keh-rem vi-djen el ... Kérem, vigyen el ...

How much does it cost to
go to ...?
meny-nyi-be ke-rül ... ig? Mennyibe kerül ... ig?

Instructions

Here is fine, thank you.
itt joh les, ker-ser-nerm Itt jó lesz, köszönöm.

The next corner, please.
ah ker-vet-ke-zoer shah-
rok-naal, le-djen see-vesh

A következő saroknál, legyen
szíves.

The next street to the left/right.

ah ker-vet-ke-zoer ut-tsaa-naal bahl-rah/yobb-rah — A következő utcánál balra/jobbra.

Stop here!

aall-yon meg itt! — Álljon meg itt!

Please slow down.

keh-rem, lash-sheet-shon le — Kérem, lassítson le.

Please wait here.

keh-rem, vaar-yon itt — Kérem, várjon itt.

Some Useful Phrases

The train is delayed.

ah vo-naht keh-shik — A vonat késik.

The train is cancelled.

ah vo-naht nem yaar — A vonat nem jár.

How long will it be delayed?

meny-nyit fogh kehsh-ni? — Mennyit fog késni?

There is a delay of ... hours.

... oh-raat keh-shik — ... órát késik.

Can I reserve a place?

fogh-lahl-hah-tok edj he-yet? — Foglalhatok egy helyet?

How long does the trip take?

meny-nyi i-de-igh tahrt ahz u-tah-zaash? — Mennyi ideig tart az utazás?

Is it a direct route?

ez edj kerz-vet-len oot-vo-nahl? — Ez egy közvetlen útvonal?

Is that seat taken?
fogh lahlt ahz uh hey?   Foglalt az a hely?
I want to get off at ...
se-ret-nehk le-saall-ni ...   Szeretnék leszállni ...
Where can I hire a bicycle?
hol beh-rel-he-tek edj   Hol bérelhetek egy kerékpárt?
ke-rehk-paart?

Car

DETOUR	KERÜLŐÚT
FREEWAY	SZABADÚT
GARAGE	GARÁZS
MECHANIC	SZERELŐ
NO ENTRY	NEM BEJÁRAT
NO PARKING	TILOS A PARKOLÁS
NORMAL	NORMÁL
ONE WAY	EGYIRÁNYÚ
REPAIRS	JAVÍTÁSOK
SELF SERVICE	ÖNKISZOLGÁLÓ
SUPER	SZUPER
UNLEADED	ÓLOMMENTES

HUNGARIAN

Where can I rent a car?
hol beh-rel-he-tek edj   Hol bérelhetek egy autót?
ahu-toht?
How much is it ...?
meny-nyi-be ke-rül ...?   Mennyibe kerül ...?
daily/weekly
nah-pon-tah/he-ten-te   naponta/hetente

Does that include insurance/
mileage?
> *ahz aar tahr-tahl-mahz-*
> *zah ah biz-to-shee-taasht/*
> *ki-loh-meh-tert?*

Az ár tartalmazza a
biztosítást/kilómétert?

What make is it?
> *mi-yen djaart-maa-nyoo*
> *ahz ahu-toh?*

Milyen gyártmányú az autó?

Where's the next petrol
station?
> *hol vahn ah legh-ker-ze-*
> *leb-bi ben-zin-koot?*

Hol van a legközelebbi
ben zinkút?

Please fill the tank.
> *keh-rem terl-che megh ah*
> *ben-zin-tahr-taayt*

Kérem töltse meg a
benzintartályt.

I want ... litres of petrol (gas).
> *keh-rek ... li-ter ben-zint*

Kérek ... liter benzint.

Please check the oil and
water.
> *keh-rem el-le-noer-riz-ze*
> *ahz o-lah-yaht ehsh*
> *ah vi-zet*

Kérem, ellenőrizze
az olajat és a vizet.

How long can I park here?
> *med-digh pahr-kol-hah-*
> *tok itt?*

Meddig parkolhatok itt?

Does this road lead to...?
> *ez ahz oot ve-zet ...?*

Ez az út vezet ...?

air (for tyres)	*le-ve-ghoer*	levegő
battery	*ahk-ku-mu-laa-tor*	akkumulátor

brakes	*fehk*	fék
clutch	*kup-lungh*	kuplung
driver's licence	*yo-gho-sheet-vaany*	jogosítvány
engine	*mo-tor*	motor
lights	*vi-laa-ghee-taash*	világítás
oil	*o-lahy*	olaj
puncture	*de-fekt*	defekt
radiator	*hüü-toer*	hűtő
road map	*ahu-tohsh tehr-kehp*	autós térkép
tyres	*ke-rėhk-gu-mi*	kerékgumi
windscreen	*sehl-veh-doer*	szélvédő

Car Problems

I need a mechanic.
sük-sheh-ghem vahn edj se-re-loer-re — Szükségem van egy szerelőre.

The battery is flat.
le-me-rült ahz akku-mu-laa-tor — Lemerült az akkumulátor.

The radiator is leaking.
fo-yik ah hüü-toer — Folyik a hűtő.

I have a flat tyre.
de-fek-tet kahp-tahm — Defektet kaptam.

It's overheating.
tool-füüt — Túlfűt.

It's not working.
nem müü-ker-dik — Nem működik.

HUNGARIAN

Accommodation

CAMPING GROUND	KEMPING
GUEST HOUSE	VENDÉGHÁZ
HOTEL	SZÁLLODA
MOTEL	MOTEL
YOUTH HOSTEL	IFJÚSÁGI SZÁLLÓ

Where is a ...?
  hol vahn edj ...?   Hol van egy ...?

cheap hotel	*ol-choh saal-lo-dah*	olcsó szálloda
good hotel	*yoh saal-lo-dah*	jó szálloda
nearby hotel	*ker-ze-li saal-lo-dah*	közeli szálloda
clean hotel	*tis-tah saal-lo-dah*	tiszta szálloda

What is the address?
  mi ah tseem?   Mi a cím?
Could you write the address,
please?
  le-eer-naa ah tsee-met   Leírná a címet kérem?
  keh-rem?

At the Hotel
Do you have any rooms
available?
  vahn sah-bahd   Van szabad szobájuk?
  so-baa-yuk?

I would like ...

se-ret-nehk edj ...		Szeretnék egy ...
a single room	*edj-aa-djahsh so-baat*	egyágyas szobát
a double room	*keht-aa-djahsh so-baat*	kétágyas szobát
a room with a bathroom	*für-doer-so-baash so-baat*	fürdőszobás szobát
to share a dorm	*aa-djaht edj haa-loh-te-rem-ben*	ágyat egy hálóteremben
a bed	*edj aa-djaht*	egy ágyat

I want a room ...

se-ret-nehk edj so-baat ...		Szeretnék egy szobát ...
with a bathroom	*für-doer-so-baa-vahl*	fürdőszobával
with a shower	*zu-hah-nyo-zoh-vahl*	zuhanyozóval
with a television	*te-le-vee-zioh-vahl*	televízióval
with a window	*ahb-lahk-kahl*	ablakkal

I'm going to stay for ...

... mah-rah-dok		... maradok
one day	*edj nah-pigh*	egy napig
two days	*keht nah-pigh*	két napig
one week	*edj heh-tigh*	egy hétig

Do you have identification?

vahn vah-lah-mi-yen ah se-mehy-ah-zo-nosh-shaa-ghaat i-ghah-zo-loh pah-peer-yah?	Van valamilyen a személyazonosságát igazoló papírja?

Your membership card,
please.

keh-rem ah tahgh-shaa-ghi   Kérem a tagsági igazolványát
i-ghah-zol-vaa-nyaat

Sorry, we're full.

shahy-naa-lom de te-le   Sajnálom, de tele vagyunk.
vah-djunk

How long will you be
staying?

med-digh mah-rahd?   Meddig marad?

How many nights?

haany ehy-sah-kaat   Hány éjszakát marad?
mah-rahd?

It's ... per day/per person.

... ft nah-pon-tah/   ... Ft naponta/személyenként
se-meh-yen-kehnt

How much is it per night/
per person?

meny-nyi-be ke-rül   Mennyibe kerül éjszakánként
ehy-sah-kaan-kehnt/   személyenként?
se-meh- yen-kehnt?

Can I see it?

megh-nehz-he-tem ah so-   Megnézhetem a szobát?
baat?

Are there any others?

vahn edj maa-shik so-bah?   Van egy másik szoba?

Are there any cheaper
rooms?

vahn edj ol-chohbb   Van egy olcsóbb szoba?
so-bah?

Can I see the bathroom?
meg-nehz-he-tem ah
für-doer-so-baat?

Megnézhetem a fürdőszobát?

Is there a reduction for
students/children?
vahn ked-vez-mehny
di-aa-kok-nahk/
dje-re-kek-nek?

Van kedvezmény diákoknak/
gyerekeknek?

Does it include breakfast?
ahz aar tahr-tahl-
mahz-zah ah regh-ghe-lit?

Az ár tartalmazza a reggelit?

It's fine, I'll take it.
ez yoh les

Ez jó lesz.

I don't know how long I'm
staying.
mehgh nem tu-dom
pon-to-shahn hodj
med-digh mah-rah-dok

Még nem tudom pontosan,
hogy meddig maradok.

Is there a lift?
lift vahn?

Lift van?

Where is the bathroom?
hol vahn ah für-doer-
so-bah?

Hol van a fürdőszoba?

Is there hot water all day?
e-ghehs nahp vahn
me-legh veez?

Egész nap van meleg víz?

Do you have a safe where I
can leave my valuables?
vahn er-nerk-nehl sehf,
ah-hol ahz ehr-teh-ke-
i-met hahdj-hah-tom?

Van önöknél széf, ahol az
értékeimet hagyhatom?

Is there somewhere to wash clothes?

vahn vah-lah-hol edj hey, ah-hol mosh-hah-tok? — Van valahol egy hely, ahol moshatok?

Can I use the kitchen?

hahs-naal-hah-tom ah kony-haat? — Használhatom a konyhát?

Can I use the telephone?

hahs-naal-hah-tom ah te-le-font? — Használhatom a telefont?

Requests & Complaints

Please wake me up at ...

keh-rek ehb-res-tehsht ... oh-rah-kor — Kérek ébresztést ... órakor.

The room needs to be cleaned.

ah so-baat ki kell tah-kah-ree-tah-ni — A szobát ki kell takarítani.

Please change the sheets.

keh-rem che-rehl-ye ki ah le-pe-doert — Kérem, cseréljc ki a lepedőt.

I can't open/close the window.

nem tu-dom ki-nyit-ni/ be-chuk-ni ahz ahb-lah-kot — Nem tudom kinyitni/ becsukni az ablakot.

I've locked myself out of my room.

ki-zaar-tahm mah-ghahm ah so-baam-bohl — Kizártam magam a szobámból.

The toilet won't flush.
ah veh tseh nem erb-leet   A WC nem öblít.

I don't like this room.
ez ah so-bah nem tet-sik   Ez a szoba nem tetszik.
It's too small.
tool ki-chi   Túl kicsi.
It's noisy.
zah-yosh   Zajos.
It's too dark.
tool sher-teht   Túl sötét.
It's expensive.
draa-ghah   Drága.

Some Useful Words & Phrases

I am/We are leaving ...
    ... *me-djek el/me-djünk el*   ... megyek el/megyünk el
now/tomorrow
    mosht/hol-nahp   most/holnap

I would like to pay the bill.
    se-ret-nehk fi-zet-ni   Szeretnék fizetni.

name	*nehv*	név
surname	*ve-ze-tehk-nehv*	vezetéknév
room number	*so-bah-saam*	szobaszám
address	*tseem*	cím
air-conditioned	*lehgh-kon-di-tsi-o-naalt*	légkondicionált

HUNGARIAN

balcony	*er-kehy*	erkély
bathroom	*für-doer-so-bah*	fürdőszoba
bed	*aadj*	ágy
bill	*saam-lah*	számla
blanket	*tah-kah-roh*	takaró
candle	*djer-tyah*	gyertya
chair	*sehk*	szék
clean	*tis-tah*	tiszta
cupboard	*sek-rehny*	szekrény
dark	*sher-teht*	sötét
dirty	*pis-kosh*	piszkos
double bed	*dup-lah aadj*	dupla ágy
electricity	*e-lekt-ro-mosh-shaagh*	elektromosság
excluded	*ki-veh-te leh-vel*	kivételével
fan	*ven-til-laa-tor*	ventillátor
included	*be-le-ehrt-ve*	beleértve
key	*kulch*	kulcs
lift (elevator)	*lift*	lift
light bulb	*eh-goer*	égő
lock (n)	*zaar*	zár
mattress	*maht-rats*	matrac
mirror	*tü-ker*	tükör
padlock	*lah-kaht*	lakat
pillow	*paar-nah*	párna
quiet	*chen-desh*	csendes
room (in hotel)	*so-bah*	szoba
sheet	*le-pe-doer*	lepedő
shower	*zu-hah-nyo-zoh*	zuhanyozó
soap	*sahp-pahn*	szappan
suitcase	*boer-rernd*	bőrönd

swimming pool	*u-so-dah*	uszoda
table	*ahs-tahl*	asztal
toilet	*veh tseh*	WC
toilet paper	*veh tseh pah-peer*	WC papír
towel	*ter-rül-ker-zoer*	törülköző
water	*veez*	víz
cold water	*hi-degh veez*	hideg víz
hot water	*me-legh veez*	meleg víz
window	*ahb-lahk*	ablak

Around Town

What time does it open?
  mi-kor nyit ki?   Mikor nyit ki?
What time does it close?
  mi-kor zaar be?   Mikor zár be?

I'm looking for ...
  ke-re-shem ...   Keresem ...

the art gallery	*ah gah-leh-ri-aat*	a galériát
a bank	*edj bahn-kot*	egy bankot
the church	*ah temp-lo-mot*	a templomot
the city centre	*ah vaa-rosh-kerz-pon-tot*	a városközpontot
the ... embassy	*ah/ahz ... ker-vet-sheh-ghet*	a/az ... követséget
my hotel	*ah saal-lo-daa-maht*	a szállodámat
the market	*ah pi-ah-tsot*	a piacot
the museum	*ah moo-ze-u-mot*	a múzeumot
the police	*ah ren-doer-sheh-ghet*	a rendőrséget

the post office	*ah posh-taat*	a postát
a public toilet	*edj nyil-vaa-nosh veh tseht*	egy nyilvános WC
the telephone centre	*ah te-le-fon-kerz-pon-tot*	a telefonközpontot
the tourist information office	*ah tu-rish-tah in-for-maa-tsi-ohsh i-ro-daat*	a turista információs irodát

What ... is this?
  me-yik ... ez?   Melyik ... ez?

street	*ut-tsah*	utca
suburb	*ke-rü-let*	kerület

For directions, see the Getting Around section, page 244-246

At the Post Office

I would like some stamps.
  beh-ye-ghe-ket se-ret-nehk ven-ni.   Bélyegeket szeretnék venni.

How much is the postage?
  meny-nyi-be ke-rül ah beh-yegh?   Mennyibe kerül a bélyeg?

How much does it cost to send ... to ...?
  meny-nyi-be ke-rül el-kül-de-ni ...?   Mennyibe kerül elküldeni ...?

I would like to send ...
  se-ret-nehk el-kül-de-ni ...   Szeretnék elküldeni ...

a letter	*edj le-ve-let*	egy levelet
a postcard	*edj keh-pesh-lah-pot*	egy képeslapot
a parcel	*edj cho-mah-ghot*	egy csomagot
a telegram	*edj taa-vi-rah-tot*	egy táviratot
aerogram	*ern-bo-ree-teh-ko-loh*	önborítékoló
	leh-ghi-posh-tah	légi posta levél
	le-vehl	
air mail	*leh-ghi-posh-tah*	légiposta
envelope	*bo-ree-tehk*	boríték
mail box	*posh-tah-laa-dah*	postaláda
registered mail	*ah-yaan-lott*	ajánlott küldemény
	kül-de-mehny	
surface mail	*shi-mah posh-tah*	síma posta

Telephone

I want to ring ...
   se-ret-nehk ...   Szeretnék ... telefonálni.
   te-le-fo-naal-ni.

The number is ...
   ah saam ...   A szám ...

I want to speak for three minutes.
   haa-rom per-tsigh   Három percig
   se-ret-nehk be-sehl-ni. szeretnék beszélni.

How much does a three-minute call cost?
   meny-nyi-be ke-rül   Mennyibe kerül egy három
   edj haa-rom-per-tsesh perces hívás?
   hee-vaash?

HUNGARIAN

How much does each extra
minute cost?
   meny-nyi-be ke-rül
   min-den to-vaab-bi edj
   perts?

Mennyibe kerül minden
további egy perc?

I would like to speak to
Mr Perez.
   pe-rez oor-rahl
   se-ret-nehk be-sehl-ni

Perez úrral szeretnék beszélni

I want to make a reverse-
charges phone call.
   er be-sehl-ghe-tehsht
   se-ret-nehk

R beszélgetést szeretnék.

It's engaged.
   fog-lahlt

Foglalt.

I've been cut off.
   meg-sah-kahdt ah vo-nahl

Megszakadt a vonal.

At the Bank

I want to exchange some
money/travellers' cheques.
   se-ret-nehk pehnzt/utah-
   zaa-shi chek-ket vaal-
   tah-ni

Szeretnék pénzt/utazási
csekket váltani.

What is the exchange rate?
   meny-nyi ahz
   aar-fo-yahm?

Mennyi az árfolyam?

How many forints per dollar?
   haany fo-rint edj dol-laar?

Hány forint egy dollár?

Can I have money transferred
here from my bank?
   aat-u-tahl-hah-tok pehnzt   Átutalhatok pénzt ide
   i-de ah bahn-kom-bohl?   a bankomból?
How long will it take to
arrive?
   meny-nyi idoer ah-lahtt   Mennyi idő alatt
   ehr-ke-zik megh ah   érkezik meg a pénz?
   pehnz?
Has my money arrived yet?
   megh-ehr-ke-zett maar   Megérkezett már a pénzem?
   ah pehn-zem?

bankdraft	*bahnk-in-tehz-vehny*	bankintézvény
bank notes	*bahnk-ye-djek*	bankjegyek
cashier	*pehnz-taar*	pénztár
coins	*ehr-mehk*	érmék
credit card	*hi-tel-kaar-tyah*	hitelkártya
exchange	*vaal-taash*	váltás
loose change	*ahp-roh*	apró
signature	*ah-laa-ee-raash*	aláírás

HUNGARIAN

Sightseeing

Do you have a guidebook/
local map?
   vahn ooti-kerny-vük/   Van útikönyvük/térképük?
   tehr-keh-pük?
What are the main attractions?
   me-yek ah foerbb   Melyek a főbb látnivalók?
   laat-ni-vah-lohk?

What is that?
mi ahz?   Mi az?

How old is it?
mi-yen reh-ghi?   Milyen régi?

Can I take photographs?
fehny-keh-pez-he-tek?   Fényképezhetek?

What time does it open/close?
mi-kor nyit ki/zaar be?   Mikor nyit ki/zár be?

ancient	*oer-shi*	ősi
archaeological	*reh-gheh-se-ti*	régészeti
beach	*shtrahnd*	strand
building	*eh-pü-let*	épület
castle	*vaar*	vár
cathedral	*seh-kesh-edj haaz*	székesegyház
church	*temp-lom*	templom
concert hall	*hahngh-ver-sheny-te-rem*	hangversenyterem
library	*kernyv-taar*	könyvtár
main square	*foer tehr*	fő tér
market	*pi-ahts*	piac
monastery	*ko-losh-tor*	kolostor
monument	*em-lehk-müü*	emlékmű
mosque	*me-chet*	mecset
old city	*reh-ghi vaa-rosh*	régi város
palace	*pah-lo-tah*	palota
opera house	*o-pe-rah-haaz*	operaház
ruins	*ro-mok*	romok
stadium	*shtah-di-on*	stadion
statues	*sob-rok*	szobrok
synagogue	*zhi-nah-ghoh-ghah*	zsinagóga

| temple | *temp-lom* | templom |
| university | *e-dje-tem* | egyetem |

Entertainment

What is there to do in the evenings?
 mit le-het chi-naal-ni esh-tehn-kehnt? — Mit lehet csinálni esténként?

Are there any discos?
 vahn-nahk dis-kohk? — Vannak diszkók?

Are there places where you can hear local folk music?
 vah-nahk o-yahn he-yek, ah-hol he-yi nehp-ze-neht le-het hahll-ghaht-ni? — Vannak olyan helyek, ahol helyi népzenét lehet hallgatni?

How much does it cost to get in?
 meny-nyi-be ke-rül ah be-leh-poer? — Mennyibe kerül a belépő?

cinema	*mo-zi*	mozi
concert	*kon-tsert*	koncert
discotheque	*dis-koh*	diszkó
theatre	*seen-haaz*	színház

HUNGARIAN

In the Country
Weather

What's the weather like?
 mi-yen ahz i-doer? — Milyen az idő?

The weather is ... today.

ahz i-doer ... mah	Az idő ... ma.

Will it be ... tomorrow?

... les hol-nahp?	... lesz holnap?

cloudy	*fel-hoersh*	felhős
cold	*hi-degh*	hideg
foggy	*ker-dersh*	ködös
frosty	*hüü-versh*	hűvös
hot	*me-legh*	meleg
raining	*e-shoer*	esős
snowing	*hah-vah-zaash*	havazás
sunny	*nah-posh*	napos
windy	*se-lesh*	szeles

Camping

Am I allowed to camp here?

itt le-het kem-pin-ghez-ni?	Itt lehet kempingezni?

Is there a campsite nearby?

vahn itt vah-lah-hol ah	Van itt valahol a
ker-zel-ben edj kem-pingh?	közelben egy kemping?

backpack	*haa-ti-zhaak*	hátizsák
can opener	*kon-zerv-nyi-toh*	konzervnyitó
compass	*i-raany-tüü*	iránytű
crampons	*yehgh-segh*	jégszeg
firewood	*tüü-zi-fah*	tűzifa
gas cartridge	*gaaz-paht-ron*	gázpatron
hammock	*fügh-ghoer-aadj*	függőágy
ice axe	*yehgh-chaa-kaany*	jégcsákány
mattress	*maht-rats*	matrac

)enknife	*zheb-kehsh*	zsebkés
ope	*ker-tehl*	kötél
ent	*shaa-tor*	sátor
ent pegs	*shaa-tor tser-ler-perk*	sátor cölöpök
orch		
(flashlight)	*zheb-laam-pah*	zseblámpa
;leeping bag	*haa-loh-zhaak*	hálózsák
;tove	*kem-pingh-foer-zoer*	kempingfőző
.vater bottle	*vi-zesh-pah-lahtsk*	vizespalack

Food

As befits a country that has been at the crossroads of history for
:enturies, Hungarian cuisine is a special mixture of foods from
nany cultures, such as Balkan, Czech, German and Austrian.
Add to this traditional regional specialities and the visitor will
1ot be disappointed in the wide range of spicy, sweet, sour and
;moky flavours. Many dishes contain the famous Hungarian
)aprika, ranging from biting hot 'csípős' to the sweet 'rose
)aprika'. Sour cream is also a favourite and accompanies a vast
·ange of dishes. Pork is the most common meat, found in most
establishments along with poultry dishes. Fish is often fresh and
excellent, particularly around Lake Balaton, the Danube or the
fisza rivers; beef and lamb are not as common. Do not miss the
game dishes if you find a restaurant specialising in such. Hungarian wines are famed throughout the world, and some of the
ocal beers are excellent too. It is not a great country for
vegetarians who wish to eat out, although things are changing
fast in the cities; however in the summer, vegetables and fruit are
)lentiful and cheap.

HUNGARIAN

The main types of restaurants can be classified as:
Vendéglő – smaller with good food at reasonable prices;
Étterem – wide variety of dishes, wide variations in service;
Csárda – country cooking, limited menu but usually good;
Önkiszolgáló – self service, cheap and filling. No prizes
for *haute cuisine*.

breakfast	*regh-ghe-li*	reggeli
lunch	*e-behd*	ebéd
dinner	*vah-cho-rah*	vacsora

Table for ..., please.
se-ret-nehk edj   Szeretnék egy asztalt ...
ahs-tahlt ... se-mehy-re   személyre.
Can I see the menu please?
megh-nehz-he-tem ahz   Megnézhetem az étlapot?
eht-lah-pot?
I would like the set lunch.
me-nüt keh-rek   Menüt kérek.
What does it include?
mi vahn ben-ne?   Mi van benne?
Is service included in the bill?
ahz aar tahr-tahl-   Az ár tartalmazza
mahz-zah ah   a felszolgálást?
fel-sol-ghaa-laasht?
Not too spicy please.
nem tool füü-se-re-shen,   Nem túl fűszeresen, kérem.
keh-rem

ashtray	*hah-mu-tahr-toh*	hamutartó
the bill	*ah saam-lah*	a számla

a cup	*edj cheh-se*	egy csésze
dessert	*eh-desh-shehgh*	édesség
a drink	*edj i-tahl*	egy ital
a fork	*edj vil-lah*	egy villa
fresh	*frish*	friss
a glass	*edj po-haar*	egy pohár
a knife	*edj kehsh*	egy kés
a plate	*edj taa-nyehr*	egy tányér
spicy	*füü-se-resh*	fűszeres
a spoon	*edj kah-naal*	egy kanál
stale	*nem frish*	nem friss
sweet	*eh-desh*	édes
teaspoon	*teaash-kah-naal*	teáskanál
toothpick	*fogh-pis-kaa-loh*	fogpiszkáló

HUNGARIAN

Vegetarian Meals

I am a vegetarian.
*ve-ghe-taa-ri-aa-nush   *Vegetáriánus vagyok.
vah-djok

I don't eat meat.
*nem e-sem hoosht   *Nem eszem húst.

I don't eat chicken fish or
ham.
*nem e-sem chir-keht,   *Nem eszem csirkét,
*hah-laht, shon-kaat   *halat, sonkát.

Starters   Előételek

Hortobágyi húsos palacsinta
  Pancake stuffed with stewed and minced meat and herbs, and
  covered with a sauce of gravy and sour cream.

Libamáj
  Goose liver; a particular delicacy in Hungary. May be cooke
  in several ways, either in a light meat stock, with onion an
  water, in milk, or fried. Often served cold with bread as
  starter.

Rántott gomba
  Fried mushrooms in breadcrumbs, generally served with ric
  and tartar sauce or mayonnaise.

Rántott sajt
  Fried cheese in breadcrumbs, served like *rántott gomba*.

Soups   Levesek

Bableves
  Bean soup with turnip, carrot and sour cream.

Gombaleves
  A delicious mushroom soup with seasoning, onion, sou
  cream and parsley.

Gulyásleves
  Goulash soup, chopped meat fried in onions and paprika, an
  added to water or stock, with potatoes and a dash of whit
  wine.

Halászlé
  A strong and rich broth of usually several kinds of fish (bu
  always containing carp) in large pieces, with tomatoes, gree
  paprika and paprika. Beware, this soup can have a bite to i
  Usually brought to the table in a small cauldron, 'bogrács', o
  a tripod.

Hideg gyümölcsleves
  Cold fruit soup, often cherry 'meggy', prepared with cream
  lemon peel, cinnamon and red wine.

Káposzta leves
    Cabbage soup; comes in several variations. A popular one is
    'Hangover' soup: korhelyleves with sauerkraut, smoked
    sausage, onion, paprika and sour cream.

Újházy Tyúkhúsleves
    Chicken and meat stock soup with root vegetables and
    vermicelli.

Dishes of the Day   Készételek

Lecsó
    A delicious thick stew of onions, tomatoes, green peppers and
    lard. Can be served either as a vegetarian dish with rice, or
    with smoked sausage.

Pörkölt
    Beef 'marha', pork 'sertés', veal 'borjú', game 'vad' stew
    cooked in lard with onions, bacon and paprika, plus the
    obligatory sour cream.

Töltött káposzta
    Similar to töltött paprika, but the meat filling is stuffed in
    cabbage leaves or cooked as meat balls in the sauce.

Töltött paprika
    Green peppers stuffed with a mixture of minced meat, bacon,
    egg, onion, rice, and baked in a sauce of sour cream.

Meat   Hús

Aprópecsenye
    Braised cutlets of pork with paprika, onion and sour cream.
    Served with vinegar or lemon juice.

HUNGARIAN

Bécsi szelet
Wiener schnitzel veal cutlet deep fried in a coating of flour beaten eggs and breadcrumbs.

Köménymagos sertéshús
Pork stew with rice, onion, lard, tomato purée and caraway seeds.

Natúrszelet
Leg of veal dipped into flour and fried.

Párizsi szelet
As above, except that the final coating of breadcrumbs i substituted by another layer of flour.

Rántott szelet sertéshús
Pork chops in breadcrumbs, fried in a coating of flour, beaten eggs and breadcrumbs.

Sült csülök
Knuckle of pork boiled, then coated in flour and fried. Serve with horseradish.

Fish   Hal

Gombás fogas
Pike-perch, sometimes known as 'süllő', braised with mushrooms and a sauce of white wine, butter, lemon juice, egg and bone stock.

Rántott hal
Fish in breadcrumbs. May be carp 'ponty' or catfish 'harcsa or one of several other freshwater types, rolled in flour, egg and breadcrumbs, and fried.

Poultry   Baromfi

Becsinált csirke
Chicken fricassee fried with cauliflower, kohlrabi, celery root, carrot, turnip and mushrooms then braised in stock with lemon juice. Flavoured with egg yolks.

Pirított liba máj
Fried goose liver, first boiled in milk and then fried without seasoning.

Rántott csirke
Deep-fried chicken in breadcrumbs.

Tejfölös csirke
Chicken braised in a sour cream, lemon and butter sauce.

Game   Vad

Fácán narancsos mártással
Pheasant in orange sauce, cooked with carrots, onions, mushrooms, lemon peel and smoked meat. Before serving it is boiled in stock and sugar and orange peel added.

Nyúl vörös borban
Hare braised in red wine, with butter, pork cubes and an onion.

Őzgerinc 'remek' módon
Saddle of venison roast in a rich sauce of sour cream, lemon juice and butter with smoked bacon, carrots, turnips and mustard.

Vaddisznókotlett
Wild-boar cutlets fried in a coating of egg, spices and crispy breadcrumbs with a dressing of mustard sauce.

Salads **Saláták**

Salads are very frequently mixed with a vinegar dressing o
pickled, and include:

cabbage	*káposzta*
gherkin	*uborka*
lettuce	*fejes saláta*
tomato	*paradicsom*

Vegetables & Garnishes **Köretek & Főzelékek**

cabbage	*káposzta*
green beans	*zöld bab*
onion	*hagyma*
potato	*burgonya/krumpli*
boiled potatoes	*főtt krumpli*
roast potatoes	*sült krumpli*
chips	*hasábburgonya*

Pasta **Tészták**

Káposztás kocka

Cabbage, fried and mixed with sour cream, then added t
rolled and chopped pasta.

Lángos

An institution in Hungary, light dough mixed with puréc
potato, quick-fried in deep fat and served sweet (with jams o
sugar) or salty (with cheese or sour cream).

Túrós csusza

Fine white noodles mixed with cottage cheese or curds, an
lashings of sour cream. Comes in two general variations: wit
bacon pieces, or sweet with powdered sugar.

Desserts   Édességek

Dobostorta
  A sponge cake with layers of buttered cocoa and topped with
  a hard brown caramel coating.

Gesztenyepüré
  Mashed and sieved sweet chestnuts cooked in milk with
  vanilla and served with cream and/or rum.

Rétes
  Strudel pastry filled with a variety of fruits such as sour-
  cherry 'meggy', apple 'alma', walnut 'dió', poppy seed
  'mák', or a particular Hungarian favourite, cottage cheese
  'túró'.

Drinks – Nonalcoholic
drinks	*italok*
ice	*jég*
mineral water	*ásványvíz*
sparkling mineral water	*kristályvíz*
soft drinks	*üditők*
orange	*narancs*
lemon	*citrom*
apple	*alma*

Drinks – Alcoholic
beer	*sör*
bottled	*üveges*
draught	*csapolt*
champagne	*pezsgő*
wine	*bor*
white	*fehér*

HUNGARIAN

red	*vörös*
dry	*száraz*
sweet	*édes*

Shopping

How much is it?
  meny-nyi-be ke-rül?   Mennyibe kerül?

bookshop	*kerny-vesh-bolt*	könyvesbolt
camera shop	*fo-toh-üz-let*	fotóüzlet
clothing store	*ru-haa-zah-ti bolt*	ruházati bolt
delicatessen	*de-li-kaat-üz-let*	delikátüzlet
general store, shop	*aa-ru-haaz*	áruház
laundry	*pah-tyo-laht*	patyolat
market	*pi-ats*	piac
newsagency	*ooy-shaa-ghosh*	újságos
stationer's	*pah-peer-üz-let*	papírüzlet
pharmacy	*djohdj-ser-taar*	gyógyszertár
shoeshop	*tsi-poer-üz-let*	cipőüzlet
souvenir shop	*ah-yaan-dehk-bolt*	ajándékbolt
supermarket	*eh-lel-mi-ser-aa-ru-haaz*	élelmiszeráruház
vegetable shop	*zerld-sheh-ghesh*	zöldséges

I would like to buy ...
  se-ret-nehk ... t ven-ni   Szeretnék ...t venni
Do you have others?
  vahn vah-lah-mi maash?   Van valami más?

I don't like it.
ez nem tet-sik

Ez nem tetszik.

Can I look at it?
megh-nehz-he-tem ezt?

Megnézhetem ezt?

I'm just looking.
chahk neh-ze-loer-derm

Csak nézelődöm.

Can you write down the price?
le-eer-naa ahz aa-raat?

Leírná az árát?

Do you accept credit cards?
el-fo-ghahd-nahk hi-tel-kaar-tyaat?

Elfogadnak hitelkártyát?

Could you lower the price?
tud-naa cherk-ken-te-ni ahz aa-raht?

Tudná csökkenteni az árat?

I don't have much money.
ninch shok pehn-zem

Nincs sok pénzem.

Can I help you?
she-gheet-he-tek?

Segíthetek?

Will that be all?
ez min-den?

Ez minden?

Would you like it wrapped?
be-cho-mah-ghol-yuk?

Becsomagoljuk?

Sorry, this is the only one.
shay-nosh chahk ez ahz edj vahn

Sajnos csak ez az egy van.

How much/many do you want?
meny-nyit/haany dah-rah-bot se-ret-ne?

Mennyit/hány darabot szeretne?

Souvenirs

earrings	*fül-be-vah-loh*	fülbevaló
handicraft	*keh-zi-mun-kah*	kézimunka
necklace	*nyahk-laants*	nyaklánc
pottery	*ah-djagh-aa-ru*	agyagáru
ring	*djüü-rüü*	gyűrű
rug	*ki-shebb soer-nyegh*	kisebb szőnyeg

Clothing

clothing	*ru-haa-zaht*	ruházat
coat	*kah-baat*	kabát
dress	*ru-hah*	ruha
jacket	*zah-koh*	zakó
jumper (sweater)	*pu-loh-ver*	pulóver
shirt	*ingh*	ing
shoes	*tsi-poer*	cipő
skirt	*sok-nyah*	szoknya
trousers	*nahd-raagh*	nadrág

It doesn't fit.
nem yoh meh-ret   Nem jó méret.

It is too ...
ez tool ...   Ez túl ...

big	*nadj*	nagy
small	*kichi*	kicsi
short	*rer-vid*	rövid
long	*hos-soo*	hosszú
tight	*so-rosh*	szoros
loose	*boer*	bő

Materials

cotton	*pah-mut*	pamut
handmade	*keh-zi-mun-kah*	kézimunka
leather	*boer*	bőr
brass	*rehz*	réz
gold	*ah-rahny*	arany
silver	*e-züsht*	ezüst
pure alpaca	*tis-tah ahl-pah-kah*	tiszta alpaka
silk	*she-yem*	selyem
wool	*djahp-yoo*	gyapjú

Colours

black	*fe-ke-te*	fekete
blue	*kehk*	kék
brown	*bahr-nah*	barna
green	*zerld*	zöld
orange	*nah-rahnch-shaar-ghah*	narancssárga
pink	*roh-zhah-seen*	rózsaszín
red	*pi-rosh*	piros
white	*fe-hehr*	fehér
yellow	*shaar-ghah*	sárga

Toiletries

comb	*feh-shüü*	fésű
condoms	*ko-ton*	koton
deodorant	*de-zo-dor*	dezodor
hairbrush	*hahy-ke-fe*	hajkefe
moisturising cream	*krehm* *saa-rahz boer-re*	krém száraz bőrre

HUNGARIAN

razor	*bo-rot-vah*	borotva
sanitary napkins	*e-ghehs-shehgh-üdji be-teht*	egészségügyi betć
shampoo	*shahm-pon*	sampon
shaving cream	*bo-rot-vaal-ko-zoh krehm*	borotválkozókrén
soap	*sahp-pahn*	szappan
sunblock cream	*nahp-o-lahy*	napolaj
tampons	*tahm-pon*	tampon
tissues	*pah-peer-zheb-ken-doer*	papírzsebkendő
toilet paper	*veh tseh pah-peer*	WC papír
toothbrush	*fogh-ke-fe*	fogkefe
toothpaste	*fogh-krehm*	fogkrém

Stationery & Publications

map	*tehr-kehp*	térkép
newspaper	*ooy-shaagh*	újság
newspaper in English	*ahn-ghol nyel-vüü ooy-shaagh*	angol nyelvű újság
novels in English	*ahn-ghol nyel-vüü re-gheh-nyek*	angol nyelvű regények
paper	*pah-peer*	papír
pen (ballpoint)	*go-yohsh-toll*	golyóstoll
scissors	*ol-loh*	olló

Photography

How much is it to process this film?

meny-nyi-be ke-rül eloer-heev-ni ezt ah fil-met?

Mennyibe kerül előhívni ezt a filmet?

When will it be ready?

mi-kor les kehs?

Mikor lesz kész?

I'd like a film for this camera.

edj fil-met se-ret-nehk eb-be ah fehny-keh-pe-zoer-ghehp-be

Egy filmet szeretnék ebbe a fényképezőgépbe.

B&W (film)	*fe-ke-te fe-hehr-film*	fekete-fehér film
camera	*fehny-keh-pe-zoer-ghehp*	fényképezőgép
colour (film)	*see-nesh-film*	színesfilm
film	*film*	film
flash	*vah-ku*	vaku
lens	*len-che*	lencse
light meter	*fehny-meh-roer*	fénymérő

Smoking

A packet of cigarettes, please.

edj cho-mahgh tsi-ghah-ret-taat keh-rek

Egy csomag cigarettát kérek.

Are these cigarettes strong/mild?

ez ah tsi-ghah-ret-tah e-roersh/djen-ghe?

Ez a cigaretta erős/gyenge?

HUNGARIAN

Do you have a light?
vahn tü-ze? Van tüze?

cigarette papers	*tsi-ghah-ret-tah pah-peer*	cigaretta papír
cigarettes	*tsi-ghah-ret-tah*	cigaretta
filtered	*füsht-süü-roersh*	füstszűrős
lighter	*ern-djooy-toh*	öngyújtó
matches	*dju-fah*	gyufa
menthol	*men-to-losh*	mentolos
pipe	*pi-pah*	pipa
tobacco (pipe)	*pi-pah-do-haany*	pipadohány

Sizes & Comparisons

small	*ki-chi*	kicsi
big	*nahdj*	nagy
heavy	*ne-hehz*	nehéz
light	*kerny-nyüü*	könnyű
more	*terbb*	több
less	*ke-ve-shebb*	kevesebb
too much/many	*tool shok*	túl sok
many	*shok*	sok
enough	*e-lehgh*	elég
also	*sin-tehn*	szintén
a little bit	*edj ki-chi*	egy kicsi

HUNGARIAN

Health

Where is ...?

hol vahn ...?		Hol van ...?
the doctor	*ahz or-vosh*	az orvos
the hospital	*ah kohr-haaz*	a kórház
the chemist	*ah djohdj-ser-taar*	a gyógyszertár
the dentist	*ah fogh-or-vosh*	a fogorvos

I am sick.
  ros-sul vah-djok   Rosszul vagyok.

My friend is sick.
  ah bah-raa-tom ros-sul   A barátom rosszul van.
  vahn

Could I see a female doctor?
  edj dok-tor-noert   Egy doktornőt keresek?
  ke-re-shek?

What's the matter?
  mi ah prob-leh-mah?   Mi a probléma?

Where does it hurt?
  hol faay?   Hol fáj?

It hurts here.
  itt faay   Itt fáj.

My ... hurts.
  ah/ahz ... faay   A/az ... fáj.

Parts of the Body

ankle	*bo-kaam*	bokám
arm	*kah-rom*	karom
back	*haa-tahm*	hátam

HUNGARIAN

chest	*mell-kah-shom*	mellkasom
ear	*fü-lem*	fülem
eye	*se-mem*	szemem
finger	*uy-yahm*	ujjam
foot	*laab-fe-yem*	lábfejem
hand	*ke-zem*	kezem
head	*fe-yem*	fejem
heart	*see-vem*	szívem
leg	*laa-bahm*	lábam
mouth	*saam*	szám
nose	*or-rom*	orrom
ribs	*bor-daam*	bordám
skin	*boer-rerm*	bőröm
spine	*ghe-rin-tsem*	gerincem
stomach	*djom-rom*	gyomrom
teeth	*fo-ghahm*	fogam
throat	*tor-kom*	torkom

Ailments

(I have ...)

an allergy	*ahl-ler-ghi-aash vah-djok*	Allergiás vagyok.
a blister	*hoh-yahgh vahn rahy-tahm*	Hólyag van rajtam
a burn	*megh-eh-ghet-tem mah-ghahm*	Megégettem magam.
a cold	*megh-faaz-tahm*	Megfáztam.
constipation	*sehk-re-ke-deh-shem vahn*	Székrekedésem va
cough	*ker-her-gherk*	köhögök

diarrhoea	*hahsh-me-neh-shem vahn*	Hasmenésem van.
fever	*laa-zahm vahn*	Lázam van.
a headache	*faay ah fe-yem*	Fáj a fejem.
hepatitis	*maay-djul-lah-daa-shom vahn*	Májgyulladásom van.
influenza	*in-flu-en-zaash va-djok*	Influenzás vagyok.
low/high blood pressure	*ah-lah-chony/ mah-ghahsh ah vehr-nyo-maa-shom*	Alacsony/ Magas a vérnyomásom.
a pain	*faay dahl-mahm vahn*	Fájdalmam van.
sore throat	*faay ah tor-kom*	Fáj a torkom.
sprain	*fi-tsah-mom vahn*	Ficamom van.
a stomachache	*faay ah djom-rom*	Fáj a gyomrom.
sunburn	*le-ehgh-tem*	Leégtem.
a venereal disease	*ne-mi be-tegh-sheh-ghem vahn*	Nemi betegségem van.
worms	*ghi-lis-taam vahn*	Gilisztám van.

Some Useful Words & Phrases

(I'm ...)

diabetic	*tsu-kor-be-tegh vah-djok*	Cukorbeteg vagyok.
epileptic	*e-pi-lep-si-aash vah-djok*	Epilepsziás vagyok.
asthmatic	*ahst-maash vah-djok*	Asztmás vagyok.

I'm allergic to antibiotics/
penicillin.
> *ahl-ler-ghi-aash vah-djok*   Allergiás vagyok
> *ahz ahn-ti-bi-o-ti-kum-rah/*   az antibiotikumra/
> *ah pe-ni-tsi-lin-re*   a penicillinre.

I'm pregnant.
> *ter-hesh vah-djok*   Terhes vagyok.

I'm on the pill.
> *fo-ghahm-zaash-ghaat-loh*   Fogamzásgátlótablettát
> *tab-let-taat se-dek*   szedek.

I haven't had my period
for ... months.
> *nem yertt meg ah mensh-*   Nem jött meg a menstruációm
> *truaa-tsiohm ...*   ... hónapja.
> *hoh-nahp-yah*

I have been vaccinated.
> *be vah-djok olt-vah*   Be vagyok oltva.

I have my own syringe.
> *vahn shah-yaat tüüm*   Van saját tűm.

I feel better/worse.
> *yob-bahn/ros-sahb-bul*   Jobban/rosszabbul vagyok.
> *vah-djok*

accident	*bah-le-shet*	baleset
addiction	*kaa-rosh sen-ve-dehy*	káros szenvedély
antibiotics	*ahn-ti-bi-o-ti-kum*	antibiotikum
antiseptic	*fer-toer-zehsh-ghaat-loh*	fertőzésgátló
aspirin	*as-pi-rin*	aszpirin
bandage	*ker-tehsh*	kötés

bite	*hah-rah-paash*	harapás
blood test	*vehr-vizh-ghaa-laht*	vérvizsgálat
contraceptive	*fo-ghahm-zaash-ghaat-loh*	fogamzásgátló
injection	*in-yek-tsi-oh*	injekció
injury	*sheh-rü-lehsh*	sérülés
medicine	*or-vosh-shaagh*	orvosság
menstruation	*mensht-ru-aa-tsioh*	menstruáció
vitamins	*vi-tah-mi-nok*	vitaminok
wound	*sheb*	seb

At the Chemist

I need medication for ...
   djohdj-ser-re vahn sük-sheh-ghem ...   Gyógyszerre van szükségem ...
I have a prescription.
   vahn edj re-tsep-tem   Van egy receptem.

At the Dentist

I have a toothache.
   faay ah fo-ghahm   Fáj a fogam.
I've lost a filling.
   ki-e-shett ah ter-mehsh   Kiesett a tömés.
I've broken a tooth.
   el-tert edj fo-ghahm   Eltört egy fogam.
My gums hurt.
   faay ahz ee-nyem   Fáj az ínyem.
I don't want it extracted.
   nem ah-kah-rom ki-hoo-zaht-ni   Nem akarom kihúzatni.

Please give me an anaesthetic.
keh-rem ahd-yon   Kérem adjon
ehr-zehsh-te-le-nee-toert   érzéstelenítőt.

Time & Dates

What time is it?
haany oh-rah?   Hány óra?
What date is it today?
haa-nyah-di-kah vahn   Hányadika van ma?
mah?

It is ... o'clock.
... oh-rah vahn   ... óra van.

in the morning	*regh-ghel*	reggel
in the afternoon	*deh-lu-taan*	délután
in the evening	*esh-te*	este

Days of the Week

Monday	*heht-foer*	hétfő
Tuesday	*kedd*	kedd
Wednesday	*ser-dah*	szerda
Thursday	*chü-ter-terk*	csütörtök
Friday	*pehn-tek*	péntek
Saturday	*som-baht*	szombat
Sunday	*vah-shaar-nahp*	vasárnap

HUNGARIAN

Months

January	*yah-nu-aar*	január
February	*feb-ru-aar*	február
March	*maar-tsi-ush*	március
April	*aap-ri-lish*	április
May	*maa-yush*	május
June	*yoo-ni-ush*	június
July	*yoo-li-ush*	július
August	*ah-u-ghus-tush*	augusztus
September	*sep-tem-ber*	szeptember
October	*ok-toh-ber*	október
November	*no-vem-ber*	november
December	*de-tsem-ber*	december

Seasons

summer	*nyaar*	nyár
autumn	*oers*	ősz
winter	*tehl*	tél
spring	*tah-vahs*	tavasz

Present

today	*mah*	ma
this morning	*mah regh-ghel*	ma reggel
tonight	*mah esh-te*	ma este
this week	*e-zen ah heh-ten*	ezen a héten
year	*eb-ben ahz ehv-ben*	ebben az évben
now	*mosht*	most

HUNGARIAN

HUNGARIAN

Past

yesterday	*tegh-nahp*	tegnap
day before yesterday	*tegh-nahp-e-loertt*	tegnapelőtt
last night	*tegh-nahp esh-te*	tegnap este
last week/year	*moolt heh-ten/ moolt ehv-ben*	múlt héten/ vbenmúlt évben

Future

tomorrow	*hol-nahp*	holnap
day after tomorrow	*hol-nahp-u-taan*	holnapután
tomorrow evening	*hol-nahp esh-te*	holnap este
next week	*yer-voer heh-ten*	jövő héten
next year	*yer-voer-re*	jövőre

During the Day

afternoon	*deh-lu-taan*	délután
dawn, very early morning	*hahy-nahl*	hajnal
day	*nahp*	nap
early	*ko-raan*	korán
midnight	*ehy-fehl*	éjfél
morning	*regh-ghel*	reggel
night	*ehy-yel*	éjjel
noon	*dehl*	dél
sundown	*nahp-le-men-te*	naplemente
sunrise	*nahp-fel-kel-te*	napfelkelte

Numbers & Amounts

0	*nul-lah*	nulla
1	*edj*	egy
2	*ket-toer*	kettő
3	*haa-rom*	három
4	*nehdj*	négy
5	*ert*	öt
6	*haht*	hat
7	*heht*	hét
8	*nyolts*	nyolc
9	*ki-lents*	kilenc
10	*teez*	tíz
20	*hoos*	húsz
30	*hahr-mints*	harminc
40	*nedj-ven*	negyven
50	*ert-ven*	ötven
60	*haht-vahn*	hatvan
70	*het-ven*	hetven
80	*nyolts-vahn*	nyolcvan
90	*ki-lents-ven*	kilencven
100	*saaz*	száz
1000	*e-zer*	ezer
one million	*edj mil-li-oh*	egy millió
1st	*el-shoer*	első (1.)
2nd	*maa-sho-dik*	második (2.)
3rd	*hahr-mah-dik*	harmadik (3.)

HUNGARIAN

¼	*edj-ne-djed*	egynegyed
⅓	*edj-hahr-mahd*	egyharmad
½	*fehl*	feål
¾	*haa-rom-ne-djed*	haåromnegyed

Some Useful Words

a little (amount)	*edj ke-vehsh*	egy kevés
double	*dup-lah*	dupla
a dozen	*edj tu-tsaht*	egy tucat
Enough!	*e-lehgh!*	Elég!
few	*neh-haany*	néhány
less	*ke-ve-shebb*	kevesebb
many	*shok*	sok
more	*terbb*	több
once	*edj-ser*	egyszer
a pair	*edj paar*	egy pár
per cent	*saa-zah-lehk*	százalék
some	*vah-lah-meny-nyi*	valamennyi
too much	*tool shok*	túl sok
twice	*keht-ser*	kétszer

Abbreviations

db	piece
de./du.	am/pm
É/D	Nth/Sth
EK	UK
EU	EU
ENSZ	UN
gr/kg	gm/kg

id.	snr
ifj.	jnr
i.sz./i.e.	AD/BC
kb.	approx.
Oszt./Közp.	Dept/HQ
stb.	etc
u.i./ford.	ps/pto
u/ú/krt/k	St/Rd/Blvd/Lane
l.Vh/2.Vh	WWI/WWII

ITALIAN

Italian

Introduction

Italian is a Romance language, related to French, Spanish, Portuguese and Romanian. The Romance languages belong to the larger Indo-European group of languages, which include English. Indeed, as English and Italian share common roots in Latin, you'll find many Italian words which you will recognise.

Modern literary Italian began to be developed in the 13th and 14th centuries, predominantly through the works of Dante, Petrarch and Boccaccio, who wrote chiefly in the Florentine dialect. The language drew on its Latin heritage, and the many dialects of Italy, to develop into the standard Italian of today. While many and varied dialects are spoken in everyday conversation, standard Italian is the national language of schools, media and literature, and is understood throughout the country.

There are 57 million speakers of Italian in Italy, half a million in Switzerland, where Italian is one of the four official languages, and 1.5 million speakers in France and Yugoslavia. As a result of migration, Italian is also widely spoken in the USA, Argentina, Brazil and Australia.

Opera, film, and literature, from the great Renaissance works to modern writers such as Umberto Eco, Alberto Moravia and Primo Levi, to name a few, have all contributed to portraying Italian as the vibrant, melodic and rich language that it is. It is not, however, a difficult language for English-speakers to learn and Italians will welcome your attempts to communicate with them.

Italians are often more demonstrative than you may be accustomed – gesticulations and raised voices abound in Italy – and you may find you need to reduce the physical space you're used to when communicating with people. It is difficult, however, to offend anyone if you stick to the etiquette of your homeland.

Italian words are expressed in either feminine or masculine forms. In this chapter, the feminine form is given first, the masculine second. Informal forms of words are given within brackets after the formal word, or indicated with (inf).

Pronunciation

Italian is not difficult to pronounce. Although some of the more clipped vowels, and stress on double letters, require careful practice for English speakers, it is easy enough to make yourself understood.

Vowels

Vowels are generally more clipped than in English.

a	as the second 'a' in 'camera'
e	as the 'ay' in 'day', although without the 'i' sound
i	as in 'see'
o	as in 'dot'
u	as in 'too'

Consonants

The pronunciation of many consonants is similar to English. The following sounds depend on certain rules:

c	like 'k' before **a**, **o** and **u**
	like the 'ch' in 'choose' before **e** and **i**
ch	a hard 'k' sound
g	a hard 'g' as in 'get' before **a**, **o** and **u**
	before **e** and **i**, like the 'j' in 'job'

gh	a hard 'g' as in 'get'
gli	as the 'lli' in 'million'
gn	as the 'ny' in 'canyon'
h	always silent
r	a rolled 'rrr' sound
sc	before before **e** and **i**, like the 'sh' in 'sheep' before **h**, **a**, **o** and **u**, a hard sound as in 'school'
z	as in 'zoo', as the 'ts' in 'lights' or as the 'ds' in 'beds'

Note that when **ci**, **gi** and **sci** are followed by **a**, **o** or **u**, unles the accent falls on the **i**, it is not pronounced. Thus the nam 'Giovanni' is pronounced *joh-***vahn**-*nee*, with no 'i' sound.

Stress
Double consonants are pronounced as a longer, often mor forceful sound than a single consonant.

Stress often falls on the next to last syllable, as in *spa-***ghet**-t When a word has an accent, the stress is on that syllable, as i *cit-***tà**, 'city'.

Greetings & Civilities
Top Useful Phrases
Hello.
  chahw   Ciao.
Goodbye.
  *ah-rree-ve-***dair**-*chee/chahw*   Arrivederci/Ciao.
Yes./No.
  see/no   Sì./No.
Excuse me.
  mee **skoo**-*zee*   Mi scusi.
May I? Do you mind?
  pos-*so? vee dis-pee-***ah**-   Posso? Vi dispiace?
  chei?

Sorry. (excuse me, forgive me)
mee **skoo**-*zee/mee per-***do***-
    nee   Mi scusi. Mi perdoni.
Please.
    *per fah-***vor***-rei/per pee-ah-*
    chair-*rei*   Per favore./Per piacere.
Thank you.
    ghrah-*tsee-e*   Grazie.
Many thanks.
    ghrah-*tsee-e* **mee**-
    *lei/***ghrah***-tsee-e* **tahn**-*to* Grazie mille. Grazie tanto.
That's fine. You're welcome.
    prei-*gho*   Prego.

Greetings

Good morning.
    *bwon-***jor***-no*   Buongiorno.
Good evening/night.
    *bwo-na-***sair***-rah/***not***-tei* Buonasera/notte.
How are you?
    ko-mei **stah***?*   Come sta?
    ko-mei **stah***-ee?*   Come stai? (inf)
Well, thanks.
    be-*ne,* **ghrah**-*tsee-e*   Bene, grazie.

Forms of Address

Madam/Mrs/Ms	*see-***nyor***-ra*	Signora
Sir/Mr	*see-***nyor***-rei*	Signorc
companion, friend	*ah-***mee***-kah/o*	amica/o

ITALIAN

Small Talk
Meeting People
What is your name?

koh-mei see kee-ah-mah?   Come si chiama?

koh-mei tee kee-ah-mee?   Come ti chiami? (inf)

My name is …

mee kee-ah-mo …   Mi chiamo …

I'd like to introduce you to …

vo-rrei pre-sen-tar-lah   Vorrei presentarla

(pre-sen-tar-tee) ah …   (presentarti) a …

I'm pleased to meet you.

pee-ah-chair-rei/lee-e-to   Piacere. Lieto di conoscerla

dee ko-nosh-air-lah   (conoscerti).

(ko-nosh-air-tee)

Nationalities
Where are you from?

dah doh-vei vee-e-nee?   Da dove viene?

dee doh-vei sei?   Di dove sei?

I am from …

vehng-gho dah …   Vengo da …

so-no dee …   Sono di …

Australia	*(l')ahw-strah-lee-yah*	(l')Australia
Canada	*(eel) kah-nah-dah*	(il) Canada
England	*(l')eeng-ghil-tair-rrah*	(l')Inghilterra
Ireland	*(l')eer-lahn-dah*	(l') Irlanda
New Zealand	*(lah) nwo-vah tze-lahn-dah*	(la) Nuova Zelanda
Scotland	*(lah) sko-tzee-ah*	(la) Scozia

ITALIAN

the USA	*lyee **stah**-tee*	gli Stati Uniti
	*oo-**nee**-tee*	
Wales	*(eel) **ghahl**-les*	(il) Galles

Age

How old are you?
kwahn-tee **ahn**-nee ah (ah-ee)?   Quanti anni ha (hai)?

I am … years old.
o … **ahn**-nee   Ho … anni.

Occupations

What (work) do you do?
*kei lah-**vor**-ro fah (fah-ee)?*   Che lavoro fa (fai)?

I am a/an …
so-no oo-nah/oon …   Sono una/un …

artist	*ahr-**tee**-stah*	artista
business person	***don**-nah/**wo**-mo*	donna (f)/uomo (m)
	dee ahf-fah-ree	di affari
doctor	*do-tor-**es**-sa*	dottoressa (f)
	*do-**tor**-rei*	dottore (m)
	***me**-dee-ko*	medico
engineer	*een-jen-**yair**-rei*	ingegnere
farmer	*ah-ghree-kol-**tor**-rei*	agricoltore
journalist	*jor-nah-**lees**-tah*	giornalista
lawyer	*ahv-vo-kah-**tess**-ah*	avvocatessa (f)
	*ahv-vo-**kah**-to*	avvocato (m)
manual worker	*mah-no-vah-lei*	manovale
mechanic	*me-**kah**-nee-kah/ko*	meccanica/o
nurse	*een-feer-mee-**air**-rei*	infermiera/e

office worker	*eem-pee-e-**ghah**-tah/o*	impiegata/o
scientist	*shee-en-tzee-**ah**-tah/o*	scienziata/o
student	*stoo-den-**tes**-sah*	studentessa (f)
	*stoo-**den**-tei*	studente (m)
teacher	*een-seh-**nyahn**-tei*	insegnante
waiter	*kah-mair-ree-**air**-rah/ei*	cameriera/e
writer	*skreet-**tor**-rei*	scrittore

Religion

What is your religion?
*dee **kei** rei-lee-**jo**-nei ei lei (sei)?*
Di che religione è lei (sei)?

I am not religious.
*non **so**-no re-lee-**jo**-sah/o*
Non sono religiosa/o.

I am …
so-no …
Sono …

Buddhist	*boo-**dee**-stah*	buddista
Catholic	*kaht-**to**-lee-kah/o*	cattolica/o
Christian	*kree-stee-**ah**-nah/o*	cristiana/o
Hindu	*een-**doo***	indù
Jewish	*e-**brei**-ah/o*	ebrea/o
Muslim	*mu-sul-**mah**-nah/o*	mussulmana/o

Family

Are you married?
*ei spo-**sah**-tah/o lei?*
È sposata/o lei?

I am (not) married.
*(non) **so**-no spo-**sah**-tah/o*
(Non) Sono sposata/o.

ITALIAN

How many children do you have?
kwahn-tee fee-**lyee** ah (ahee)?

Quanti figli ha (hai)?

I don't have any children.
non oh fee-lyee

Non ho figli.

I have a daughter/a son.
oh **oo**-nah fee-lyah/oon fee-lyo

Ho una figlia/un figlio.

How many sisters/brothers do you have?
kwahn-tei so-**rehl**-lei/ **kwahn**-tee frah-**tehl**-lee ah (ahee)?

Quante sorelle/Quanti fratelli ha (hai)?

Is your wife/husband here?
soo-ah **moh**-lyee-e/soo-o mah-**ree**-to ei kwee kon lei?

Sua moglie/Suo marito è qui con lei?

Are you alone?
ei (sei) so-lah/o?

È (Sei) sola/o?

Do you have a girlfriend/boyfriend?
ah (ahee) **oo**-nah rah-**ghah**-tsah/oon rah-**ghah**-tso?

Ha (Hai) una ragazza/un ragazzo?

brother	frah-**tehl**-lo	fratello
children	fee-lyee/bahm-**bee**-nee	figli/bambini
daughter	fee-lyah	figlia
family	fah-**mee**-lyah	famiglia
father	**pah**-drei	padre
grandfather	**non**-no	nonno
grandmother	**non**-nah	nonna

husband	mah-**ree**-to	marito
mother	**mah**-drei	madre
sister	sor-**rrel**-lah	sorella
son	**fee**-lyo	figlio
uncle	**dzee**-o	zio
wife	**mo**-lyei	moglie

Feelings

I (don't) like …
    *(non) mee pee-**ah**-chei …* (Non) Mi piace …
I am sorry. (condolence)
    *kon-do-**lyahn**-tzei* Condoglianze.
I am grateful.
    *lah reen-**ghrah**-tsee-o* La ringrazio.

I am …
    o … Ho …

cold/hot	**fred**-do/**kahl**-do	freddo/caldo
hungry/thirsty	**fah**-mei/se-tei	fame/sete
in a hurry	**fret**-tah	fretta
right	rah-**jo**-nei	ragione
sleepy	**son**-no	sonno
wrong	**tor**-to	torto

I am …
    so-no … Sono …

angry	ah-rah-bee-**ah**-ta/o	arrabbiata/o
happy/sad	fei-**lee**-chei/**tree**-stei	felice/triste
tired	**stahn**-kah/o	stanca/o
worried	prei-o-koo-**pah**-tah/o	preoccupata/o
I'm well.	sto **be**-nei	Sto bene.

Language Difficulties

Do you speak English?
pahr-lah (pahr-lee)
*eeng-**ghlei**-zei?*

Parla (Parli) inglese?

Does anyone speak English?
*chei kwahl-**koo**-no kei*
***pahr**-lah eeng-**ghlei**-zei?*

C'è qualcuno che parla
inglese?

I speak a little Italian.
pahr-lo un po
*dee-tah-lee-**ah**-no*

Parlo un po' d'italiano.

I don't speak ...
*non **pahr**-lo ...*

Non parlo ...

I (don't) understand.
*(non) kah-**pees**-ko*

(Non) Capisco.

Could you speak more slowly
please?
*pwo pahr-**lah**-rei pee-oo*
*len-tah-**men**-tei, pair*
*fah-**vor**-rei?*

Può parlare (più)
lentamente, per favore?

Could you repeat that?
*pwo ree-pe-**tair**-lo, pair*
*fah-**vor**-rei?*

Può ripeterlo, per favore?

How do you say ...?
*ko-mei see **dee**-chei ...?*

Come si dice ...?

What does ... mean?
*kei (ko-zah) see-**nyee**-fee-*
*kah/vwol **dee**-rei ...?*

Che (cosa) significa/vuole
dire ...?

ITALIAN

I speak …
pahr-lo …   Parlo …

English	*eeng-**ghlei**-zei*	inglese
French	*frahn-**chei**-zei*	francese
German	*te-**des**-ko*	tedesco

Some Useful Phrases

Sure.
   ***chair**-to*   Certo.

Just a minute.
   *oon mee-**noo**-to*   Un minuto.

It's (not) important.
   *non eem-**por**-tah*   Non importa.

It's (not) possible.
   *(non) eh pos-**see**-bee-lei*   (Non) È possibile.

Wait!
   *ah-**spet**-tee! (ah-**spet**-ta!)*   Aspetti! (Aspetta! – inf)

Good luck!
   *bwo-nah for-**too**-na!*   Buona fortuna!

Signs

BAGGAGE COUNTER	DEPOSITO BAGAGLI
CUSTOMS	LA DOGANA
EMERGENCY EXIT	USCITA DI SICUREZZA
ENTRANCE	INGRESSO/ENTRATA
EXIT	USCITA
FREE ADMISSION	INGRESSO GRATUITO
HOT/COLD	CALDO/FREDDO
INFORMATION	INFORMAZIONI
NO ENTRY	VIETATO ENTRARE

ITALIAN

NO SMOKING	VIETATO FUMARE
OPEN/CLOSED	APERTO/CHIUSO
PROHIBITED	PROIBITO/VIETATO
RESERVED	PRENOTATO/IN RISERVA
TELEPHONE	TELEFONO
TOILETS	GABINETTI

Emergencies

POLICE	POLIZIA/CARABINIERI
POLICE STATION	QUESTURA/CASERMA

Help!
  ah-yoo-to!   Aiuto!
It's an emergency!
  ei oon e-mer-jen-tsah!   È un emergenza!
There's been an accident!
  chei stah-to un een-chee-den-tei!   C'è stato un incidente!
Call a doctor!
  kee-ah-mah un dot-tor-rei/un me-dee-ko!   Chiama un dottore/un medico!
Call an ambulance!
  kee-ah-mah un ahm-bu-lahn-tsah!   Chiama una ambulanza!

ITALIAN

I've been raped.
*so-no stah-tah vee-o-len-**tah**-tah/o*

Sono stata/o violentata/o.

I've been robbed!
*mee **ahn**-no de-roo-**bah**-tah/o*

Mi hanno derubata/o.

Call the police!
*kee-**ah**-mah lah po-lee-**tsee**-ah!*

Chiama la polizia!

Go away!
*vah-ee **vee**-ah! mee **lah**-shee een pah-chei!*

Vai via! Mi lasci in pace!

I'll call the police!
*kee-ah-**mair**-ro lah po-lee-**tsee**-ah!*

Chiamerò la polizia!

Thief!
*ahl **lah**-dro!*

Al ladro!

I am ill.
*so-no mah-**lah**-ta/o*

Sono malata/o.

My friend is ill.
*lah mee-ah ah-**mee**-kah ei mah-**lah**-tah*

La mia amica è malata. (f)

*eel mee-o ah-**mee**-ko ei mah-**lah**-to*

Il mio amico è malato. (m)

Where is the police station?
*do-**vei** lah kwes-**doo**-rah?*

Dov'è la questura?

Where are the toilets?
*do-**ve** so-no ee ghah-bee-**net**-tee?*

Dove sono i gabinetti?

I am lost.
*mee so-no **pair**-so*

Mi sono perso.

Could you help me please?
mee pwo ah-yoo-tah-rei?
mee ah-yoo-tee, pair fah-vor-rei

Mi può aiutare?
Mi aiuti, per favore.

Could I please use the telephone?
pos-so fah-rei oo-nah tei-lei-fo-nah-tah?

Posso fare una telefonata?

I'm sorry. I apologise.
mee skoo-zee. mee dee-spee-ah-chei

Mi scusi. Mi dispiace.

I didn't realise I was doing anything wrong.
non sah-pei-vo kei fah-chei-vo kwahl-ko-zah dee mah-lei

Non sapevo che facevo qualcosa di male.

I didn't do it.
non lo faht-to

Non l'ho fatto.

I wish to contact my embassy/consulate.
vo-rrei met-tair-mee een kon-taht-to kon lah mee-ah ahm-bah-shah-tah/eel mee-o kon-so-lah-to

Vorrei mettermi in contatto con la mia ambasciata/ il mio consolato.

I speak English.
pahr-lo eeng-ghlei-zei

Parlo inglese.

I have medical insurance.
o lahs-see-koo-rah-tsee-o-nei (lah-sees-den-tsah) me-dee-kah

Ho l'assicurazione (l'assistenza) medica.

ITALIAN

My possessions are insured.
lah mee-ah ro-bah ei   La mia roba è assicurata.
ahs-see-koo-rah-tah

My … was stolen.
mee ahn-no roo-bah-to …   Mi hanno rubato …
I've lost …
o pair-so …   Ho perso …

my bags	*ee mee-ei-ee bah-**ghah**-lyee*	i miei bagagli
my handbag	*lah mee-ah bor-sah*	la mia borsa
my money	*ee mee-ei-ee sol-dee/ eel mee-o de-nahr-ro*	i miei soldi/il mio denaro
my travellers' cheques	*ee mee-ei-ee 'travellers' cheques'*	i miei travellers' cheques
my passport	*eel mee-o pahs-sah-por-to*	il mio passaporto
my wallet	*eel mee-o por-tah-fo-lyo*	il mio portafoglio

Paperwork

form	*mo-doo-lo*	modulo
name	*no-mei*	nome
address	*een-dee-reets-o*	indirizzo
date of birth	*dah-tah dee nah-shee-tah*	data di nascita
place of birth	*lwo-gho dee nah-shee-tah*	luogo di nascita
age	*e-tah*	età
sex	*ses-so*	sesso
nationality	*nah-tsee-o-nah-lee-tah*	nazionalità

ITALIAN

religion	*rei-lee-jo-nei*	religione
reason for travel	*mo-tee-vee dee vee-ahj-jo*	motivi di viaggio
profession	*pro-fes-see-o-nei*	professione
married	*spo-zah-tah/o*	sposata/o
divorced	*dee-vor-tsee-ah-tah/o*	divorziata/o
single	*noo-bee-lei*	nubile (f)
	che-lee-bei	celibe (m)
passport	*pahs-sah-por-to*	passaporto
passport number	*noo-mair-ro del pahs-sah-por-to*	numero del passaporto
visa	*vee-zah kon-so-lah-rei*	visto consolare
identification (card)	*(kahr-tah d)ee-den-tee-fee-kah-tsee-o-nei*	(carta d')identi-ficazione
birth certificate	*chair-tee-fee-kah-to dee nah-shee-tah*	certificato di nascita
driver's licence	*pah-ten-tei*	patente
car owner's title	*tee-to-lo dee pro-pree-e-tah*	titolo di proprietà
car registration	*re-jee-strah-tsee-o-nei*	registrazione
customs	*do-ghah-nah*	dogana
immigration	*ee-mee-ghrah-tsee-o-nei*	immigrazione
border	*fron-tee-air-rah*	frontiera

Getting Around

ARRIVALS	ARRIVI
BUS STOP	FERMATA DELL'AUTOBUS
DEPARTURES	PARTENZE
STATION	STAZIONE
SUBWAY	METRÒ (METROPOLITANA)
TICKET OFFICE	BIGLIETTERIA
TIMETABLE	ORARIO
TRAIN STATION	STAZIONE F.S.(FERROVIA DELLO STATO)

What time does … leave/
arrive?
*ah kei **or**-rah pahr-**tei**/ah-**ree**-vah …?*   A che ora parte/arriva …?

the (air)plane	*lah-**air**-re-o*	l'aereo
the boat	*lah **bahr**-kah*	la barca
the ferry	*eel trah-**ghet**-to*	il traghetto
the bus	***lahw**-to-boos*	l'autobus
the train	*eel **trei**-no*	il treno

Directions
Where is …?
*do-**vei** …?*   Dov'è …?
How do I get to …?
*mee pwo **dee**-rei lah* **strah**-dah pair …?*   Mi può dire la strada per …
Is it far from/near here?
*ei lon-**tah**-no/vee-**chee**-no?*   È lontano/vicino?

Can I walk there?
*chee pos-so ahn-**dah**-rei ah
pee-e-dee?*   Ci posso andare a piedi?

Can you show me (on the
map)?
*mee **mo**-stree (sool-lah
kahr-tah/pee-ahn-**tee**-nah)?*   Mi mostri (sulla
carta/piantina).

Are there other means of
getting there?
*chee so-no ahl-tree mo-dee
pair ahr-ree-**vahr**-chee?*   Ci sono altri modi per
arrivarci?

I want to go to …
***vor**-rei ahn-**dah**-rei ah …*   Vorrei andare a …

Go straight ahead.
*see vah (vah-ee) **sem**-prei
dee-**reet**-to*   Si va sempre diritto.

Turn left …
*jee-rah ah see-**nee**-strah …*   Gira a sinistra …

Turn right …
*jee-rah ah **de**-strah …*   Gira a destra …

at the next corner
*ahl **pros**-see-mo
ahng-gho-lo*   al prossimo angolo

at the traffic lights
*ah-ee se-**mah**-for-ree*   ai semafori

behind	*dee-e-tro*	dietro
in front of	*dah-**vahn**-tee*	davanti
far	*lon-**tah**-no*	lontano
near	*vee-**chee**-no*	vicino
opposite	*dee **fron**-te ah*	di fronte a

Buying Tickets

Excuse me, where is the ticket office?
skoo-zee, do-vei lah bee-lyet-ter-ree-ah?

Scusi, dov'è la biglietteria?

Where can I buy a ticket?
do-vei pos-so/see pwo kom-prah-rei oon bee-lyet-to?

Dove posso/si può comprare un biglietto?

I want to go to …
vor-rei ahn-dah-rei ah …

Vorrei andare a …

Do I need to book?
see de-vei/bee-zo-nyah prei-no-tah-rei (oon po-sto)?

Si deve/Bisogna prenotare (un posto)?

You need to book.
see, de-vei prei-no-tah-rei/ fah-rei oo-nah prei-no-ta-tsee-o-nei

Sì, deve prenotare/fare una prenotazione.

I would like to book a seat to …
vo-rrei prei-no-tah-rei oon po-sto pair …

Vorrei prenotare un posto per …

I would like …
vo-rrei …

Vorrei …

a one-way ticket
(oon bee-lyet-to dee) so-lo ahn-dah-tah

(Un biglietto di) Solo andata.

a return ticket
(oon bee-lyet-to dee) ahn-dah-tah ei ree-tor-no

(Un biglietto di) Andata e ritorno.

two tickets
*doo-ei bee-**lyet**-tee*
due biglietti

tickets for all of us
*bee-**lyet**-tee pair **toot**-tee noy*
biglietti per tutti noi

a student's/child's fare
*oo-nah tah-**reef**-ah/oo-no **skon**-to pair stoo-**den**-tee/bahm-**bee**-nee*
una tariffa/uno sconto per studenti/bambini

1st class
*pree-mah **klahs**-sei*
prima classe

2nd class
*se-**kon**-dah **klahs**-sei*
seconda classe

It is full.
*ei pee-**e**-no*
È pieno/tutto occupato.

Is it completely full?
*ei kom-ple-tah-**men**-tei pee-**e**-no?*
È completamente pieno?

Can I get on the waiting (stand-by) list?
*pos-so **met**-tair-mee nel-lah **lee**-stah dah-**tei**-zah?*
Posso mettermi nella lista d'attesa?

Air

CHECKING IN	POSTO/BANCO DI CONTROLLO
LEFT-LUGGAGE OFFICE	DEPOSITO BAGAGLI
REGISTRATION	REGISTRAZIONE

Is there a flight to …?
chei oon vo-lo pair …?　　C'è un volo per …?

When is the next flight to …?
ah kei or-rah pahr-tei eel　　A che ora parte il prossimo
pross-ee-mo vo-lo pair …?　　volo per ...?

How long does the flight take?
kwahn-to tem-po door-rah　　Quanto tempo dura il volo
eel vo-lo?

What is the flight number?
kwahl ei eel noo-mair-ro　　Qual'è il numero di volo?
dee vo-lo?

boarding pass	*kahr-tah deem-bahr-ko*	carta d'imbarco
customs	*do-ghah-nah*	dogana

Bus

BUS/TRAM STOP	FERMATA DELL'AUTOBUS/DEL TRAM

Where is the bus/tram stop?
doh-vei lah fair-mah-tah　　Dov'è la fermata
del-ahw-to-bus/del trahm?　　dell'autobus/del tram?

Which bus goes to …?
kwah-lei ahw-to-bus vah　　Quale autobus va a …?
ah …?

Does this bus go to …?
kwest ahw-to-bus vah a …?　　Quest'autobus va a …?

How often do buses pass by?
*o-nyee **kwahn**-to tem-po*
***pahss**-ah-no lyee*
***ahw**-to-bus?*

Ogni quanto tempo
passano gli autobus?

What time is the … bus?
*ah kei **or**-rah **pahs**-sah …*
***ahw**-to-bus?*

A che ora passa … autobus?

next	*eel **pross**-ee-mo*	il prossimo
first	*eel **pree**-mo*	il primo
last	***lool**-tee-mo*	l'ultimo

Could you let me know when
we get to …?
*mee pwo **deer**-rei kwahn-*
*do see ah-**ree**-vah ah …?*
I want to get off!
*deh-vo **shen**-dair-rei!*

Mi può dire quando si
arriva a …?

Devo scendere!

Train

DINING CAR	VAGONE RISTORANTE
EXPRESS	RAPIDO
PLATFORM NO	BINARIO No.
SLEEPING CAR	VAGONE LETTO

Is this the right platform
for …?
*ei **kwes**-do eel bee-**nah**-ree-*
o pair …?

È questo il binario per …?

Passengers must …
*ee pahs-sej-**jair**-ree **deh**-vo-no …/bee-**zo**-nyah …* — I passeggeri devono …/ Bisogna …

change trains — *kam-bee-**ahr**-rei **trei**-nee* — cambiare treni

change platforms — *kam-bee-**ahr**-rei bee-**nah**-ree* — cambiare binari

The train leaves from platform …
*eel **trei**-no **pahr**-tei dahl bee-**nah**-ree-o …* — Il treno parte dal binario …

dining car — *vah-**gho**-nei rees-tor-**rahn**-tei* — vagone ristorante

express — *rah-pee-do* — rapido

local — *lo-**kah**-lei* — locale

sleeping car — *vah-**gho**-nei **let**-to* — vagone letto

Metro

METRO/UNDERGROUND	METRO
CHANGE (for coins)	SPICCIOLI
WAY OUT	USCITA

Which line takes me to …?
*kwah-**lei** lah **lee**-nei-ah pair ahn-**dah**-rei ah …?* — Qual'è la linea per andare a …?

ITALIAN

What is the next station?
*kwah-**lei** lah **pros**-see-mah stah-tsee-o-nei?*

Qual'è la prossima stazione?

Taxi

Can you take me to ...?
*mee pwo por-**tahr**-rei ah ...?*

Mi può portare a ...?

Please take me to ...
*mee **por**-tee ah ..., pair pee-ah-**chair**-rei*

Mi porti a ..., per piacere.

How much does it cost to go to ...?
*kwahn-to kos-dah ahn-**dah**-rei ah ...?*

Quanto costa andare a ...?

Instructions

Here is fine, thank you.
*kwee vah be-**nees**-see-mo, **ghrah**-tsee-e*

Qui va benissimo, grazie.

The next corner, please.
*ahl **pros**-see-mo **ahn**-gho-lo, pair fah-**vor**-rei*

Al prossimo angolo, per favore.

Continue!
*ah-**vahn**-tee!*

Avanti!

The next street to the left/right.
*ei lah **pros**-see-mah **strah**-dah ah see-**nee**-strah/**des**-tra*

È la prossima strada a sinistra/destra.

Stop here!
*see **fair**-mee kwah!*

Si fermi qua!

Please slow down.
*pwo rahl-len-**tahr**-rei, pair fah-**vor**-rei*

Può rallentare, per favore.

Please wait here.
*mee ahs-**spet**-tee kwee*

Mi aspetti qui.

Some Useful Phrases

The train is delayed/cancelled.
*eel **trei**-no ei een ree-**tahr**-do/kahn-chel-**lah**-to*

Il treno è in ritardo/cancellato.

There is a delay of … hours.
*chee sah-**rah** oon ree-**tahr**-do dee … **or**-rei*

Ci sarà un ritardo di … ore.

Can I reserve a place?
*pos-so pre-no-**tah**-rei oon pos-do?*

Posso prenotare un posto?

How long does the trip take?
***kwahn**-to doo-rah eel vee-**ahj**-jo?*

Quanto dura il viaggio?

Is it a direct route?
*ei oon ee-tee-nair-**rah**-ree-o dee-**ret**-to?*

È un itinerario diretto?

Is that seat taken?
*ei ok-koo-**pah**-to kwel **pos**-do?*

È occupato quel posto?

I want to get off at …
***vo**-lyo **shen**-dair-rei ah …*

Voglio scendere a …

Excuse me. (to get off)
*pair-**mes**-so*

Permesso.

Where can I hire a bicycle?
do-vei pos-so no-lej-jahr-rei oo-nah bee-chee-klet-tah?

Dove posso noleggiare una bicicletta?

Car

DETOUR	DEVIAZIONE
FREEWAY	AUTOSTRADA
PETROL STATION	STAZIONE DI SERVIZIO
GIVE WAY	DARE LA PRECEDENZA
MECHANIC	MECCANICO
NO ENTRY	DIVIETO DI TRANSITO
NO PARKING	DIVIETO DI SOSTA
NORMAL	NORMALE
ONE WAY	SENSO UNICO
REPAIRS	RIPARAZIONI
SELF SERVICE	SELF SERVICE
STOP	STOP
SUPER	SUPER
UNLEADED	SENZA PIOMBO

Where can I rent a car?
do-vei pos-so no-lej-jahr-rei oo-nah mah-kee-nah?

Dove posso noleggiare una macchina?

How much is it daily/weekly?
kwahn-to kos-dah ahl jor-no/ ahl-lah set-tee-mah-nah?

Quanto costa al giorno/alla settimana?

ITALIAN

Does that include
insurance/mileage?

ei kom-prei-zo lahs-see-koor-ra-tsee-o-nei/eel kos-do pair kee-lo-me-tro?

È compreso l'assicurazione, il costo per kilometro?

Where's the next petrol
station?

doh-vei lah pros-see-mah stah-tsee-o-nei dee sair-vee-tsee-o?

Dov'è la prossima stazione di servizio?

Please fill the tank.

eel pee-e-no, pair fah-vor-rei

Il pieno, per favore.

I want ... litres of petrol (gas).

vo-lyo ... lee-tree (dee behn-zee-nah)

Voglio ... litri (di benzina).

Please check the oil and water.

pwo kon-trol-lahr-rei lo-lyo ei lah-kwah, pair fah-vor-rei?

Può controllare l'olio e l'aqua, per favore?

How long can I park here?

pair kwahn-to tem-po pos-so pahr-kej-jahr-rei kwee?

Per quanto tempo posso parcheggiare qui?

Does this road lead to?

kwes-dah strah-dah chee por-tair-rah ah ...?

Questa strada ci porterà a ...?

air (for tyres)	*ah-ree-ah*	aria
battery	*bah-tair-ree-ah*	batteria
brakes	*frei-nee*	freni
clutch	*free-tsee-o-nei*	frizione

ITALIAN

driver's licence	*pah-**tehn**-tei (dee **ghwee**-dah*	patente (di guida)
engine	*mo-**tor**-rei*	motore
high beam lights	*ah-bah-lyee-**ahn**-tee*	abbaglianti
headlights	***ahn**-ah-bah-lyee-ahn-tee*	anabbaglianti
tail lights	*fah-nah-**lee**-nee dee **ko**-dah*	fanalini di coda
oil	*o-lyo*	olio
puncture	*for-rah-**too**-rah*	foratura
radiator	*rah-dee-ah-**tor**-rei*	radiatore
road map	*kar-tah strah-**dah**-lei*	carta stradale
tyres	***ghohm**-mei*	gomme
windscreen	*pah-rah-**bre**-tsah*	parabrezza

Car Problems

I need a mechanic.
*oh bee-**zo**-nyo dee oon me-**kah**-nee-ko* — Ho bisogno di un meccanico.

What make is it?
*kei **tee**-po dee **mah**-kee-nah ei?* — Che tipo di macchina è?

The battery is flat.
*lah ba-tair-**ree**-ah ei **skah**-ree-kah* — La batteria è scarica.

The radiator is leaking.
*eel rah-dee-ah-**tor**-rei pair-dei ah-kwah* — Il radiatore perde acqua.

I have a flat tyre.
*oh lah **ghom**-muh boo-**kah**-tah* — Ho la gomma bucata.

It's overheating.
see stah soo-rree-skahl-dahn-do Si sta surriscaldando.

It's not working.
non foon-tsee-o-nah Non funziona.

Accommodation

CAMPING GROUND	CAMPING/CAMPEGGIO
GUESTHOUSE	PENSIONE
HOTEL	ALBERGO
YOUTH HOSTEL	OSTELLO DELLA GIOVENTÙ

I am looking for …
sto chair-kahn-do … Sto cercando …

Where is a … hotel?
do-vei un ahl-bair-gho …? Dov'è un albergo …?

cheap	*kei kos-dah po-ko*	che costa poco
good	*bwo-no*	buono
nearby	*vee-chee-no*	vicino
clean	*pu-lee-to*	pulito

What is the address?
kwah-lei leen-dee-reets-o? Qual'è l'indirizzo?

Could you write the address, please?
mee pwo skree-vair-rei leen-dee-reets-o, pair fah-vor-rei? Mi può scrivere l'indirizzo, per favore?

At the Hotel

Do you have any rooms
available?
   ah del-lei kah-mair-rei   Ha delle camere libere?
   lee-bair-rei?

I would like …
   vo-rrei …   Vorrei …

a single room	*oo-nah kah-mair-rah seeng-gho-lah*	una camera singola
a double room	*oo-nah kah-mair-rah dop-pee-ah/pair doo-ei*	una camera doppia/per due
a room with a bathroom	*oo-nah kah-mair-rah kon bah-nyo*	una camera con bagno
to share a room	*dee-vee-dair-rei oo-nah stahn-tsa*	dividere una stanza
a bed	*un let-to*	un letto

I want a room with a …
   vo-rrei oo-nah kah-mair-rah kon …   Vorrei una camera con …

bathroom	*bah-nyo*	bagno
shower	*lah doch-chah*	la doccia
television	*te-lei-vee-zee-o-nei/ te-lei-vee-zor-rei*	televisione/ televisore
window	*fee-nes-tra*	finestra

I'm going to stay for …
   res-do pair …   Resto per…

one day	*oon jor-no*	un giorno

ITALIAN

two days	*doo-ei jor-nee*	due giorni
one week	*oo-nah set-tee-mah-nah*	una settimana

Do you have identification?
ah oo-nah kar-tah dee-den-tee-tah?
Ha una carta d'identità?

Your membership card, please.
lah soo-ah tes-sair-ah, pair fah-vor-rei
La sua tessera, per favore.

Sorry, we're full.
mee dees-pee-ah-chei, ei pee-e-no/non chei pos-do
Mi dispiace, è pieno/non c'è posto.

How long will you be staying?
kwahn-to tem-po vwo-lei res-dahr-rei?
Quanto tempo vuole restare

How many nights?
kwahn-tei not-tee?
Quante notti?

It's … per day/per person.
kos-dah … ahl jor-no/ pair pair-so-nah
Costa … al giorno/per persona.

How much is it per night/per person?
kwahn-to kos-dah … pair oo-nah not-tei/pair chahs-koo-nah/o
Quanto costa … per una notte/per ciascuna/o?

Can I see it?
pos-so ve-dair-lah?
Posso vederla?

Are there any others?
chei nei so-no ahl-trei?
Ce ne sono altre?

Are there any cheaper rooms?
*chee so-no **ahl-trei**
kah-mair-rei kei
kos-dah-no dee **me**-no?*

Ci sono altre camere che
costano di meno?

Can I see the bathroom?
***pos**-so ve-**dair**-rei eel
bah-nyo?*

Posso vedere il bagno?

Is there a reduction for
students/children?
*chei oo-no **scon**-to pair
stoo-**den**-tee/bahm-**bee**-
nee?*

C'è uno sconto per
studenti/bambini?

Does it include breakfast?
*lah ko-**lats**-ee-o-nei ei
kom-**prei**-zah (nel **pre**-tso)?*

La colazione è compresa
(nel prezzo)?

It's fine, I'll take it.
*vah **be**-nei, lah **pren**-do.*

Va bene, la prendo.

I'm not sure how long I'm
staying.
*non **so**-no see-**koo**-rah/o
kwahn-to **tem**-po chee
res-tair-**ro***

Non sono sicura/o quanto
tempo ci resterò.

Is there a lift?
*chei oon ah-chen-**sor**-rei?*

C'è un ascensore?

Where is the bathroom?
*do-vei eel **bah**-nyo?*

Dov'è il bagno?

Is there hot water all day?
*chei lah-kwah kahl-dah
toot-to eel **jor**-no?*

C'è l'aqua calda tutto il
giorno?

Do you have a safe where I
can leave my things?
   *chei oo-nah cahs-set-tah
   dee see-koo-re-tsah pair
   lah ro-bah dee va-lor-rei?*

C'è una cassetta di
sicurezza per la roba di
valore?

Is there somewhere to wash
clothes?
   *chei kwal-kei pos-do pair
   lah-vahr-rei ee ves-tee-tee?*

C'è qualque posto per
lavare i vestiti?

Can I use the kitchen?
   *pos-so oo-zar-rei lah
   koo-chee-nah?*

Posso usare la cucina?

Can I use the telephone?
   *pos-so oo-zar-rei eel
   te-le-fo-no?*

Posso usarc il telefono?

Requests & Complaints

Please wake me up at …
   mee sve-lyee ah …

Mi svegli a …

The room needs to be cleaned.
   *lah kah-mair-rah dev-ess-
   sair-rei poo-lee-tah*

La camera dev'essere pulita

Please change the sheets.
   *kahm-bee lei len-zwo-lah,
   pair pee-ah-chair-rei*

Cambi le lenzuola, per
piacere.

I can't open/close the window.
   *non pos-so ah-pree-rei/
   kyoo-dair-rei lah
   fee-nes-strah*

Non posso aprire/chiudere
la finestra.

I've locked myself out of my room.
*mee so-no **kyoo**-zah/o fwor-ree dahl-lah mee-ah **kah**-mair-rah*
Mi sono chiusa/o fuori dalla mia camera.

The toilet won't flush.
*eel ghah-bee-**net**-to non fun-tsee-o-nah*
Il gabinetto non funziona.

I don't like this room.
*kwes-dah kah-**mair**-rah non mee pee-**ah**-chei*
Questa camera non mi piace.

It's too small.
*ei **trop**-po **pee**-ko-lah*
È troppo piccola.

It's noisy.
*chei **trop**-po roo-**mor**-rei*
C'è troppo rumore.

It's too dark.
*ei **trop**-po **skoo**-rah*
È troppo scura.

It's expensive.
*ei **trop**-po **kah**-rah*
È troppo cara.

Some Useful Phrases

I am/We are leaving now.
***pahr**-to/pahr-tee-**ah**-mo ah-**des**-so*
Parto/Partiamo adesso.

I would like to pay the bill.
*vo-**rrei** pah-**ghah**-rei eel kon-to*
Vorrei pagare il conto.

name	*no-mei*	nome
surname	*ko-nyo-mei*	cognome
room number	*noo-mair-ro del-lah kah-mair-rah*	numero della camera

Some Useful Words

address	*een-dee-**reets**-o*	indirizzo
air-conditioned	***ahr**-ree-ah kon-dee-tsee-o-**nah**-tah*	aria condizionata
balcony	*bahl-**ko**-nei*	balcone
bathroom	***bah**-nyo*	bagno
bed	***let**-to*	letto
bill	***kon**-to*	conto
blanket (wool)	*ko-**pair**-tah (dee **lah**-nah)*	coperta (di lana)
candle	*kahn-**de**-lah*	candela
chair	*se-**dee**-ah*	sedia
clean	*pu-**lee**-tah/to*	pulita/o
cupboard	*kre-**den**-tsah*	credenza
dark	*skoo-**rah**/o*	scura/o
dirty	***spor**-kah/o*	sporca/o
double bed	*let-to mah-tree-mo-nee-**ahl**-lei*	letto matrimoniale
electricity	*e-let-tree-chee-**tah***	elettricità
excluded	*es-**kloo**-zah/o*	esclusa/o
fan	*ven-tee-lah-**tor**-rei*	ventilatore
included	*een-**kloo**-zah/o*	inclusa/o
key	*kee-**ah**-vei*	chiave
lift (elevator)	*ah-chen-**sor**-rei*	ascensore
light bulb	*lahm-pah-**dee**-nah*	lampadina
lock (n)	*ser-rah-**too**-rah*	serratura
mattress	*mah-tair-**rahs**-so*	materasso
mirror	***spek**-kee-o*	specchio
padlock	*loo-**ket**-to*	lucchetto
pillow	*koo-**shee**-no*	cuscino
quiet	*trahn-**kweel**-lah/o*	tranquilla/o

room (in hotel)	*kah-mair-rah*	camera
sheet	*len-zwo-lo*	lenzuolo
shower	**doch**-ah	doccia
soap	*sah-po-nei*	sapone
suitcase	*vah-lee-jah*	valigia
swimming pool	*pee-shee-nah*	piscina
table	*tah-vo-lah*	tavola
toilet	*ghah-bee-net-to*	gabinetto
toilet paper	*kahr-tah ee-jen-ee-kah*	carta igienica
towel	*ah-shu-ghah-mah-no*	asciugamano
wardrobe	*ahr-mahr-dee-o*	armadio
water	*ah-kwah*	acqua
cold water	*ah-kwah fred-dah*	acqua fredda
hot water	*ah-kwah kahl-dah*	acqua calda
window	*fee-nes-trah*	finestra

Around Town

I'm looking for ...
  sto chair-kahn-do ...   Sto cercando ...

the art gallery	*ghah-lair-ree-ah dar-tei/pee-nah-ko-te-kah*	la galleria d'arte/pinacoteca
a bank	*lah bahn-kah*	la banca
the church	*lah kee-ei-zah*	la chiesa
the city centre	*eel chen-tro (chee-tah)*	il centro (città)
the ... embassy	*lahm-bah-shah-tah ...*	l'ambasciata ...

my hotel	*eel **mee**-o ahl-**bair**-gho*	il mio albergo
the market	*eel mair-**kah**-to*	il mercato
the museum	*eel moo-**zei**-o*	il museo
the police	*lah po-lee-**tzee**-ah*	la polizia
the post office	*lah **pos**-dah/oo-**fee**-chee-o pos-**dah**-lei*	la posta/ufficio postale
a public toilet/ restrooms	*un ghah-bee-**net**-to/ **bah**-nyo pu-blee-ko/ sair-**vee**-tsee ee-je-nee-chee*	un gabinetto/ bagno pubblico/ servizi igienici
the telephone centre	*chen-tro te-lei-fo-nee-ko*	centro telefonico
the tourist information office	*len-tei del too-**reez**-mo/oo-**feech**-o deen-for-**mah**-tsee-o-nei*	l'Ente del Turismo/ufficio d'informazione

What time does it open?
   *ah **kei** or-rah (see) **ah**-prei?*   A che ora (si) apre?
What time does it close?
   *ah **kei** or-rah (see) kee-oo-dei?*   A che ora (si) chiude?

What ... is this?
   *kei ... ei **kwes**-dah/o?*   Che ... è questa/o?

street	***strah**-dah*	strada
suburb	*kwar-tee-**air**-rei*	quartiere

For directions, see the Getting Around section, page 316.

At the Bank

I want to exchange some money/traveller's cheques.
*vo-**rrei** kahm-bee-**ah**-rei del de-**nah**-ro/dei 'travellers' cheques.*

Vorrei cambiare del denaro/dei travellers' cheques.

What is the exchange rate?
*kwahn-**tei** eel **kahm**-bee-o?*

Quant'è il cambio?

How many lire per dollar?
*kwan-tei lee-rei ahl **do**-lah-ro?*

Quante lire al dollaro?

Can I have money transferred here from my bank?
*po-sso trahs-fair-**ree**-rei del de-**nah**-ro **dahl**-lah mee-ah **bahn**-kah ah **kwes**-dah?*

Posso trasferire del denaro dalla mia banca a questa?

How long will it take to arrive?
*kwahn-to tem-po chee vo-**rrah** pair trahs-fair-**reer**-lo?*

Quanto tempo ci vorrà per trasferirlo?

Has my money arrived yet?
*ei ahr-ree **vah**-to eel mee-o de-**nah**-ro?*

È arrivato il mio denaro?

bank draft	*bahn-ko no-tah*	banco-nota
cashier	*lah **kahs**-sah*	la cassa
coins	***spee**-cho-lee*	spiccioli
credit card	***kahr**-tah dee **kre**-dee-to*	carta di credito
exchange	***kahm**-bee-o*	cambio
signature	***feer**-mah*	firma

ITALIAN

At the Post Office

I would like to send ...

	*vo-**rrei** mah-**dah**-rei ...*	Vorrei mandare ...
a letter	*oo-nah **let**-tair-rah*	una lettera
a postcard	*oo-nah kar-to-**lee**-nah*	una cartolina
a parcel	*un pah-**ket**-to*	un pacchetto
a telegram	*un te-lei-**ghrahm**-mah*	un telegramma

I would like some stamps.

    *vo-**rrei** dei frahn-ko-**bol**-lee*   Vorrei dei francobolli.

How much does it cost to
send this to ...?

    *kwahn-**tei** lahf-frahn-kah-*   Quant'è l'affrancatura per
    ***too**-rah puir **kwes**-do,*   questo, per ...?
    pair ...?

air mail	*vee-ah ah-**air**-ree-ah*	via aerea
envelope	***boo**-sdah*	busta
mailbox	*kahs-**set**-tah*	cassetta postale
	*pos-**dah**-lei*	
parcel	*pah-**ket**-to*	pachetto
registered mail	*(**pos**-dah) rah-ko-*	(posta)
	*mahn-**dah**-tah*	raccomandata
surface mail	***pos**-dah **non**-ah-air-*	posta non-aerea/
	*ree-ah/or-dee-**nah**-*	ordinaria
	ree-ah	

Telephone

I want to ring ...

    *vo-**rrei** te-lei-fo-**nah**-rei*   Vorrei telefonare ...

The number is …
*eel **noo**-mair-ro ei …*
Il numero è …

I want to speak for three minutes.
*vo-lyo pahr-**lah**-re pair trei mee-**noo**-tee*
Voglio parlare per tre minuti.

How much does a three-minute call cost?
*kwahn-to kos-dah oo-nah te-lei-fo-**nah**-tah dee trei mee-**noo**-tee?*
Quanto costa una telefonata di tre minuti?

How much does each extra minute cost?
***kwahn**-to kos-da o-nyee mee-**noo**-to een pyoo?*
Quanto costa ogni minuto in più?

I would like to speak to Mr Perez.
*vo-rrei pahr-**lah**-rei kon eel see-nyor Per-rez*
Vorrei parlare con il signor Perez.

I want to make a reverse-charges phone call.
*vo-lyo fah-rei oo-nah kee-ah-**mah**-tah ah **kah**-ree-ko del de-stee-nah-**tah**-ree-o*
Voglio fare una chiamata a carico del destinatario.

It's engaged.
*lah **lee**-ne-ah ei ok-koo-**pah**-tah*
La linea è occupata.

I've been cut off.
*ei kah-**doo**-tah lah **lee**-nei-ah*
È caduta la linea.

Sightseeing

Do you have a guidebook/
local map?

*ah oo-nah **ghwee**-dah too-*   Ha una guida turistica/
rees-tee-kah/pee-ahn-tah   pianta locale?
*lo-**kah**-lei?*

What are the main attractions?

kwah-lei so-no lei ah-trah-   Quali sono le attrazioni più
*tsee-**o**-nee pee-oo sah-lee-*   salienti?
en-ti?

What is that?

***ko**-zei?*   Cos'è?

How old is it?

*kwahn-tee **ahn**-nee ah? dee*   Quanti anni ha? Di che
*ke e-**po**-kah ei?*   epoca è?

Can I take photographs?

pos-so fah-rei fo-to-ghrah-   Posso fare fotografie?
***fee**-ei?*

What time does it open/close?

*ah **kei** or-rah (see)*   A che ora (si) apre/chiude?
***ah**-prei/kee-oo-dei?*

ancient	***ahn**-tee-kah/ko*	antica/o
archaeological	*ahr-kee-o-**lo**-jee-kah/ko*	archeologica/o
beach	*spee-**ahj**-jah*	spiaggia
building	*e-dee-**fee**-cho*	edificio
castle	*kah-**stel**-lo*	castello
cathedral	*kah-tei-**drah**-lei/**dwo**-mo*	cattedrale/duomo
church	*kee-**ei**-zah*	chiesa

concert hall	*sah-lah pair kon-chair-tee/tei-ah-tro ko-moo-nah-lei*	sala per concerti/ teatro comunale
library	*beeb-lee-o-te-kah*	biblioteca
main square	*pee-ah-tsah preen-chee-pah-lei*	piazza principale
market	*mair-kah-to*	mercato
monastery	*mon-ahs-dair-o*	monastero
monument	*mon-oo-men-to*	monumento
mosque	*mos-kei-ah*	moschea
old city	*cheet-tah-del-lah*	cittadella
palace	*pah-lah-tso*	palazzo
opera house	*tei-ah-tro*	teatro dell'opera
ruins	*ro-vee-nei*	rovine
stadium	*stah-dee-o*	stadio
statues	*stah-too-ei*	statue
synagogue	*see-nah-gho-gha*	sinagoga
temple	*tem-pee-o*	tempio
university	*oo-nee-vair-see-tah*	università

Entertainment

What's there to do in the evenings?
ko-zah chei dah fah-rei ahl-lah sair-rah? Cosa c'è da fare alla sera?

Are there any discos?
chee so-no del-lei dee.s-ko-te-kei kwah? Ci sono delle discoteche qua?

How much does it cost to get in?

*len-**trah**-tah, kwahn-to cos-dah?*

Quanto costa l'entrata?

cinema	*chee-nei-mah*	cinema
concert	*kon-chair-to*	concerto
discotheque	*dees-ko-te-kah*	discoteca
theatre	*tei-ah-tro*	teatro

In the Country
Weather

What's the weather like?

*ko-**mei** eel tem-po?*

Com' é il tempo?

The weather is ... today.

oj-jee e ...

Oggi é ...

Will it be ... tomorrow?

*sah-**rah** ... do-**mah**-nee?*

Sarà ...domani?

cloudy	*noo-vo-lo-so*	nuvoloso
cold	***fred**-do*	freddo
foggy	*neb-bee-o-so*	nebbioso
frosty	*je-lee-do*	gelido
hot	***kahl**-do*	caldo

It's raining.	*pee-o-vei*	Piove.
It's snowing.	***ne**-vee-kah*	Nevica.
It's good weather.	*fah bel tem-po*	Fa bel tempo.
It's windy.	*tee-rah ven-to*	Tira vento.

Camping

Am I allowed to camp here?
*see **pwo** pee-ahn-**tah**-rei lah ten-dah kwee?*   Si può piantare la tenda qui?

Is there a campsite nearby?
*chei oon kahm-**pej**-jo kwee vee-**chee**-no?*   C'è un campeggio qui vicino?

backpack	*dzah-**ee**-no*	zaino
can opener	*ah-pree-**skah**-to-lei*	apriscatole
compass	***boos**-so-lah*	bussola
crampons	*rahm-**po**-nee*	ramponi
firewood	*le-nyah pair eel **fwo**-ko/dah **ahr**-dair-rei*	legna per il fuoco/da ardere
gas cartridge	***bom**-bo-lah del ghahs*	bombola del gas
hammock	***ah**-mah-kah*	amaca
mattress	*mah-tair-**rahs**-so*	materasso
penknife	*tem-pair-**ee**-no*	temperino
rope	***kor**-dah*	corda
tent	***ten**-dah*	tenda
tent pegs	*pee-**ket**-tee (pair lah **ten**-dah)*	picchetti (per la tenda)
torch (flashlight)	*lah **tor**-chah*	la torcia
sleeping bag	***sah**-ko ah pe-lo*	sacco a pelo
stove (portable)	***stoo**-fah (ah **ghahs**)*	stufa (a ghas)
water bottle/flask	*lah bor-**rah**-cha*	la borraccia

Food

breakfast	*(pree-mah) ko-la-tsee-o-nei*	(prima) colazione
lunch	*prahn-zo/ko-la-tsee-o-nei*	pranzo/colazione
dinner	*che-nah*	cena

Table for ..., please.
 oon tah-vo-lo pair ..., pair fah-vor-rei
Un tavolo per ..., per favor

Can I see the menu?
 pos-so ve-dair-rei eel me-noo?
Posso vedere il menù?

I would like the set lunch, please.
 vo-rrei eel me-noo too-ree-stee-co, pair fah-vor-rei
Vorrei il menù turistico, per favore.

What does it include?
 ko-zah kom-pren-dei?
Cosa comprende?

Is service included in the bill?
 eel sair-vee-tsee-o ei kom-prei-zo nel kon-to?
Il servizio è compreso nel conto?

Not too spicy please.
 non trop-po pee-kahn-tei, pair fah-vor-rei
Non troppo piccante, per favore.

ashtray	*por-tah-che-nair-rei*	portacenere
bill	*kon-to*	conto
cup	*tah-tsah*	tazza
dessert	*dol-chei*	dolce
drink	*be-vahn-dah*	bevanda
fork	*for-ket-tah*	forchetta

ITALIAN

fresh	*fre-skah/o*	fresca/o
glass	*bee-kee-air-rei*	bicchiere
knife	*col-tel-lo*	coltello
plate	*pee-aht-to*	piatto
spicy	*pee-kahn-tei/ah-ro-mah-tee-kah/o*	piccante/aromatica/o
a spoon	*koo-kee-ah-ee-o*	cucchiaio
stale	*ve-kee-o*	vecchio
sweet	*dol-chei*	dolce
teaspoon	*koo-kee-ah-ee-no*	cucchiaino
toothpick	*stoo-tsee-kah-den-tei*	stuzzicadente

Places to Eat

Pizzerie and *ristoranti* speak for themselves, but you may like to try eating at some of these:

tavola calda – cheap self-service with a selection of hot dishes
taverna – small restaurant of a rustic nature, though not always cheap
trattoria, (h)osteria – offering simple local dishes, they generally cater for locals rather than tourists
rosticceria – grilled meat, often takeaway only

Vegetarian Meals

I am a vegetarian.
  so-no ve-je-tah-ree-ah-nah/o   Sono vegetariana/o.
I don't eat meat.
  non mahn-jo kar-nei   Non mangio carne.

ITALIAN

I don't eat chicken, or fish, or
pork.

> *non mahn-jo nei **pol**-lo, nei*   Non mangio né pollo, né
> ***pe**-shei, nei mah-ee-**ah**-lei*   pesce, né maiale.

Appetisers — Antipasti

antipasto misto	Assortment of cold appetisers.
caponata (alla siciliana)	Eggplant dish from Sicily, with capers, olives, onion and anchovies.
ceci con oregano	Marinated chickpeas with oregano.
condimento al pepe	Pepper relish.
melone con prosciutto	Melon with cured ham.
sottaceti	Pickled vegetables.

Soup — Zuppa/Brodo

capelletti	A form of ravioli, with various stuffings, i broth.
minestrone	Vegetable soup, often with beef stock and pork.
stracciatella	Chicken and vegetable soup.
zuppa pavese	Pavian soup: bread, butter, chicken broth and eggs.
paparot	Spinach soup. (Istria)

Pasta & Rice — Pastasciutta e Riso

Pastasciutta is the collective name for over 500 varieties products made from flour, water and sometimes eggs. If y want your pasta to be cooked to perfection, ask for it to be *a den-tei*, 'al dente'. Note that pasta dishes are generally larg than the 'main' course, so this is the course to fill up on if you're very hungry.

agnolotti	Small pasta pockets stuffed with meat sauce. (Turin/Piedmont)
bomba di riso	Rice with pigeon. (Parma)
cannelloni	Wide strips of pasta rolled around meat or spinach-and-cheese.
gnocchi	Flour and potato dumplings.
lasagne	Sheets of pasta, layered alternately with minced meat, tomato sauce, and cheese or béchamel sauce.
polenta	Cornmeal, often sliced and deep-fried.
ravioli	Square pockets of pasta, filled with meat paste.
risi e bisi	Risotto with green peas. (Venice/Veneto)
risotto in capro roman	Risotto with mutton. (Venice)
sartù	Savoury rice dish. (Naples)
spaghetti	Needs no introduction.
supplì	Deep-fried balls of rice with mozzarella cheese and tomato sauce inside.
tagliatelle & fettucine	Ribbon pasta.
tortellini	Small envelopes of pasta wrapped around meat.
tuoni e lampo	Varieties of pasta, with chick peas and tomato sauce. (Capri)

ITALIAN

Sauces
Italian sauces are delicious, and it is quite acceptable to use th
unsalted bread provided to mop up your sauce.

aglio e olio	Garlic and olive oil.
alfredo	Butter, cream, Parmesan cheese and parsley.
alla checca	Cold summer sauce of ripe tomatoes, olives, basil, capers and oregano. (Rome)
bolognese/al ragù	Minced beef, tomatoes, onions and herbs.
carbonara	Cured bacon *(pancetta)*, cream, paprika, egg and parmesan cheese.
matriciana	Spicy tomato and bacon.
misto di mare	Mixed seafood, often in cream and wine.
pescatore/ marinara	Mixed seafood, often in tomato sauce.
pesto	Basil, pine nuts and garlic.
puttanesca	Spicy tomato sauce with anchovies, olives and basil.
siciliana	Eggplant, anchovies, olives, capers, tomate and garlic.
tonno e funghi	Tuna and mushrooms in tomato and cream sauce.

Meat	**Carne**
beef	*manzo*
pork	*maiale*
hare	*lepre*
kid	*capretto*
lamb	*agnello*
liver	*fegato*

mutton	*montone*
tripe	*trippa*
veal	*vitello*

Seafood **Frutti di Mare**

anelletti gratinati	Crumbed fried cuttlefish rings. (Sicily)
baccalà montecato	Purée of salt cod, served with polenta. (Venice/Veneto)
bottarga	Fish roe. (Sicily)
burrida/ciuppa/ zimmo	Fish stews. (Genoa/Liguria)
cuscucu	Fish soup. (Sicily)
sfogie in saòr	Sole with herbs and garlic. (Venice/Veneto)

anchovies	*acciughe*
cockles	*vongole*
cod	*baccalà/merluzzo/ stoccafisso*
crayfish	*gambero*
fish	*pesce*
lobster	*aragosta*
mussels	*cozze*
oysters	*ostriche*
prawns	*gamberoni*
red mullet	*triglia*
shrimp	*scampi*
spider crabs	*granevole/granceole*

Poultry & Wildfowl **Pollame & Selvaggina**

chicken	*pollo*
duck	*anitra*
partridges	*pernici*

ITALIAN

pigeons	*piccioni*
quail	*quaglia*
turkey	*tacchino*

Vegetables — Verdure

You usually need to order vegetables or salad as extras. *Insala* is simply lettuce. *Insalata mista* is a tossed salad.

artichokes	*carciofi*
beans	*fagioli(ni)*
cabbage	*cavoli*
chickpeas	*ceci*
eggplant (aubergine)	*melanzane*
mushrooms	*funghi*
onion	*cipolla*
peas	*piselli*
tomatoes	*pomodori*
capsicum	*peperoni*

Specific Dishes — Piatti Speciali

abbacchio	Young lamb. (Rome/Lazio)
bistecca alla fiorentina	Huge grilled T-bone steak. Often priced *all'etto*, 'per hundred weight'. Ask how much an average steak would be: *Di solito quanto costa una bistecca fiorentina?* (Florence)
bollito	Various meats boiled together in one pot and served with vegetables. (Turin/ Piedmont)
bruschetta	Crisp baked bread slices in oil, often with tomato brushed on top. (Florence/Tuscany)
busella	Tripe dish. (Milan/Lombardy)

ITALIAN

calzone	Folded pizza. (Naples)
capon magro	Salad of vegetables and fish. (Genoa/Liguria)
cima	Cold veal, stuffed with pork, sweetbreads, nuts, peas and eggs. (Genoa)
cotechino	Sausage, stuffed with raw spiced pork. (Emiglia-Romagna)
fasœil al fùrn	Oven-baked beans. (Piedmont)
finocchiona	Spicy salami, with fennel seeds. (Florence/Tuscany)
grissini	Slender bread sticks. (Turin/Piedmont)
involtini	Stuffed veal rolls. (Bologna/Emiglia-Romagna)
mostarda	Candied fruits in mustard. (Cremona)
polenta e osei	Small roasted birds, served with polenta. (Milan/Lombardy)
rane dorate	Fried frogs legs. (North)
saltimbocca	Veal rolled with ham and sage, cooked in wine or Marsala. (Rome)
tacchino con sugo di melagrana	Turkey with pomegranate sauce. (Venice/Veneto)
testarelle di abbacchio	Lamb's heads. (Rome/Lazio)
tortino	Flat omelette with vegetables. (Florence/Tuscany)
zampone	Pig's foot, stuffed with raw spiced sausage. (Modena)

Condiments & Staples

bread	*pane*
butter	*burro*

eggs	*uova*
garlic	*aglio*
oil	*olio*
pepper	*pepe*
salt	*sale*

Fruit — **Frutta**

apple	*mela*
apricot	*albicocca*
cherries	*ciliegie*
grapes	*uva*
orange	*arancia*
plum	*prugna/susina*
raspberries	*lamponi*
strawberries	*fragole*

Desserts — **Dolci**

bignè alla cioccolata	Puff pastry filled with cream and covered with chocolate.
cassata	Pudding of sponge, cream, fruit and chocolate. Also an ice-cream flavour. (Sicily)
crema inglese	Custard.
granita di limone	Lemon-water ice.
macedonia	Fruit salad.
panettone	Large, dry yeast cake.
zabaglione/ zabaione	Egg yolks whipped with sugar and Marsala.
zuccotto	Almond and hazelnut cake with brandy and liqueur.
zuppa inglese	Trifle.

ITALIAN

Cheese — Formaggio

fontina	Creamy kind of Gruyère. (Piedmont)
gorgonzola	Soft, rich, blue-veined cheese.
mozzarella	Traditionally made from buffalo's milk.
parmigiano	Parmesan – often simply called *grana*.
pecorino	Hard cheese, usually made from ewe's milk, popular at the end of a meal.
ricotta	Soft ewe's-milk cheese.

Drinks – Nonalcoholic — Bevande

milk	*latte*
tea	*tè*
mineral water	*acqua minerale*
orange juice	*succo d'arancia*
soft drink	*gassosa/gazzosa*

caffè latte	Coffee with milk.
caffè macchiato	Strong coffee with a little milk.
cappuccino	Named after the Capuchin monks who wore robes of chocolate and cream colours, cappuccino is considered a morning drink by Italians.
espresso	Very strong black coffee served in small cups and taken at any time of the day.
latte macchiato	Hot milk with a little coffee.

Drinks – Alcoholic

beer	*birra*
brandy	*acquavite*
wine	*vino*
bitter or very dry	*amaro*
dry	*secco/asciutto*

ITALIAN

red	*rosso*
semi-sparkling	*frizzante*
slightly sweet	*abboccato*
sparkling	*spumante*
sweet	*amabile*
white	*bianco*

Shopping

How much is it?
kwahn-to kos-dah?   Quanto costa?

bookshop	lee-brair-**ree**-ah	libreria
camera shop	fo-**to**-ghrah-fo	fotografo
clothing store	ne-**gho**-tsee-o dee ah-bee-lyee-ah-**men**-to	negozio di abbigliamento
greengrocer	froo-tee-**ven**-do-lo	fruttivendolo
grocery store	ne-**gho**-tsee-o dee ah-lee-men-**tah**-ree/ dro-ghair-**ree**-ah	negozio di alimentari/ drogheria
laundry	lah-vahn-dair-**ree**-ah	lavanderia
market	mair-**kah**-to	mercato
newsagency/ stationers	e-**dee**-ko-lah/kahr-to-**lah**-yo	edicola/cartolaio
pharmacy	fahr-mah-**chee**-ah	farmacia
shoeshop	kahl-tso-lair-**ree**-ah	calzoleria
souvenir shop	ne-**gho**-tsee-o dee 'souvenir'	negozio di souvenir
supermarket	soo-pair-mair-**kah**-to	supermercato

ITALIAN

would like to buy …	vo-rrei kom-**prah**-rei …	Vorrei comprare …
Do you have others?	chee so-no **ahl**-trei/ee?	Ci sono altre/i?
don't like it.	non mee pee-**ah**-chei	Non mi piace.
Can I look at it?	**pos**-so dah-rei oon o-kee-**ah**-tah?	Posso dare un'occhiata?
I'm just looking.	(sto) so-lo ghwahr-**dahn**-do	Sto solo guardando.
Can you write down the price?	pwo skree-vair-rei eel **pre**-tso?	Può scrivere il prezzo?
Do you accept credit cards?	ah-**chet**-tah lah **kahr**-tah dee **kre**-dee-to?	Accetta la carta di credito?
Could you lower the price?	pwo **fahr**-mee lo **skon**-to?	Può farmi lo sconto?
don't have much money.	non o **mol**-tee **sol**-dee	Non ho molti soldi.
Can I help you?	**pos**-so ah-yoo-**tahr**-lah? ko-zah dei-**zee**-dair-rah?	Posso aiutarla? Cosa desidera?
Will that be all?	nee-ent-**ahl**-tro?	Nient'altro?
Would you like it wrapped?	lah/lo vwo-lei een-kahr-**tah**-tah/o?/eem-bahl-**lah**-tah/o?	La/Lo vuole incartata/o?/ imballata/o?

ITALIAN

Sorry, this is the only one.
> *mee dee-spee-**ah**-chei, ei loo-nee-kah/o*

Mi dispiace, è l'unica/o.

How much/many do you want?
> ***kwahn**-to/ee nei vwo-lei?*

Quanto/i ne vuole?

Souvenirs

blown glass	*ve-tro so-fee-**ah**-to*	vetro soffiato
earrings	*o-re-**kee**-nee*	orecchini
handicraft	*lah-**vor**-ro ahr-tee-jah-**nah**-lei*	lavoro artigianale
jewellery	*joy-**el**-lee*	gioielli
leather handbag, bag	*bor-**set**-tah/**bor**-sah dee **kwoy**-o/een **pel**-lei*	borsetta/borsa di cuoio/in pelle
miniature statue	*stah-too-ah een mee-nee-ah-**too**-rah*	statua in miniatura
necklace	*kol-**lah**-nah*	collana
pottery	*oj-**jet**-tee een chair-**ah**-mee-kah*	oggetti in ceramica
ring	*ah-**nel**-lo*	anello
rug	*tah-**pet**-to*	tappetto

Clothing

clothing	***ah**-bee-tee/ves-**tee**-tee*	abiti/vestiti
coat	*kah-**pot**-to*	cappotto
dress	*ve-**stee**-to*	vestito
jacket	***jah**-kah*	giacca
jumper (sweater)	*mah-lyee-**o**-nei, ghol-**fee**-no*	maglione, golfino

shirt	*kah-**mee**-chah*	camicia
shoes	***skar**-pei*	scarpe
skirt	***ghon**-nah*	gonna
trousers	*pahn-tah-**lo**-nee*	pantaloni

It doesn't fit.
*non mee vah **be**-nei*   Non mi va bene.

It is too …/They are too …
*ei **trop**-po …/so-no*   È troppo …/Sono
trop-pei/ee …   troppe/i …

big	***ghrahn**-dei*	grande,
	***ghrahn**-dee*	grandi (pl)
small	***pee**-ko-lah/o,*	piccola/o,
	***pee**-ko-lei/ee*	piccole/i (pl)
short	*kor-**tah**/o,*	corta/o,
	*kor-**tei**/ee*	corte/i (pl)
long	***loong**-ghah/o,*	lunga/o,
	***loong**-ghei/ee*	lunghe/i (pl)
tight	*ah-dair-**ren**-tei/*	aderente/
	***stret**-tah/o*	stretta/o
	***stret**-tei/ee*	strette/i (pl)
loose	***lahr**-gha/o,*	larga/o,
	***lahr**-ghei/ee*	larghe/i (pl)

Materials

cotton	*ko-**to**-nei*	cotone
handmade	***faht**-to ah **mah**-no*	fatto a mano
leather	*pel-**lei**/**kwoy**-o*	pelle/cuoio
of brass	*dee ot-**to**-nei*	di ottone
of gold	***dor**-ro*	d'oro

of silver	*dahr-jen-to*	d'argento
silk	*se-tah*	seta
wool	*lah-nah*	lana

Toiletries

comb	*pet-tee-nei*	pettine
condoms	*prei-zair-vah-tee-vee*	preservativi
deodorant	*dei-o-dor-rahn-tei*	deodorante
hairbrush	*spah-tso-lah (pair ee kah-pel-lee)*	spazzola (per i capelli)
moisturising cream	*krei-mah ee-drah-tahn-tei*	crema idratante
razor	*rah-zoy-o*	rasoio
sanitary napkins	*ahs-sor-ben-tee ee-je-nee-chee*	assorbenti igienici
shampoo	*shahm-poo*	shampoo
shaving cream	*krei-mah dah bahr-bah*	crema da barba
soap	*sah-po-nei*	sapone
sunblock cream	*krei-mah so-lah-rei*	crema solare
tampons	*tahm-po-nee*	tamponi
tissues	*fah-tso-let-tee dee kahr-tah*	fazzoletti di carta
toilet paper	*kahr-tah ee-je-nee-kah*	carta igienica
toothbrush	*spah-tso-lee-no dah den-tee*	spazzolino da denti
toothpaste	*den-tee-free-cho*	dentifricio

Stationery & Publications

map	*kahr*-tah/pee-*ahn*-tah	carta/pianta
newspaper	jor-*nah*-lei	giornale
newspaper in English	jor-*nah*-lei een eeng-*ghlei*-zei	giornale in inglese
novels in English	ro-*mahn*-tsee een eeng-*ghlei*-zei	romanzi in inglese
paper	*kahr*-tah	carta
pen (ballpoint)	*pen*-nah (ah *sfair*-rah)	penna (a sfera)
scissors	*for*-bee-chee	forbici

Photography

How much is it to process this film?

kwahn-to *kos*-dah pair svee-loo-*pah*-rei kwes-dah pel-*lee*-ko-lah?

Quanto costa per sviluppare questa pellicola?

When will it be ready?

kwahn-do sah-*rahn*-no *pron*-tei, lei fo-to?

Quando saranno pronte le foto?

I'd like a film for this camera.

vo-rrei oo-nah pel-*lee*-ko-lah/oon rol-*lee*-no pair kwes-dah *mah*-kee-nah fo-to-*ghrah*-fee-kah

Vorrei una pellicola/un rollino per questa macchina fotografica.

B&W (film)	bee-*ahn*-ko ei *nair*-ro	bianco e nero
camera	*mah*-kee-nah fo-to-*ghrah*-fee-kah	macchina fotografica
colour (film)	ko-*lor*-rei	colore

film	*pel-lee-ko-lah/* *rol-lee-no*	pellicola/rollino
flash	*flahsh*	flash
lens	*o-bee-e-tee-vo*	obiettivo
light meter	*e-spo-zee-me-tro*	esposimetro

Smoking

A packet of cigarettes, please.
oon pah-ket-to dee see-ghah-ret-tei, pair fah-vor-rei   Un pachetto di sigarette, pe favore.

Are these cigarettes strong/mild?
kwes-dei see-ghah-ret-tei (non) so-no for-tee?   Queste sigarette (non) sono forti?

Do you have a light?
ah dah-chen-dair-rei?   Ha d'accendere?

cigarette papers	*kahr-tee-nei (pair see-ghah-ret-tei)*	cartine (per sigarette)
cigarettes	*see-ghah-ret-tei*	sigarette
filtered	*kon feel-tro*	con filtro
lighter	*ah-chen-dee-no*	accendino
matches	*fee-ahm-mee-fair-ree*	fiammiferi
menthol	*ah-lah men-tah*	alla menta
pipe	*pee-pah*	pipa
tobacco (pipe)	*tah-bah-ko dah pee-pah*	tabacco da pipa

Colours

| black | *nair-rah/o* | nera/o |
| blue (dark) | *bloo* | blu |

blue (light)	che-**le**-stei/ah-**tsoo**-rro	celeste/azzurro
brown	mah-**rro**-nei	marrone
green	**vair**-dei	verde
orange	ah-**rahn**-cho-nei	arancione
pink	**ro**-zah	rosa
purple	vee-**o**-lah	viola
red	**ros**-sah/o	rossa/o
white	bee-**ahn**-kah/o	bianca/o
yellow	**jahl**-lah/o	

Sizes & Comparisons

small	**pee**-ko-lah/o	piccola/o
big	**ghrahn**-dei	grande
heavy	pe-**zahn**-tei	pesante
light	lej-**jair**-rah	leggera/o
more	(dee) pyoo	(di) più
less	(dee) **me**-no	(di) meno
too much/many	**trop**-po	troppo/i
many	**tahn**-tei/ee	tante/i
enough	ah-bah-**stahn**-tzah	abbastanza
also	**ahn**-kei	anche
a little bit	oon po	un po'

Health

Where is …?		
do-**vei** …?		Dov'è …?
the doctor	lah dot-tor-**res**-sah/ eel dot-**tor**-rei/ eel me-dee-ko	la dottoressa/il dottore/il medico
the hospital	lo-spe-**dah**-lei	l'ospedale

ITALIAN

| the chemist | *lah/eel fahr-mah-**chee**-stah* | la/il farmacista |
| the dentist | *lah/eel den-**tee**-stah* | la/il dentista |

I am sick
   *mee sen-to **mah**-lei* — Mi sento male.

My friend is sick. (f)
   *lah mee-ah ah-**mee**-kah ei mah-**lah**-tah* — La mia amica è malata.

My friend is sick. (m)
   *eel mee-o ah-**mee**-ko ei mah-**lah**-to* — Il mio amico è malato.

Could I see a female doctor?
   *pos-so ve-**dair**-rei oo-nah dot-tor-**res**-sah?* — Posso vedere una dottoressa?

What's the matter?
   ko-zah chei? — Cosa c'è?

Where does it hurt?
   *do-vei tee fah **mah**-lei?* — Dove ti fa male?

It hurts here.
   *mee fah **mah**-lei kwee* — Mi fa male qui.

My ... hurts.
   *mee fah **mah**-lei lah/eel ...* — Mi fa male la/il ...

Parts of the Body

ankle	*kah-**vah**-lyee-ah*	caviglia
arm	***brah**-cho*	braccio
back	*skee-**eh**-nah/**dor**-soh*	schiena/dorso
chest	***pet**-to*	petto
ear	*o-**re**-kee-o*	orecchio
eye	*o-**kee**-o*	occhio

finger	*dee-to*	dito
foot	*pee-e-dei*	piede
hand	*mah-no*	mano
head	*tes-tah*	testa
heart	*kwor-rei*	cuore
knee	*jee-no-kee-o*	ginocchio
leg	*ghahm-bah*	gamba
mouth	*bok-kah*	bocca
nose	*nah-zo*	naso
shoulder	*spah-lah*	spalla
skin	*pel-lei*	pelle
stomach	*sto-mah-ko*	stomaco
teeth	*den-tee*	denti
throat	*gho-lah*	gola

Ailments

I have …		
o …	Ho …	
an allergy	*oo-nah-lair-jee-ah*	un'allergia
a blister	*ve-shee-kah*	vescica
a burn	*skot-tah-too-rah*	scottatura
a cold	*rahf-fre-dor-rei*	raffreddore
constipation	*stee-tee-ke-tsah*	stitichezza
a cough	*tos-sei*	tosse
diarrhoea	*dee-ah-rei-ah*	diarrea
fever	*feb-brei*	febbre
a headache	*mahl dee tes-tah*	mal di testa
hepatitis	*e-pah-tee-tei*	epatite
indigestion	*een-dee-jes-tee-o-nei*	indigestione
an infection	*een-fe-tsee-o-nei*	infezione
influenza	*een-floo-en-zah*	influenza

ITALIAN

lice	*pee-**do**-kee*	pidocchi
low/high blood pressure	*pres-see-**o**-nei **bahs**-sah/**ahl**-tah (dee **sahn**-ghwei)*	pressione bassa/alta (di sangue)
pain	*do-**lor**-rei*	dolore
sore throat	*mahl dee **gho**-lah*	mal di gola
sprain	***strah**-po moo-sko-**lahr**-rei*	strappo muscolare
stomachache	*mahl dee **sto**-mah-ko*	mal di stomaco
sunburn	*sko-tah-**too**-rah (dahl **so**-lei)*	scottatura (dal sole)
venereal disease	*mah-laht-**tee**-ah ve-**nair**-ree-ah*	malattia venerea
worms	***vair**-mee*	vermi

Some Useful Words & Phrases

I'm ...
   so-no ...   Sono ...

diabetic	*dee-ah-**be**-tee-kah/o*	diabetica/o
epileptic	*e-pee-**let**-tee-kah/o*	epilettica/o
asthmatic	*ahs-**mah**-tee-kah/o*	asmatica/o

I'm allergic to antibiotics.
   *so-no ah-**lair**-jee-kah/o ah-lyee ahn-tee-bee-o-tee-chee*   Sono allergica/o agli antibiotici.

I'm allergic to penicillin.
   *so-no ah-**lair**-jee-kah/o ah-lah pe-nee-chee-**lee**-nah*   Sono allergica/o alla penicillina.

I'm pregnant.
   *so-no een-**cheen**-tah*   Sono incinta.

ITALIAN

I'm on the pill.
*pren-do lah **peel**-lo-lah* Prendo la pillola.

I haven't had my period for
… months.
*non o ah-**voo**-to lei* Non ho avuto le
mes-troo-ah-tsee-o-nee mestruazioni per … mesi.
*pair … **mei**-zee*

I have been vaccinated.
so-no stah-tah/o vah-chee- Sono stata/o vaccinata/o.
***nah**-tah/o*

I have my own syringe.
o con mei lah mee-ah Ho con me la mia siringa.
*see-reeng-**ghah***

I feel better/worse.
*mee sen-to **me**-lyo/**pej**-jo* Mi sento meglio/peggio.

accident	*een-chee-**den**-tei*	incidente
addiction	*to-sse-ko-mah-**nee**-ah*	tossicomania
antibiotics	*ahn-tee-bee-**o**-tee-chee*	antibiotici
antiseptic	*ahn-tee-**set**-tee-ko*	antisettico
aspirin	*ah-spee-**ree**-nah*	aspirina
bandage	***ben**-dah*	benda
blood pressure	*pres-see-**o**-nei (del **sahng**-ghwei*	pressione (del sangue)
blood test	*ah-**nah**-lee-zee del **sahng**-ghwei*	analisi del sangue
contraceptive	*ahn-tee-kon-che-tsee-o-**nahl**-lei*	anticoncezionale
injection	*een-eeye-tsee-**o**-nei*	iniezione
injury	*fair-**ree**-tah*	ferita

medicine	*me-dee-**chee**-nah*	medicina
menstruation	*me-stroo-a-tsee-**o**-nee*	mestruazioni
oxygen	*o-**ssee**-je-no*	ossigeno
vitamins	*vee-tah-**mee**-nei*	vitamine

At the Chemist

I need medication for ...
*o bee-**zo**-nyah/o dee oo-nah
me-dee-cah-tsee-o-nei
pair ...*

Ho bisogna/o di una
medicazione per ...

I have a prescription.
*o oo-nah ree-**chet**-tah*

Ho una ricetta.

At the Dentist

I have a toothache.
*o oun mahl dee **den**-tee*

Ho un mal di denti.

I've lost a filling.
*o pair-so oon o-too-ra-tsee-
o-nei*

Ho perso un otturazione.

I've broken a tooth.
*mee see ei **rot**-to oon **den**-tei*

Mi si è rotto un dente.

My gums hurt.
*mee fahn-no mah-lei lei
jen-**jee**-vei*

Mi fanno male le gengive.

I don't want it extracted.
*non lo **vo**-lyo **to**-lyair-rei*

Non lo voglio togliere.

Please give me an anaesthetic.
*mee dee-ah oon ahn-e-ste-
tee-ko, pair fah-**vor**-fei*

Mi dia un anestetico, per
favore.

Time & Dates

What date is it today?
*kei **jor**-no ei **oj**-jee?*
kwahn-tee nei ahb-bee-**ah**-
mo **oj**-jee?

Che giorno è oggi?
Quanti ne abbiamo oggi?

What time is it?
*kei **or**-rei **so**-no? kei **or**-rah
ei?*

Che ore sono?/Che ora è?

It is …
so-no lei …   Sono le …
in the morning   *dee maht-**tee**-nah*   di mattina
in the afternoon   *dee po-mair-**ree**-jo*   di pomeriggio
in the evening   *dee **sair**-rah*   di sera

Days of the Week

Monday   *loo-nei-**dee***   lunedì
Tuesday   *mahr-te-**dee***   martedì
Wednesday   *mair-ko-lei-**dee***   mercoledì
Thursday   *jo-ve-**dee***   giovedì
Friday   *ve-nair-**dee***   venerdì
Saturday   ***sah**-bah-to*   sabato
Sunday   *do-**me**-mee-kah*   domenica

Months

January   *jen-**nah**-ee-o*   gennaio
February   *feb-**brah**-ee-o*   febbraio
March   ***mahr**-tso*   marzo
April   *ah-**pree**-lei*   aprile
May   ***mahj**-jo*   maggio
June   ***joo**-nyo*   giugno

July	*loo*-lyo	luglio
August	ah-*ghos*-to	agosto
September	set-*tem*-brei	settembre
October	ot-*to*-brei	ottobre
November	no-*vem*-brei	novembre
December	dee-*chem*-brei	dicembre

Seasons

summer	e-*stah*-tei	estate
autumn	ahw-*toon*-no	autunno
winter	een-*vair*-no	inverno
spring	pree-mah-*vair*-rah	primavera

Present

today	*oj*-jee	oggi
this morning	stah-maht-*tee*-nah	stamattina
tonight	stah-*sair*-rah	stasera
this week/year	kwes-dah set-tee-*mah*-nah/kwes-*dahn*-no	questa settimana/quest'anno
now	ah-*des*-so	adesso

Past

yesterday	ee-*air*-ree	ieri
day before yesterday	lahl-tro ee-*air*-ree	l'altro ieri
yesterday morning	ee-*air*-ree maht-*tee*-nah	ieri mattina
last night	ee-*air*-ree sair-rah	ieri sera
last week/year	lah set-tee-*mah*-nah skor-sah/*lahn*-no pahs-*sah*-to/*skor*-so	la settimana scorsa/l'anno passato/scorso

Future

tomorrow	*do-**mah**-nee*	domani
day after tomorrow	*do-po-do-**mah**-nee*	dopodomani
tomorrow morning	*do-**mah**-nee maht-**tee**-nah*	domani mattina
tomorrow afternoon/evening	*do-**mah**-nee po-mair-**reej**-jo/**sair**-rah*	domani pomeriggio/sera
next week	*lah set-tee-**mah**-nah **pros**-see-mah*	la settimana prossima
next year	***lahn**-no pros-**see**-mo*	l'anno prossimo

During the Day

afternoon	*po-mair-**reej**-jo*	pomeriggio
dawn, very early morning	***ahl**-bah*	alba
day	***jor**-no*	giorno
early	***pres**-do*	presto
midnight	*me-tsah-**not**-tei*	mezzanotte
morning	*maht-**tee**-nah*	mattina
night	***not**-tei*	notte
noon	*me-tso-**jor**-no*	mezzogiorno
sundown	*trah-**mon**-to*	tramonto

Numbers & Amounts

0	***tsair**-ro*	zero
1	***oo**-no*	uno
2	***doo**-ei*	due
3	*trei*	tre
4	***kwaht**-tro*	quattro
5	***cheen**-kwei*	cinque

ITALIAN

6	*sei*	sei
7	***set**-tei*	sette
8	***ot**-to*	otto
9	***no**-vei*	nove
10	*dee-**ei**-chee*	dieci
11	***oon**-dee-chee*	undici
12	***do**-dee-chee*	dodici
13	***trei**-dee-chee*	tredici
14	*kwah-**tor**-dee-chee*	quattordici
15	***kween**-dee-chee*	quindici
16	***sei**-dee-chee*	sedici
17	*dee-chah-**set**-tei*	diciassette
18	*dee-**chot**-to*	diciotto
19	*dee-chah-**no**-vei*	diciannove
20	***ven**-tee*	venti
21	*ven-**too**-no*	ventuno
22	*ven-tee-**doo**-ei*	ventidue
30	***tren**-tah*	trenta
40	*kwah-**rahn**-tah*	quaranta
50	*cheen-**kwahn**-tah*	cinquanta
60	*ses-**sahn**-tah*	sessanta
70	*set-**tahn**-tah*	settanta
80	*ot-**tahn**-tah*	ottanta
90	*no-**vahn**-tah*	novanta
100	***chen**-to*	cento
1000	***meel**-lei*	mille
one million	*oon mee-lee-o-nei*	un milione
1st	***pree**-mo*	primo
2nd	*se-**kon**-do*	secondo
3rd	***tair**-tso*	terzo

ITALIAN

¼	*oon kwar-to*	un quarto
⅓	*oon tair-tso*	un terzo
½	*oon me-tso/lah me-tah*	un mezzo/la metà
¾	*trei kwahr-tee*	tre quarti

a little (amount)	*(oon) po-ko, oon po'*	(un) poco, un po'
double	*dop-pee-ah*	doppio
dozen	*oo-nah do-tsee-nah*	una dozzina
Enough!	*bahs-dah!*	Basta!
few	*po-kei/po-kee*	poche/pochi
less	*me-no*	meno
many	*tahn-tei/ee*	tante/i
more	*pyoo*	più
once	*oo-nah vol-tah*	una volta
a pair	*oon pah-ee-o*	un paio
per cent	*pair-chen-to*	percento
some	*kwal-kei*	qualche
too much	*trop-po*	troppo
twice	*doo-ei vol-tei*	due volte

Abbreviations

A.A. – Assistenza Automobilistica	Automobile Association
a.c. – anno corrente	this year
ANAS	National Road Board
ANSA	Italian News Agency
C.C. – Carabinieri	police
C/F – caldo/freddo	hot/cold
c.m.	the present month
c.p.	postcard

Dr, dott (m)/dr.ssa (f)	Dr – Doctor
ENIT	Tourist Information Office
ferr.	railway
F.S. – Ferrovia dello Stato	National Railway
p.p.	parcel post
P.za – Piazza	(city) square
S.	Saint
SS. – Santi/Santissimi	very holy
S/O/N/E	South/West/North/East
sec.	century
Sig./Sig.a	Mr/Mrs, Miss
R.U. (Regno Unito)	UK
v/v.le – via/viale	street/boulevard
WL	Sleeping Car

SLOVAK

Slovak

Introduction

The Slovak language belongs to the Western branch of t[he] Slavonic languages, and is the standard language of the s[ix?] million people living in Slovakia, as well as nearly two milli[on] people living beyond the country's borders.

Slovak evolved into a separate Slavonic language betwee[n] the 9th and the 15th centuries, and was associated with t[he] development of a national Slovak culture at a time when Slov[a]kia's territory and the surrounding regions were dominated [by] Latin at religious, administrative and literary level. In the 17[th] century Slovakia found itself at the eastern border of Christi[an] Europe, and the rules of Slovak were written down for the fi[rst] time. However, Slovak emerged only in the mid-19th century [in] the course of a national revival as a uniform literary langua[ge].

Of all Slavonic languages the one which bears the close[st] resemblance to Slovak is Czech. This should come as [no] surprise, since Slovakia and the Czech lands have strong ti[es] dating back to the 9th century and the Great Moravian Empir[e] where one common language (Old Church Slavonic) was in us[e]. Modern Slovak and Czech are, in general, mutually understan[d]able, but you are well advised not to substitute one for the othe[r]. The linguistic territory of each language includes many region[al] dialects, and these form a continuum across present and pa[st] political boundaries, so that, for example, the East Slova[k] dialect is closer to the West Ukrainian dialect than to t[he] standard Czech language.

SLOVAK

Standard Slovak recognizes two forms of address corresponding to English 'you': formal *Vy* and more familiar *ty*. This phrasebook uses the polite form *Vy*, since in Slovak it is considered the appropriate form when initiating conversation or addressing strangers.

Pronunciation

Slovak is basically a phonetic language (ie written as it sounds) and not as difficult as it may look at first sight. It may help to remember that Slovak makes use of only four diacritical marks; the two found most frequently are the length mark (for example **é**) and the softening mark (for example **ď**), and the other two are limited to the letters **ä** and **ô**.

Vowels

The Slovak language has six short vowels **a, ä, e, i, o, u, y** and five long vowels **á, é, í, ó, ú, ý**. It is important to observe their different pronunciation, as detailed below, since vowel length may determine the meaning of a word.

a	as the 'u' in 'cup'	**á**	as the 'a' in 'father'
ä	as the 'a' in 'fat'	**é**	as the 'ea' in 'bear'
e	as in 'bed'	**í**	as the 'ee' in 'feet'
i	as the 'y' in 'sorry'	**ó**	as the 'a' in 'mall'
o	as in 'pot'	**ú**	as the 'oo' in 'choose'
u	as the 'oo' in 'book'	**ý**	as the 'ee' in 'feet'
y	as the 'i' in 'bit'		

Diphthongs

There are four diphthongs in Slovak: three diphthongs **ia, ie, i**
which are pronounced phonetically, and the diphthong **ô** whic
is pronounced 'uo' like the sound in 'swan'.

Consonants

The consonants **b, d, f, g, l, m, n, s, v, z** are pronounced more c
less as in English.

c	as the 'ts' in 'lots'
č	as the 'ch' in 'China'
ch	is similar to the Scottish 'ch' in 'loch' or German 'cl in 'Nacht'
ď, ť, n, ľ	correspond to the English sounds 'dy, ty, ny, ly' i 'during', 'tutor', 'new', 'lure'
dz	is similar to the 'ds' in 'roads' or Italian 'z' in 'zerc
dž	as the 'j' in 'jeans'
h	as the 'h' in 'hand' but pronounced more forcefull;
j	as the 'y' in 'yes'
k, p, t	are never aspirated
ĺ, ŕ	long ĺ and ŕ are given as a test piece for students o the Slovak language; they are semi-vowels, founc in words such as *stĺp*, *vŕba*, *tŕň*
q, w, x	only exist in words of foreign origin and are pronounced approximately as in their original language.
r	is rolled as in Scottish
š	as the 'sh' in 'shoe'

Slovak speakers refer to their language lovingly as *l'úbozvučná slovenčina* ('sweet sounding Slovak') in recognition of its melodious quality which, for example, does not allow two consecutive long syllables, and avoids heavy emphasis on any word. Stress always falls on the first syllable, but is far less strong than in other languages, including English.

Greetings & Civilities
Top 10 Useful Phrases

Hello.
  doh-bree dyeny   Dobrý deň
Goodbye.
  doh vidyeny-nyiah   Do videnia.
Yes./No.
  aa-noh/nyieh   Áno./Nie.
Excuse me.
  prepaach-tyeh   Prepáčte.
May I? Do you mind?
  smyiem? dovoh-leetyeh?   Smiem? Dovolíte?
Sorry. (Forgive me.)
  prepaach-tyeh, proh-seem Prepáčte, prosím.
Please.
  proh-seem   Prosím.
Thank you.
  dyakuh-yem   Ďakujem.
Many thanks.
  dyakuh-yem (vely-mih)   Ďakujem (veľmi) pekne.
  pek-nah
That's fine. You're welcome.
  nyieh yah zah čho   Nie je za čo.
  proh-seem   Prosím.

Greetings

Good morning.
doh-brair raano   Dobré ráno.

Good afternoon.
doh-bree dyeny   Dobrý deň.

Good evening.
doh-bree veh-cher   Dobrý večer.

Good night.
doh-broo nots   Dobrú noc.

How are you?
akoh sah maa-tyeh ?   Ako sa máte?

Well, thanks.
dyakuh-yem dobreh   Ďakujem, dobre.

Forms of Address

Madam/Mrs	*pah-nyih*	Pani
Sir/Mr	*paan*	Pán
Miss	*slech-nah*	Slečna
friend	*pryiah-tyely* (m)	Priateľ
	pryiah-tyely-kah (f)	Priateľka

Small Talk

Meeting People

What is your name?
akoh sah voh-laa-tyeh?   Ako sa voláte?

My name is ...
voh-laam sah ...   Volám sa ...

I'd like to introduce you to ...
dovoly-tyeh abih som   Dovoľte, aby som
vaas predstah-vil   Vás predstavil. Toto je ...
totoh yeh ...

I'm pleased to meet you.
tyeshee mah Teší ma.

Age

How old are you?
koly-koh maa-teh rokohw? Koľko máte rokov?
I am ... years old.
maam ... rokohw Mám ... rokov.

Nationalities

Where are you from?
odkyialy styeh ? Odkiaľ ste?
I am from ...
som z ... Som z ...

Australia	*ahwstraa-lyieh*	Austrálie
Canada	*kanah-dih*	Kanady
England	*anglitz-kah*	Anglicka
Ireland	*eer-skah*	Írska
New Zealand	*novair-hoh zair-landuh*	Nového Zélandu
Scotland	*shkawht-skah*	Škótska
USA	*oo-es-ah (spoyeh-neekh shtaa-tohw ameritz-keekh)*	USA (Spojených štátov amerických)
Wales	*wheyl-suh*	Walesu

Occupations

What do you do?
choh robee-tyeh ? Čo robíte?

I am a/an ...
(yah) som ... (Ja) som ...

English	Slovak (phonetic)	Slovak
artist	*oomeh-lets* (m)	umelec
	oomel-kinya (f)	umelkyňa
business person	*podnyih-kah-tyely* (m)	podnikatel
	podnyih-kah-tyely-kah (f)	podnikatelka
doctor	*dok-tor* (m)	doktor
	dok-tor-kah (f)	doktorka
engineer	*inzhih-nyier* (m)	inžinier
	inzhih-nyier-kah (f)	inžinierka
farmer	*roly-nyeek* (m)	roľník
	roly-nyeech-kah (f)	roľníčka
journalist	*novih-naar* (m)	novinár
	novih-naar-kah (f)	novinárka
lawyer	*praav-nyik* (m)	právnik
	praav-nyich-kah	právnička
manual worker	*robot-nyeek* (m)	robotník
	robot-nyeech-kah (f)	robotníčka
mechanic	*mekhah-nik* (m)	mechanik
	mekhah-nich-kah (f)	mechanička
nurse	*osheh-trovah-tyely* (m)	ošetrovateľ
	osheh-trovah-tyely-kah (f)	ošetrovateľka
office worker	*oorad-nyeek* (m)	úradník
	oorad-nyeech-kah (f)	úradníčka
scientist	*vedyets-kee pratsov-nyeek* (m)	vedecký pracovník
	vedyets-kaa pratsov-nyeech-kah (f)	vedecká pracovníčka

student	*shtuh-dent* (m)	študent
	shtuh-dent-kah (f)	študentka
teacher	*oochih-tyely* (m)	učiteľ
	oochih-tyely-kah (f)	učiteľka
waiter	*chash-nyeek* (m)	čašník
	chash-nyeech-kah (f)	čašníčka
writer	*spisoh-vah-tyely* (m)	spisovateľ
	spisoh-vah-tyely-kah (f)	spisovateľka

Religion

What is your religion?

   akair-hoh styeh (vyieroh)   Akého ste (viero-)vyznania?
   viznah-nyiah ?

I am not religious.

   som bez viznah-nyiah   Som bez vyznania.

I am ...

   (yah) som ...   (Ja) som ...

Buddhist	*boodhih-stah* (m)	budhista
	bood-hist-kah (f)	budhistka
Catholic	*kahtoh-leek* (m)	katolík
	kahtoh-leech-kah (f)	katolička
Protestant	*evanyieh-lik* (m)	evanjelik
	evanyieh-lich-kah (f)	evanjelička
Christian	*kres-tyan* (m)	kresťan
	kres-tyan-kah (f)	kresťanka
Hindu	*hindoo-istah* (m)	hinduista
	hindoo-ist-kah (f)	hinduistka
Jewish	*zhid* (m)	žid
	zhidohv-kah (f)	židovka

| Muslim | *mos-lim* (m) | moslim |
| | *mos-lim-kah* (f) | moslimka |

Family

Are you married?
    steh zhenah-tee? (m)   Ste ženatý?
    steh vidah-taa? (f)   Ste vydatá ?
I am single.
    som slobod-nee (m)   Som slobodný.
    som slobod-naa (f)   Som slobodná.
I am married.
    som zhenah-tee (m)   Som ženatý.
    som vidah-taa (f)   Som vydatá.
How many children do you have?
    koly-koh maa-tyeh   Koľko máte detí?
    dyeh-tyee?
I don't have any children.
    nye-maam (zhiad-neh)   Nemám (žiadne) deti.
    dyeh-tih
I have a daughter/a son.
    maam tsair-ruh/sinah   Mám dcéru/syna.
How many brothers/sisters do you have?
    koly-koh maa-teh   Koľko máte bratov/sestier?
    brah-tohw/seh-styier?
Is your husband/wife here?
    vaash man-zhel/vaa-shah   Váš manžel/Vaša manželka
    man-zhel-kah yeh tuh?   je tu?

Do you have a boyfriend/
girlfriend?

   maa-teh priah-tyeh-lyah/   Máte priateľa/priateľku?
   priah-tyely-kuh?

brother	*braht*	brat
daughter	*tsair-rah*	dcéra
family	*rodyih-nah*	rodina
father	*oh-tyets*	otec
grandfather	*stah-ree oh-tyets*	starý otec
grandmother	*stah-raa mat-kah*	stará matka
husband	*man-zhel*	manžel
mother	*mat-kah*	matka
sister	*seh-strah*	sestra
son	*sin*	syn
wife	*manzhel-kah*	manželka

Feelings

I like .../I don't like ...

   maam raad ... (m)   Mám rád ...
   maam radah ... (f)/   Mám rada .../
   nyeh-maam raad ... (m)   Nemám rád ...
   nyeh-maam radah ... (f)   Nemám rada ...

I am ...

cold/hot	*yeh mih zimah/ tyep-loh*	Je mi zima/teplo.
hungry/thirsty	*maam hlahd/smed*	Mám hlad/smäd.
in a hurry	*ponaa-hlyam sah*	Ponáhľam sa.
right	*maam prahv-duh*	Mám pravdu.

sleepy	*som ospah-lee* (m)/ *ospah-laa* (f)	Som ospalý/ ospalá.

I am ...

angry	*hnye-vaam sah*	Hnevám sa.
happy	*som shtyast-nee* (m)	Som šťastný.
	som shtyast-naa (f)	Som šťastná.
sad	*som smut-nee* (m)	Som smutný.
	som smut-naa (f)	Som smutná.
tired	*som oonah-vehnee*(m)	Som unavený.
	som oonah-vehnaa (f)	Som unavená.
well	*tsee-tyim sah dob-reh*	Cítim sa dobre.
worried	*ohbaa-vam sah*	Obávam sa.

I am sorry. (condolence)
   lyutuh-yem   Ľutujem.
I am grateful.
   som vdyach-nee (m)/   Som vďačný/
   vdyach-naa (f)   vďačná.

Language Difficulties

Do you speak English?
   hovoh-ree-tyeh   Hovoríte po anglicky?
   poh ahnglits-kih ?
Does anyone (here) speak
English?
   hovoh-ree (tuh) nyiek-toh   Hovorí (tu) niekto
   poh ahnglits-kih ?   po anglicky?
I speak a little ...
   yah hovoh-reehm   Ja hovorím trocha (po) ...
   tro-kha (poh ...)

SLOVAK

don't speak ...		
nyeh-hovoh-reehm (poh ...)	Nehovorím (po) ...	
(don't) understand.		
rozuh-miehm/ nyeh-rozuh-miehm	Rozumiem./Nerozumiem.	
Could you speak more slowly please?		
muoh-zhetyeh proh-seem hoh-vohrity pohmal-shyieh ?	Môžete prosím hovoriť pomalšie?	
Could you repeat that?		
muoh-zhetyeh toh zo pa-kovaty ?	Môžete to zopakovať?	
How do you say ...?		
akoh sah povyieh ?	Ako sa povie ...?	
What does ... mean?		
choh znameh-naa ?	Čo znamená ...?	

I speak ...		
hovoh-reehm poh ...	Hovorím po ...	
Arabic	*arab-skih*	arabsky
Danish	*daan-skih*	dánsky
Dutch	*holand-skih*	holandsky
English	*anglits-kih*	anglicky
Finnish	*feen-skih*	finsky
French	*fran-tsooz-kih*	francúzsky
German	*nyemetz-kih*	nemecky
Italian	*talyian-skih*	taliansky
Japanese	*yapon-skih*	japonsky

Some Useful Phrases

Sure.
oorchih-tyeh — Určite!

Just a minute.
ohkam-zhik — Okamžik.

It's (not) important.
toh (nyieh) yeh duole-zhitair — To (nie) je dôležité.

It's (not) possible.
toh (nyieh) yeh mozh-nair — To (nie) je možné.

Wait!
pochkay (sing)/ — Počkaj!/
pochkay-tyeh (pl) — Počkajte!

Good luck!
fshet-koh naylep-shyieh — Všetko najlepšie!

Signs

BAGGAGE COUNTER	PODAJ BATOŽÍN
CHECK-IN COUNTER	ODBAVOVANIE CESTUJÚCICH
CUSTOMS	COLNICA (COLNÁ KONTROLA)
EMERGENCY EXIT	NÚDZOVÝ VÝCHOD
ENTRANCE	VCHOD
EXIT	VÝCHOD
FREE ADMISSION	VOĽNÝ (BEZPLATNÝ) VSTUP

SLOVAK

HOT/COLD (WATER)	HORÚCA/STUDENÁ (VODA)
INFORMATION	INFORMÁCIE
NO ENTRY	ZÁKAZ VSTUPU/VSTUP ZAKÁZANÝ
NO SMOKING	ZÁKAZ FAJČENIA
OPEN/CLOSED	OTVORENÉ/ ZATVORENÉ
OPENING HOURS	OTVÁRACIE HODINY
PROHIBITED	ZAKÁZANÉ
RESERVED	REZERVOVANÉ
TELEPHONE	TELEFÓN
TOILETS	ZÁCHODY/WC/ TOALETY

Emergencies

POLICE	POLÍCIA
POLICE STATION	STANICA POLÍCIE

Help!
pomots   Pomoc!
It's an emergency!
potreh-buyem pomots!   Potrebuje pomoc!
There's been an accident!
stalah sah nyeh-hodah!   Stala sa nehoda!

SLOVAK

Call a doctor!
   zahvolai-tyeh doktoh-rah/   Zavolajte doktora/lekára!
   lekaa-rah!

Call an ambulance!
   zahvolai-tyeh   Zavolajte záchranku!
   zaakhran-koo!

I've been raped.
   bolah som   Bola som znásilnená.
   znaasil-nyenaah

I've been robbed.
   ohkrad-lih mah   Okradli ma.

Call the police!
   zahvolai-tyeh polee-tsyiuh! Zavolajte políciu!

Where is the police station?
   gdyeh yeh poli-tsaynaa   Kde je policajná stanica?
   stanyih-tsa?

Go away!
   khody prech (sg)/   Choď preč!/Choďte preč!
   khody-tyeh prech (pl)

I'll call the police!
   zahvoh-laam polee-tsyiuh ! Zavolám políciu!

Thief!
   zlodyey   Zlodej!

I am ill.
   (yah) som khoree (m)   (Ja) som chorý.
   (yah) som khoraa (f)   (Ja) som chorá.

My friend is ill.
   muoy pryia-tyely yeh   Môj priateľ je chorý.
   khoree (m)
   moya pryia-tyely-kah yeh Moja priateľka je chorá.
   khoraa (f)

I am lost.
    nye-viznaahm sah tuh   Nevyznám sa tu.

Where are the toilets?
    gdyeh soo tuh zaa-khodih ?   Kde sú tu záchody?

Could you help me please?
    muo-zhotye mih (proh-   Môžete mi (prosím) pomôcť?
    seem) poh-muotsty ?

Could I please use the telephone?
    muo-zhem (proh-seem)   Môžem (prosím) použiť
    pohw-zhity teleh-fawn ?   telefón?

I'm sorry. I apologise.
    prepaach-tyeh proh-seem   Prepáčte, prosím.

I didn't realise I was doing
anything wrong.
    nyeh-oovedoh-mil (m)/   Neuvedomil/Neuvedomila
    nyeh-oovedoh-milah (f)   som si, že robím niečo
    som sih zheh roh-beam   nesprávne.
    nyíeh-cho nye-spraavneh

I didn't do it.
    yah som toh nyeh-oorobil   Ja som to neurobil/
    (m)/*nyeh-oorobilah (f)*   neurobila.

I wish to contact my embassy/
consulate.
    zhelaam sih hoh-vohrity   Želám si hovoriť so zastu-
    zoh zastuh-pityely-stvom   piteľstvom mojej krajiny.
    moyey krayih-nih

I have medical insurance.
    maam nyemotsen-skair   Mám nemocenské poistenie.
    poh-istyenyieh

My possessions are insured.
moyah batoh-zhinah yeh poh-istyenaa   Moja batožina je poistená.

My ... was stolen.
ookrad-lih mih   Ukradli mi ...

I've lost my ...
strahtyil som ... (m)   Stratil som ...
strahtyil-lah som ... (f)   Stratila som ...

bags	*batoh-zhinuh*	batožinu
handbag	*tash-kuh/kabel-kuh*	tašku/kabelku
money	*penyiah-zeh*	peniaze
travellers' cheques	*tses-tohv-nair sheh-kih*	cestovné šeky
passport	*tses-tohv-nee pahs*	cestovný pas
next of kin	*(nai-blizh-shee) pree-buznee*	(najbližší) príbuzní

My blood group is (A, B, O positive/negative).
mohyah krvnaa skupih-nah yeh (aa, bair, awh poh zi-teev-nah/neh-ga-teev-nah)   Moja krvná skupina je (A, B, O pozitívna/negatívna).

Paperwork

name/surname	*menoh/pryieh-zviskoh*	meno/priezvisko
address	*adreh-sah*	adresa
date of birth	*daatum naroh-dyenyiah*	dátum narodenia

place of birth	*myiestoh naroh-dyenyiah*	miesto narodenia
age	*vek*	vek
sex	*poh-hlavyieh*	pohlavie
nationality/ citizenship	*naarod-nosty/ shtaat-nah pree-slush-nosty*	národnosť/ štátna príslušnosť
religion	*vyieroh-vizna-nyieh*	vierovyznanie
reason for travel	*oochel tses-tih*	účel cesty
profession	*povoh-lanyieh*	povolanie
marital status	*stav (rohdyin-nee)*	stav (rodinný)
passport	*tses-tohv-nee pahs*	cestovný pas
passport number	*cheesloh tses-tohv-nairhoh pahsuh*	číslo cestovného pasu
visa	*veezum*	vízum
tourist card	*toorist- itskee preh-oo-kahz*	turistický preukaz
identification	*preh-oo-kahz totozh-nostih*	preukaz totožnosti
birth certificate	*rodnee list*	rodný list
driver's licence	*vodyich-skee preh-oo-kahz*	vodičský preukaz
car owner's title	*doklah-dih oh vlast-nyeetst-veh motoroh-vair-hoh vozid-lah*	doklady o vlastníctve motoro-vého vozidla
car registration	*reghistrach-nair doklah-dih motor oh-vairhoh vozid-lah*	registračné doklady motorového vozidla
customs	*tsol-naa pre hlyiad-kah*	colná prehliadka

| immigration | *pri-styahoh-valets-kair zaalezhi-tostyih* | prisťahovalecké záležitosti |
| border | *shtaat-nah hranyi-tsa* | štátna hranica |

Getting Around

ARRIVALS	PRÍCHODY
BUS STOP	AUTOBUSOVÁ ZASTÁVKA
DEPARTURES	ODCHODY
STATION	STANICA
SUBWAY	PODZEMNÁ DRÁHA/ METRO
TICKET OFFICE	PREDAJ CESTOVNÝCH LÍSTKOV
TIMETABLE	CESTOVNÝ PORIADOK
TRAIN STATION	ŽELEZNIČNÁ STANICA

What time does the ... leave/ arrive?

	kedih ot-khaa-dzah/ pri-khaa-dzah ...?	Kedy odchádza/prichádza ...?
aeroplane	*lyieh-tadloh*	lietadlo
boat	*lody*	loď
(city) bus	*(mest-skee) owtoh-buhs*	(mestský) autobus
(intercity) bus	*(medzih-mest-skee) owtoh-buhs*	(medzimestský) autobus

SLOVAK

| train | *vlakh* | vlak |
| tram | *elek-trich-kah* | električka |

Directions

Where is ...?
gdyeh yeh ...? — Kde je ...

How do I get to ...?
akoh sah dostah-nyem doh ...? — Ako sa dostanem do ...?

Is it far from/near here?
yeh toh od-tyialy-toh dya-lekoh/bleez-koh? — Je to odtiaľto ďaleko/blízko?

Can I walk there?
daa sah tam easty peshih? — Dá sa tam ísť peši?

Can you show me (on the map)?
muo-zhetyeh mih uh-kaazaty (nah mapeh) — Môžete mi ukázať (na mape)?

Are there other means of getting there?
akoh sah tam daa eshtyeh dos-taty? — Ako sa tam dá ešte dostať?

I want to go to ...
khtsehm easty doh — Chcem ísť do ...

Go straight ahead.
khody-tyeh rovnoh dya-lay — Choďte rovno ďalej.

It's two blocks down.
soo toh od-tyialy-toh dveh uhlih-tse — Sú to odtiaľto dve ulice.

Turn left ...
zaboch-tyeh vlya-voh — Zabočte vľavo ...

Turn right ...
zaboch-tyeh fpra-voh   Zabočte vpravo ...
at the next corner.
nah nasleh-duh-yootsom   na nasledujúcom rohu.
rohuh
at the traffic lights.
na krizho-vatkeh zoh   na križovatke so svetlami.
svetlah-mih
behind/in front of *zah/ pred*   za/pred
far/near   *dya-lehkoh/bleez-koh*   ďaleko/blízko
in front of   *pred*   pred
opposite   *oh-protyih*   oproti

Booking Tickets

Excuse me, where is the ticket
office?
gdyeh yeh pre-dai   Kde je predaj cestovných
tses-tohv-neekh least-   lístkov, prosím?
kohw proh-seem ?
Where can I buy a ticket?
gdyeh sih muo-zhem   Kde si môžem kúpiť cestovný
koo-pity tses-tohv-nee   lístok?
leas-tok ?
I want to go to ...
khtsem easty do   Chcem ísť do ...
Do I need to book?
potreh-buyem   Potrebujem miestenku?
myies-tyenkuh ?
You need to book.
potreh-buyetye   Potrebujete miestenku.
myies-tyenkuh

I would like to book a seat to ...
 myies-tyenkuh do ...   Miestenku do ... prosím.
 proh-seem

I would like ...
 proh-seem sih   Prosím si ...

a one-way ticket	*yednoh-smernee*	jednosmerny lístok
	leas-tok	
a return ticket	*spyiatoch-nee leas-tok*	spiatočný lístok
two tickets	*dvah least-kih*	dva lístky
tickets for all	*least-kih preh naas*	lístky pre nás
of us	*fshet-keekh*	všetkých

a student's fare	*shtudent-skee leas-tok*	študentský lístok
a child's fare	*dyet-skee leas-tok*	detský lístok
pensioner's fare	*leas-tok preh*	lístok pre
	duo-khod-tsohw	dôchodcov

1st class
 prvaa tryieh-dah   prvá trieda
2nd class
 dru-haa tryieh-dah   druhá trieda

It is full.
 fshet-koh yeh   Všetko je obsadené.
 obsah-dyenair
Is it completely full?
 nyieh yeh tuh nich   Nie je tu nič voľné?
 voly-nee ?
Can I get a stand-by ticket?
 muo-zhèm tuh dos-taty   Môžem tu dostať 'stand-by'
 stend-baay leas-tok ?   lístok?

Air

CHECKING IN	PREZENTÁCIA/ ODBAVOVANIE CESTUJÚCICH
LUGGAGE PICKUP	VÝDAJ BATOŽÍN
REGISTRATION	REGISTRÁCIA

Is there a flight to ...?
yeh let doh ...? Je let do ...?

When is the next flight to ...?
kedih yeh nai-blizh-shee let doh ...? Kedy je najbližší let do ...?

How long does the flight take?
akoh dlhoh tr-vaa tentoh let ? Ako dlho trvá tento let?

What is the flight number?
akair chees-loh maa tentoh let ? Aké číslo má tento let?

You must check in at ...
pred od-letom sah muh-seetye dos-tavity k prezen-taatsiyi kuh ... Pred odletom sa musíte dostaviť k prezentácii ku ...

airport tax	*letisht-nee poh-platok*	letištný poplatok
boarding pass	*palub-nee leas-tok*	palubný lístok
customs	*tsol-naa kon-trolah*	colná kontrola

Bus

BUS/TRAM STOP	ZASTÁVKA AUTOBUSOV / ELEKTRIČIEK

Where is the bus/tram stop?
  gdyeh yeh tuh zas-taavkah owtoh-buhsuh/ elek-trichkih ?
Kde je tu zastávka autobusu/ električky?

Which bus goes to ...?
  ktoh-reem owtoh-buhsom sah dos-tanyem doh ?
Ktorým autobusom sa dostanem do ...?

Does this bus go to ...?
  idyeh tentoh owtoh-buhs doh ...?
Ide tento autobus do ...?

How often do buses pass by?
  akoh chas-toh tuh yaz-dyiah owtoh-buhsih ?
Ako často tu jazdia autobusy?

What time is the ... bus?
  kedih pree-dyeh ... owtoh-buhs ?
Kedy príde ... autobus ?

next	*nasleh-duhyoo-tsih*	nasledujúci
first	*pr-vee*	prvý
last	*poh-slednee*	posledný

Could you let me know when
we get to ...?
*muo-zhetyeh mah
proh-seem upoh-zornyity
kedih buh-dyemeh v ...?*

Môžete ma prosím upozorniť,
keď budeme v ...?

I want to get off!
khtsem vih-stoopyity

Chcem vystúpiť!

Metro

METRO/UNDERGROUND	METRO/PODZEMNÁ DRÁHA
CHANGE (for coins)	DROBNÉ (MINCE)
THIS WAY TO	TÝMTO SMEROM
WAY OUT	K VÝCHODU

Which line takes me to ...?
*ktoh-rohw lin-kohw sah
dos-tahnyem doh ...?*

Ktorou linkou sa
dostanem do ...?

What is the next station?
*akoh sah volaa nah-
sleduhyoo-tsah
stanyi-tsah?*

Ako sa volá nasledujúca
stanica?

Train

DINING CAR	JEDÁLENSKÝ VOZEŇ
EXPRESS	EXPRES/ RÝCHLIK
PLATFORM NO	NÁSTUPIŠTE ČÍSLO
SLEEPING CAR	SPACÍ VOZEŇ

Is this the right platform
for ...?
   yeh toh spraav-neh   Je to správne nástupište do ...?
   naah-stupish-tyeh doh ...?
Passengers must ...
   tsestuh-yootsih muhsyiah ... Cestujúci musia ...

change trains	*pres-toopity nah*	prestúpiť na ...
change	*preysty nah inair*	prejsť na iné
platforms	*naah-stupish-tyeh*	nástupište

The train leaves from
platform ...
   vlak od-khaatzah z   Vlak odchádza z nástupišťa ...
   naah-stupish-tyah ...

dining car	*yedaa-lenskee vozeny*	jedálenský vozeň
express	*eks-pres/ reekh-lick*	expres/rýchlik
local	*lokaal-nih vlakh*	lokálny vlak
sleeping car	*spuh-tsee vozeny*	spací vozeň

Taxi

Can you take me to ...?
   muo-zhetyeh mah   Môžete ma zaviesť do ...?
   zavyiesty doh ...?
Please take me to ...   Zavezte ma prosím do ...
   zavestyeh mah proh-seem
   doh ...
How much does it cost to go to ...?
   koly-koh toh budyeh   Koľko to bude stáť do ...?
   staaty doh ...?

Instructions

Here is fine, thank you.
   potyialy-toh stachee   Potiaľto stačí.
The next corner, please.
   azh poh nai-blizh-shee   Až po najbližší roh, prosím.
   rokh proh-seem
Continue!
   poh-krachuy-tyeh   Pokračujte v jazde!
   v yaz-dyeh
The next street to the left/right.
   nah-sleduyoo-tsa ulitsa   Nasledujúca ulica vľavo/
   vlyah-voh/ fprah-voh   vpravo.
Stop here!
   zah-stavtyeh tuh   Zastavte tu, prosím.
   proh-seem
Please slow down.
   spomal-tyeh proh-seem   Spomalte, prosím.
Please wait here.
   pochkay-tyeh tuh   Počkajte tu, prosím.
   proh-seem

Some Useful Phrases

The train is delayed.
vlak maa meshkah-nyieh
Vlak má meškanie.

The train is cancelled.
vlak bol zruh-sheh-nee
Vlak bol zrušený.

How long will it be delayed?
akoh dlhoh budyeh meshkaty?
Ako dlho bude meškať?

There is a delay of ... hours.
meshkah-nyieh budyeh ...
Meškanie bude ...

Can I reserve a place?
muo-zhem sih rezer-vohvaty myiestyen-kuh?
Môžem si rezervovať miestenku?

How long does the trip take?
akoh dlhoh tr-vaa tsestah?
Ako dlho trvá cesta?

Is it a direct route?
yeh toh pryiah-meh spoyeh-nyieh?
Je to priame spojenie?

Is that seat taken?
ob-sadyenair?
Obsadené?

I want to get off at ...
khtsem vih-stoopity v ...
Chcem vystúpiť v ...

Excuse me.
preh-paachtyeh
Prepáčte.

Where can I hire a bicycle?
gdyeh sah tuh daa poh-zhichaty bih-tsih-kehl?
Kde sa tu dá požičať bicykel?

Car

DETOUR	OBCHÁDZKA
FREEWAY	DIAĽNICA
GARAGE/WORKSHOP	AUTOOPRAVOVŇA
GIVE WAY	DAJ PREDNOSŤ V JAZDE
MECHANIC	(AUTO)MECHANIK
NO ENTRY	ZÁKAZ VJAZDU
NO PARKING	ZÁKAZ PARKOVANIA
NORMAL	NORMÁL
ONE WAY	JEDNOSMERNÁ DOPRAVA
REPAIRS	AUTOOPRAVY
SELF SERVICE	SAMOOBSLUHA
STOP	STOP/ ZASTAVIŤ/ STÁŤ
SUPER	SUPER
UNLEADED	NATURAL

Where can I rent a car?
gdyeh sih muo-zhem preh-nayaty owtoh?
Kde si môžem prenajať auto?

How much is it daily/weekly?
koly-koh toh stoh-yee nah dyeny/teezh-dyeny?
Koľko to stojí na deň/týždeň?

Does that include insurance/mileage?
yeh v tse-nyeh za-hrnuh-tai poh-istyeh-nyieh/kiloh-metraazh?
Je v cene zahrnuté poistenie/kilometráž?

Where's the next petrol station?

gdyeh yeh nai-blizh-shyieh benzee-novair cher-pahd-loh ? — Kde je najbližšie benzínové čerpadlo?

Please fill the tank.

pl-noo naa-drzh proh-seem — Plnú nádrž, prosím.

I want ... litres of petrol (gas).

potreh-buyem ... lit-rohw ben-zeenuh — Potrebujem ... litrov benzínu.

Please check the oil and water.

skon-troluy-tyeh proh-seem hlah-dyinuh aw-leyah ah vodih — Skontrolujte prosím hladinu oleja a vody.

How long can I park here?

akoh dlhoh tuh muo-zhem par-kovaty? — Ako dlho tu môžem parkovať ?

Does this road lead to?

veh-dyieh taa-toh tses-tah doh? — Vedie táto cesta do ...?

air (for tyres)	*stlah-cheh-nee vz-dukh/ kom-preh-sor*	stlačený vzduch/ kompresor
battery	*bah-tair-ryiah*	batéria
brakes	*brz-dih*	brzdy
clutch	*spoy-kah*	spojka
driver's licence	*voh-dyich-skee preh-oo-kaz*	vodičský preukaz
engine	*moh-tor*	motor

lights	*sveht-laa*	svetlá
oil	*aw-ley*	olej
puncture	*preh-pikh-nootaa*	prepichnutá
	pneu-mah-tikah/	pneumatika/
	deh-fekt (fam)	defekt
radiator	*khlah-dyich*	chladič
road map	*owtoh-mapah*	automapa
tyres	*pneu-mah-tikih*	pneumatiky
windscreen	*pred-nair skloh*	predné sklo

Car Problems

I need a mechanic.
potreh-buyem pomots   Potrebujem pomoc auto-
owtoh-mekhah-nikah   mechanika.

What make is it?
akaa yeh toh znach-kah   Aká je to značka (auta)?
(owtah)?

The battery is flat.
bah-tair-ryiah yeh
vih-bihtaa   Batéria je vybitá.

The radiator is leaking.
khlah-dyich tyeh-chyieh   Chladič tečie.

I have a flat tyre.
maam preh-pikh-nutoo   Mám prepichnutú
pneu-mah-tikuh   pneumatiku.
maam deh-fekt (fam)   Mám defekt.

It's overheating.
moh-tor sah   Motor sa prehrieva.
preh-hryieh-vah

It's not working.
neh-fuhn-guhyeh toh   Nefunguje to.

Accommodation

CAMPING GROUND	KEMPING/TÁBORISKO
GUEST HOUSE	PENZIONÁT
HOTEL	HOTEL
MOTEL	MOTEL
YOUTH HOSTEL	TURISTICKÁ UBYTOVŇA MLÁDEŽE

I am looking for ...
   hlyah-daam   Hľadám ...
Where is a ...?
   gdyeh yeh ...?   Kde je ... ?

cheap hotel	*lahts-nee hoh-tel*	lacný hotel
good hotel	*kvahlit-nee hoh-tel*	kvalitný hotel
nearby hotel	*hoh-tel nah-blees-kuh*	hotel nablízku
clean hotel	*dobreh uhdr-zhyia-vah-nee hoh-tel*	dobre udržiavaný hotel

What is the address of ... ?
   ah-kaa yeh adreh-sah tohoh ...?   Aká je adresa toho ... ?
Could you write the address, please?
   muo-zhetyeh mih proh-seem nah-peesaty too adreh-suh ?   Môžete mi prosím napísať tú adresu?

SLOVAK

At the Hotel

Do you have any rooms
available?
maa-tyeh voly-nair izbih?   Máte voľné izby?

I would like ...
poh-trebuhyem ...   Potrebujem ...

a single room	*yednoh-luozhkoh-voo izbuh*	jednolôžkovú izbu
a double room	*izbuh preh dveh ohsoh-bih*	izbu pre dve osoby
a room with a bathroom	*izbuh s koo-pely-nyohw*	izbu s kúpeľňou
to share a dorm	*(spoloch-noo) izbuh nah uhbitov-nyih*	(spoločnú) izbu na ubytovni
a bed	*pos-tyely*	posteľ

I want a room with a ...
muo-zhetyeh mih daty izbuh ...   Môžete mi dať izbu ...

bathroom	*s koo-pelynyohw*	s kúpeľňou
shower	*zoh spr-khohw*	so sprchou
television	*s teleh-veeznim prih-yeemachom*	s televíznym prijímačom
window	*s oknom*	s oknom

I'm going to stay for ...
zoh-stanyem tuh ...   Zostanem tu ...

one day	*yeden dyeny*	jeden deň
two days	*dvah dnyih*	dva dni
one week	*yeden teezh-dyeny*	jeden týždeň

Slovak 407

m not sure how long I'm
aying.
  nyeh-vyiem eshtyeh akoh   Neviem ešte ako dlho tu
  dlhoh tuh zoh-stanyem   zostanem.

o you have identification?
  maa-tyeh preh-oo-kaz   Máte preukaz totožnosti?
  totozh-nostyih?

our membership card, please.
  vaash chlen-skee   Váš členský preukaz, prosím.
  preh-oo-kaz proh-seem

orry, we're full.
  zhyialy smeh pl-nee   Žiaľ, sme plní.

ow long will you be staying?
  akoh dlhoh tuh zoh-   Ako dlho tu zostanete?
  stanyeh-tyeh?

ow many nights?
  koly-koh nohtsee ?   Koľko nocí?

's ... per day/per person.
  stoh-yee toh ... nah dyeny/   Stojí to ... na deň/osobu.
  oh-sobuh

ow much is it per night/per
erson?
  koly-koh toh stoh-yee   Koľko to stojí na deň/
  nah dyeny/oh-sobuh?   osobu?

an I see it?
  muo-zhem toh (proh-seem)   Môžem to (prosím) vidieť?
  vi-dyiety?

re there any others?
  maa-tyeh eshtyeh ih-nair   Máte ešte iné na výber?
  nah vee-ber?

SLOVAK

Do you have any cheaper
rooms?
  maa-tyeh ih lats-
  nyey-shyieh izbih?   Máte aj lacnejšie izby?
Can I see the bathroom?
  muo-zhem vih-dyiety
  koo-pelynyu?   Môžem vidieť kúpeľňu?
Is there a reduction for
students/children?
  mah-yoo shtuden-tyih/
  dyetyih zlyah-vuh?   Majú študenti/deti zľavu?
Does it include breakfast?
  soo rah-nyaikih
  zahrh-nuhtair f tse-nyeh?   Sú raňajky zahrnuté v cene?
It's fine, I'll take it.
  doh-breh, beh-ryiem toh   Dobre, beriem to.
Is there a lift?
  yeh tam vee-tyakh?   Je tam výťah?
Where is the bathroom?
  gdyeh yeh koo-pelynyah?   Kde je kúpeľňa?
Is there hot water all day?
  yeh horoo-tsah vodah
  poh tselee dyeny?   Je horúca voda po celý deň?
Do you have a safe where
I can leave my valuables?
  maa-tyeh treh-zor (saife)
  nah uh-lozheh-nyieh   Máte trezor (safe) na uloženie
  tsen-nos-tyee?   cenností?
Is there somewhere to wash
clothes?
  muo-zhem sih nyiegdyeh
  opraty obleh-chenyieh?   Môžem si niekde oprať
                                         oblečenie?

can I use the kitchen?
  muo-zhem poh-uzheevaty kukhih-nyuh? Môžem používať kuchyňu?

can I use the telephone?
  muo-zhem poh-uzheevaty teleh-fawn? Môžem používať telefón?

Requests & Complaints

please wake me up at ...
  zoh-boody-tyeh mah (proh-seem) oh ... Zobuďte ma (prosím) o ...

the room needs to be cleaned.
  izbuh trebah vih-chistyity Izbu treba vyčistiť.

please change the sheets.
  vih-menytyeh (proh-seem) postyely-noo byehlih-zeny Vymeňte (prosím) posteľnú bielizeň.

can't open/close the window.
  nyeh-muo-zhem oh-tvohrity /zah-tvohrity oknoh Nemôžem otvoriť /zatvoriť okno.

I've locked myself out of my room.
  vim-kohl (m)/vim-klah (f) som sah z izbih Vymkol/Vymkla som sa z izby.

the toilet won't flush.
  zaa-khod nyeh-splah-khooyeh Záchod nesplachuje.

don't like this room.
  taa-toh izbah sah mih nyeh-paachih Táto izba sa mi nepáči.

it's too small.
  yeh pree-lish malaa Je príliš malá.

It's noisy.
> *yeh hlooch-naa* Je hlučná.

It's too dark.
> *yeh pree-lish tmah-vaa* Je príliš tmavá.

It's expensive.
> *yeh drahaa* Je drahá.

Some Useful Words & Phrases

I am leaving ...
> *ot-khaa-dzam ...* Odchádzam ...

We are leaving ...
> *ot-khaa-dzameh ...* Odchádzame ...

now/tomorrow
> *teraz/zai-trah* teraz/zajtra

I would like to pay the bill.
> *khtsel (m)/khtselah (f) bih* Chcel/Chcela by
> *som vih-rovnaty ooh-chet* som vyrovnať účet.

name	*menoh (krst-nee)*	meno (krstné)
surname	*pryieh-zviskoh*	priezvisko
room number	*chees-loh izbih*	číslo izby

address	*adreh-sah*	adresa
air-conditioned	*klimah-tih-zaatsyiah*	klimatizácia
balcony	*bal-koohn*	balkón
bathroom	*koo-pelynyah*	kúpeľňa
bed	*pos-tyely*	posteľ
bill	*ooh-chet*	účet
blanket	*prih-kreev-kah*	prikrývka

candle	*svyiech-kah*	sviečka
chair	*stolich-kah/kres-loh*	stolička/kreslo
clean	*chis-tee* (m)	čistý
	chis-taa (f)	čistá
	chis-taihr (neut)	čisté
cupboard	*ot-kladah-tsee*	odkladací priestor
	pryieh-stor	
dark	*tmah-vee* (m)	tmavý
	tmah-vaa (f)	tmavá
	tmah-vair (neut)	tmavé
dirty	*shpinah-vee* (m)	špinavý
	shpinah-vaa (f)	špinavá
	shpinah-vair (neut)	špinavé
double bed	*dvoh-yih-taa postyely*	dvojitá posteľ
electricity	*elek-trinah*	elektrina
excluded	*bez ...*	bez ...
fan	*ventih-laator*	ventilátor
included	*vraa-tah-nyeh/*	vrátane/včítane
	fchee-tah-nyeh	
key	*klyooch*	kľúč
lift (elevator)	*vee-tyakh*	výťah
light bulb	*zhyiah-rohw-kah*	žiarovka
lock (n)	*zaam-kah*	zámka
mattress	*matrats*	matrac
mirror	*zrkad-loh*	zrkadlo
padlock	*vih-satsyiah*	visacia zámka
	zaam-kah	
pillow	*van-koosh*	vankúš
quiet	*tyikhoh*	ticho
room (in hotel)	*(hohtel-ohvaa) iz-bah*	(hotelová) izba
sheet	*plakh-tah*	plachta

shower	*spr-khah*	sprcha
soap	*midloh*	mydlo
suitcase	*kufohr*	kufor
swimming pool	*bazairn*	bazén
table	*stuol*	stôl
toilet	*zaa-khod/*	záchod/
	toah-letah/vair-tsair	toaleta/WC
toilet paper	*zaa-khod-ohvee*	záchodový
	(toah-letnee)	(toaletný) papier
	pah-pyier	
towel	*utyeh-raak*	uterák
water	*vodah*	voda
cold water	*studyeh-naa vodah*	studená voda
hot water	*horoo-tsah vodah*	horúca voda
window	*oknoh*	okno

Around Town

I'm looking for ...

hlyah-daam ...		Hľadám ...
the art gallery	*galair-ryiuh*	galériu
a bank	*bankuh*	banku
the church	*kostol*	kostol
the city centre	*stred (tsen-truhm)*	stred (centrum)
	mestah	mesta
the ... embassy	*shtaat-neh zastuh-*	štátne zastu-
	pityehly-stvoh ...	piteľstvo ...
my hotel	*muoy hohtel*	môj hotel
the market	*trkh*	trh
the museum	*moo-zeum*	múzeum
the police	*polee-tsyiuh*	políciu

SLOVAK

the post office	*posh-tuh*	poštu
a public toilet	*vereih-nair zaa-khodih*	verejné záchody
the telephone centre	*teleh-fawn-nuh tsentraa-luh*	telefónnu centrálu
the tourist information office	*infor-mahchnair stredyis-koh preh turis-tohw*	informačné stredisko pre turistov

What time does it open?
od koly-kei yeh otvoh-renair? Od koľkej je otvorené ?

What time does it close?
doh koly-kei yeh otvoh-renair? Do koľkej je otvorené ?

What ... is this?
akoh sah voh-laa? Ako sa volá ...?

| street | *taa-toh uhli-tsa* | táto ulica |
| suburb | *taa-toh shtvr̄-ty* | táto štvrť |

Note: For directions, see the Getting Around section, page 393-394.

At the Post Office

I would like to send ...
khtsel (m)/*khtseh-lah* (f) Chcel/Chcela by som
bih som pos-laty ... poslať ...

| a letter | *list* | list |
| a postcard | *pohlyad-nitsu* | pohľadnicu |

SLOVAK

| a parcel | *bah-leak* | balík |
| a telegram | *teleh-grahm* | telegram |

I would like some stamps.
khtsel (m)/*khtseh-lah* (f)   Chcel/Chcela by som
bih som koo-pity znaam-kih kúpiť známky.

How much is the postage?
koly-koh yeh posh-   Kolko je poštovné ?
tohv-nair?

How much does it cost to
send ... to ...?
koly-koh stoh-yee ... doh ...? Kolko stojí ... do ... ?

an aerogram	*airoh-grahm*	aerogram
air mail	*letyets-kaa posh-tah*	letecká pošta
envelope	*obaal-kah*	obálka
mailbox	*poshtoh-vaa skhraan-kah*	poštová schránka
parcel	*bah-leak*	balík
registered mail	*dopoh-ruche-nyeh*	doporučene
surface mail	*obichai-nohw posh-tohw*	obyčajnou poštoⱳ

Telephone
I want to ring ...
khtsem teleh-fohnoh-vaty ... Chcem telefonovať ...
The number is ...
chees-loh yeh   Číslo je ...
I want to speak for three
minutes.
buh-dyem hoh-vohrity trih minoo-tih Budem hovoriť tri minúty.

How much does a three-minute
call cost?
    koly-koh stoh-yee troi-
    minoo-tohvee hoh-vor?

Koľko stojí trojminútový
hovor ?

How much does each extra
minute cost?
    koly-koh stoh-yee kazh-daa
    minoo-tah nah-vishe?

Koľko stojí každá minúta
navyše ?

I would like to speak to
Mr Perez.
    muo-zhem hoh-vohrity
    s paa-nom pe-re-zom?

Môžem hovoriť s pánom
Perezom ?

I want to make a reverse-
charges phone call.
    khtsem teleh-fohnoh-vaty
    nah ooh-chet volah-nair-
    hoh chees-lah

Chcem telefonovať na účet
volaného čísla.

It's engaged.
    yeh op-sadyeh-nair

Je obsadené.

I've been cut off.
    muoy hoh-vor bol
    preh-rushe-nee

Môj hovor bol prerušený.

At the Bank

I want to exchange some
money/traveller's cheques.
    khtsem vih-meh-nyihty
    peh-nyiah-zeh/
    tses-tohv-nair shekih

Chcem vymeniť peniaze/
cestovné šeky

What is the exchange rate?
    akee yeh vee-men-nee kurz

Aký je výmenný kurz?

SLOVAK

How many crowns per dollar?
   koly-koh koh-roohn   Koľko korún dostanem za
   dostah-nyem zah yeden   jeden dolár?
   doh-laar ?
Can I have money transferred
here from my bank?
   muo-zhem sem trahns-   Môžem sem transferovať
   feroh-vaty peh-nyiah-zeh peniaze z mojej banky?
   z mohyay bankih?
How long will it take to arrive?
   kedih toh muo-zhem   Kedy to môžem očakávať?
   ocha-kaavaty?
Has my money arrived yet?
   ob-drzha-lih styeh uzh   Obdržali ste už moje
   moyeh peh-nyiah-zeh?   peniaze?

bank draft	*bankoh-vaa zmen-kah*	banková zmenka
bank notes	*bankov-kih*	bankovky
cashier	*poklad-nyeek* (m)	pokladník
	poklad-nyeech-kah (f)	pokladníčka
coins	*min-tseh*	mince
credit card	*ooveh-rohvaa*	úverová (kreditná)
	(kredit-naa) kartah	karta
exchange	*zmeh-naa-reny*	zmenáreň
loose change	*drob-nair/min-tse*	drobné/mince
signature	*(vlastnoh-ruchnee)*	(vlastnoručný)
	pod-pis	podpis

Sightseeing

Do you have a guidebook/
local map?
   maa-tyeh tses-tohv-noo   Máte cestovnú príručku/
   pree-ruchkuh/myiest-nuh   miestnu mapu?
   mapuh ?

What are the main attractions?
   akair soo tuh turist-itskair   Aké sú tu turistické
   za-ooyee-mah-vostih ?   zaujímavosti?

What is that?
   cho yeh toh ?   Čo je to?

How old is it?
   akoh yeh toh stah-rair ?   Ako je to staré?

Can I take photographs?
   muo-zhem fotoh-gra-   Môžem fotografovať?
   foh-vaty ?

What time does it open/close?
   oh koly-kay otvaa-rahyoo/   O koľkej otvárajú /zatvárajú?
   zah-tvaa-rahyoo ?

ancient	*staroh-bilee* (m)	starobylý
	staroh-bilaa (f)	starobylá
	staroh-bilair (neut)	starobylé
archaeological	*arkheoloh-ghi-tskee* (m)	archeologický
	arkheoloh-ghi-tskaa (f)	archeologická
	arkheoloh-ghi-tskair (neut)	archeologické
beach	*plaazh*	pláž

building	*budoh-vah*	budova
castle	*hrad/zaa-mok*	hrad/zámok
cathedral	*kateh-draalah*	katedrála
church	*kostol*	kostol
concert hall	*kon-tsert-naa syieny*	koncertná sieň
library	*knyizh-nyitsa*	knižnica
main square	*hlav-nair-naa-mestyieh*	hlavné námestie
market	*trkh*	trh
monastery	*klaash-tor*	kláštor
monument	*pah-mat-nyeek*	pamätník
mosque	*meshi-tah*	mešita
old city	*stah-raa chasty mestah*	stará časť mesta
palace	*palaats*	palác
opera house	*operah*	opera
ruins	*zroo-tsa-nyihnih*	zrúcaniny
stadium	*shtah-diyawn*	štadión
statues	*sokhih*	sochy
synagogue	*sinah-gawhgah*	synagóga
temple	*khraam*	chrám
university	*uhnih-ver-zitah*	univerzita

Entertainment

What's there to do in the evenings?

> *kam sah daa easty poh vecheh-rokh?*

Kam sa dá ísť po večeroch?

Are there any discos?

> *soo tuh diskoh-taihkih?*

Sú tu diskotéky?

Are there places where you
can hear local folk music?

    daa sah tuh nyieh-gdyeh   Dá sa tu niekde ísť počúvať
    easty pochoo-vaty   ľudovú hudbu?
    lyudoh-voo hoodbuh?

How much does it cost to
get in to the ...?

    koly-koh yeh vstup-nair ...?   Koľko je vstupné ... ?

cinema	*(doh) kinah*	(do) kina
concert	*(na) kon-tsert*	(na) koncert
discotheque	*(na) diskoh-taihkuh*	(na) diskotéku
theatre	*(do) dyivah-dlah*	(do) divadla

In the Country
Weather

What's the weather like?

    akair yeh pocha-syieh?   Aké je počasie?

The weather is ... today.

    dnyes yeh ...   Dnes je ...

Will it be ... tomorrow?

    budyeh zai-trah ...?   Bude zajtra ...?

cloudy	*zamrah-chenair*	zamračené
cold	*zimah*	zima
foggy	*hmlis-toh*	hmlisto
frosty	*mraaz*	mráz
hot	*horoo-tsoh*	horúco
raining	*pr-shaty*	pršať
snowing	*snyeh-zhity*	snežiť
sunny	*sl-nyech-noh*	slnečno
windy	*vetyer-noh*	veterno

Camping

Am I allowed to camp here?
muo-zhem tuh stanoh-vaty? Môžem tu stanovať?

Is there a campsite nearby?
yeh tuh nableez-kuh Je tu nablízku táborisko?
taaboh-riskoh?

backpack	*plets-nyiak*	plecniak
can opener	*otvaa-rach nah konzer-vih*	otvárač na konzerv
compass	*kom-pahs*	kompas
crampons	*skobih*	skoby
firewood	*palivoh-vair dreh-voh*	palivové drevo
gas cartridge	*naa-plny doh plinoh-vairhoh vahrih-cha*	náplň do plynovéh variča
hammock	*(visuh-tair) luozh-koh*	(visuté) lôžko
ice axe	*horoh-lezets-kee cha-kan*	horolezecký čakan
mattress	*mah-trahts*	matrac
penknife	*vretskoh-vee nuozh*	vreckový nôž
rope	*poh-vraz/ lanoh*	povraz/lano
tent	*stahn*	stan
tent pegs	*stahno-vair kolee-kih*	stanové kolíky
torch (flashlight)	*bater-kah*	baterka
sleeping bag	*spah-tsee vahk*	spací vak
stove	*varich*	varič
water bottle	*flah-sha nah voduh*	fľaša na vodu

SLOVAK

Food

breakfast	*ranyai-kih*	raňajky
lunch	*obed*	obed
dinner	*vecheh-rah*	večera

Table for ..., please.
   stuol preh ... proh-seem   Stôl pre ... prosím.
Can I see the menu please?
   muo-zhem dos-taty   Môžem dostať jedálny lístok?
   yedaal-nih leas-tok?
I would like the set lunch,
please.
   ponuh-kuh dnyah   Ponuku dňa, prosím.
   proh-seem
What does it include?
   cho yeh ftom zahr-nuhtair?   Čo je v tom zahrnuté?
Is service included in the bill?
   yeh obslu-hah zahr-nuhtaa   Je obsluha zahrnutá v cene?
   ftse-nyeh?
Not too spicy please.
   meh-nyay koreh-nyiah   Menej korenia, prosím.
   proh-seem

Vegetarian

I am a vegetarian.
   (yah) som veghe-tahryiaan   (Ja) som vegetarián.
I don't eat meat.
   nyeh-yem masoh   Nejem mäso.

I don't eat chicken or fish
or ham.
> *nyeh-yem kurah-tsyieh
> masoh ribih ahnyih
> shun-kuh*

Nejem kuracie mäso, ryby an
šunku.

Some Useful Words

ashtray	*popol-nyeek*	popolník
the bill	*ooh-chet*	účet
a cup	*shaal-kah*	šálka
dessert	*mooch-nyik/ zaa-kuh-sok*	múčnik/zákusok
a drink	*naa-poy*	nápoj
a fork	*vidlich-kah*	vidlička
fresh (food)	*cherst-vair (yedloh)*	čerstvé (jedlo)
a glass	*poh-haar*	pohár
a knife	*nuozh*	nôž
a plate	*tah-nyier*	tanier
spicy (food)	*shtyip-lyah-vaih/ koreh-nyistair (yedloh)*	štipľavé/ korenisté (jedlo)
a spoon	*lizhi-tsah*	lyžica
stale (food)	*nyieh tselkom cherst-vair (yedloh)*	nie celkom čerstvé (jedlo)
sweet (food)	*slad-kair (yedloh)*	sladké (jedlo)
teaspoon	*lih-zhich-kah*	lyžička
toothpick	*shpahraa-tkoh*	šparátko

Slovak Cuisine

Food in Slovakia reflects the myriad of influences which ha
shaped this part of Europe. During your stay you will find dishe

which you may have learned to appreciate elsewhere, such as Austrian strudel, Czech dumplings, German sauerkraut, French crépes and Hungarian goulash, but you'll always find them prepared with a special Slovak touch. You may even have tasted a Slovak speciality without knowing: *Liptovská bryndza* (Liptauer cheese, named after the Liptov region in Central Slovakia), and *medovníky*, honey cakes with ginger, are eaten throughout the world. Less well-known but equally delicious are dishes such as *kapustnica* (sauerkraut soup), *lokše* (potato pancakes), *haruľa* (spicy potato puffs) *živánska* (marinated pork roasted with layers of onion, garlic, bacon and vegetables), and many varieties of local freshwater fish with names such as *sumec*, *zubáč*, *šťuka* and *hlavátka*.

Modern Slovak cooks have not forgotten traditional recipes – they are well worth discovering!

Dobrú chuť'!	*(doh-broo khuty)*	Bon appétit!
Na zdravie!	*(nah zdrah-vyieh)*	Cheers!

Soups / Polievky

beef soup	*hovädzí vývar*
chicken soup	*kuracia polievka*
fish soup	*rybacia polievka*
vegetable soups:	*zeleninové polievky:*
asparagus	*špargľová*
bean	*fazuľová*
cauliflower	*karfiolová*
celeriac	*zelerová*
leek	*pórová*
pea	*hrášková*

potato	*zemiaková*
spinach	*špenátová*
tomato	*rajčiaková*
with ...	*s ...*
dumplings	*knedlíčkami*
gnocchi	*haluškami*
noodles (vermicelli)	*rezancami*
rice	*ryžou*

Starters & Snacks

Predjedlá

cheese platter (including local mountain cheese varieties)	*syrový tanier (oštiepok aparenica)*
chicken salad with mayonnaise	*kurací šalát s majonézou*
goose liver with apples	*husacia pečeň s jablkam*
green salad with goat cheese	*hlávkový šalát s oštiepkor*
open sandwich	*dánsky chlebíček*
with ...	
ham	*so šunkou*
herring	*so sleďom*
smoked salmon	*s údeným lososom*
salami platter with fresh/ pickled vegetables	*salámový tanier s oblohou*
salad Niçoise	*šalátová misa Nicé*
scrambled eggs with onion	*miešane vajíčka na cibuľk*

Fish

Ryby

braised carp in red sauce	*kapor v paprikovej omáčk*
carp braised in wine	*kapor na víne*
fillet of fish fried in breadcrumbs	*vyprážané rybacie filé*
trout fried in butter	*pstruh pečený na masle*

SLOVAK

Meat

Gypsy style grilled beef	*cigánska roštenka*
roast beef with ham and eggs	*roštenka so šunkou a vajcom*
steak	*biftek*
veal escalopes with cream and mushrooms	*teľacie medailónky na smotane a hríboch*
Wiener schnitzel	*vyprážaný rezeň*

Mäso

Poultry

chicken braised in red sauce	*kurací paprikáš*
fried chicken	*vyprážané kurča*
turkey breast stuffed with mushrooms and almonds	*morčacie prsia na hríboch as mandľovou plnkou*

Hydina

Game

pheasant soup	*polievka z bažanta*
rabbit/hare in a cream sauce	*zajac na smotane*
roast partridge	*pečená jarabica*
venison in red wine	*srnčie mäso s červeným vínom*

Divina

Pasta, Rice & Vegetarian Dishes

cauliflower soufflé	*karfiolový nákyp*
fried cheese with tartare sauce	*vyprážaný syr s tatarskou omáčkou*
risotto with vegetables	*zeleninové rizoto*
spaghetti/macaroni with tomato sauce and cheese	*špagety/makaróny na taliansky spôsob*

Cestoviny, Ryža a Bezmäsité Jedlá

tagliatelle with cottage cheese and fried bacon	*široké rezance s tvarohom a slaninou*

Salads	**Šaláty**
beetroot	*cviklový*
cabbage	*kapustový*
celeriac and carrot	*zelerový s mrkvou*
cucumber	*uhorkový*
lettuce	*hlávkový*
mixed	*z miešanej zeleniny*
potato	*zemiakový*
sauerkraut	*zo sudovej (kyslej) kapusty*
tomato	*rajčiakový/paradajkový*
Wallachian/Russian (mixed vegetables, salami, eggs and mayonnaise)	*vlašský/ruský*

Side Dishes	**Prílohy**
bread and pastry	*chlieb a pečivo*
potato chips	*zemiakové hranolky*
rice	*ryža*
roast potatoes	*opekané zemiaky*

Desserts	**Múčniky**
apple strudel	*jablkový závin*
bread pudding	*žemľovka*
cherry soufflé	*čerešňová bublanina*
chestnut cream	*gaštanové pyréchocolate*
chocolate gâteau	*čokoládová torta*
doughnuts	*šišky*

SLOVAK

fruit cake	*ovocný (hiskupský) chlebíček*
pancakes with chocolate and cream	*palacinky s čokoládou ašlahačkou*
rice soufflé	*ryžový nákyp*
roulade	*čokoládová roláda*
shortbread	*maslové (drobné čajové) pečivo*

Drinks / **Nápoje**

beer (bottled/draught)	*pivo (fľaškové/čapované)*
carbonated water	*sóda*
coffee	*káva*
espresso/short black	*espresso*
fruit juice	*ovocná šťava*
hot chocolate	*kakao/varená čokoláda*
liqueurs	*likéry*
mineral water	*minerálna voda*
spirits	*destiláty*
tea	*čaj*
Turkish coffee	*turecká káva*
Vienna coffee (with cream)	*viedenská káva (so šľahačkou)*
water	*voda*
wine (white/red)	*víno (biele/červene)*
young (green) wine	*burčák/burčiak*

Shopping

How much is it?
koly-koh toh stoh-yee?   Koľko to stojí?

bookshop	*predai*	predaj kníh
camera shop	*fotoh-(potreh-bih)*	foto(potreby)
clothing store	*odyeh-vih*	odevy
delicatessen	*lahuod-kih*	lahôdky
general store	*ob-khod zoh z*	obchod so
	myiesha-neem	zmiešaným
	tovah-rom	tovarom
laundry	*praa-chov-nya*	práčovňa
market	*trkh*	trh
newsagency/	*novih-nih*	noviny
stationer's	*ah chahso-pisih/*	a časopisy/
	pahpyier-nitstvoh	papiernictvo
pharmacy	*lekaa-reny*	lekáreň
shoeshop	*obuv*	obuv
souvenir shop	*darche-kih/ suveh-*	darčeky/suveníry
	neerih	
supermarket	*samoh-obslu-hah*	samoobsluha
vegetable shop	*zele-nyinah ah*	zelenina a
	ovoh-tsyieh	ovocie

I would like to buy ...
  khtsel (m)/*khtseh-lah* (f) *bih*   Chcel/Chcela by
  som koo-pity ...   som kúpiť ...
Do you have others?
  maa-tyeh ih-nair nah vee-ber?   Máte iné na výber?
I don't like it.
  toh sah mih nyeh-pozdaa-vah   To sa mi nepozdáva.
Can I look at it?
  muo-zhem toh vih-dyiety?   Môžem to vidieť?
I'm just looking.
  len sah tahk pozeh-raam   Len sa tak pozerám.

SLOVAK

Can you write down the price?
muo-zhetyeh mih napee- saty tsenuh?   Môžete mi napísať cenu?

Do you accept credit cards?
muo-zhem plah-tyity ooveh-rovohw kar-tohw?   Môžem platiť úverovou kartou?

Could you lower the price?
muo-zhetyeh znyee-zhity tsenuh?   Môžete znížiť cenu?

I don't have much money.
nyeh-maam veh-lya penyah-zee   Nemám veľa peňazí.

Can I help you?
cho sih zhelaa-tyeh?   Čo si želáte?

Will that be all?
toh yeh fshet-koh?   To je všetko?

Would you like it wrapped?
zhelaa-tyeh sih toh zabah-lity?   Želáte si to zabaliť?

Sorry, this is the only one.
zhyialy ih-nair nyeh-maameh   Žiaľ, iné nemáme.

How much/many do you want?
koly-koh (kuh-sohw) sih zhelaa-tyeh?   Koľko (kusov) si želáte?

Souvenirs

earrings	*naa-ush-nyitse*	náušnice
handicraft	*umelets-koh-pryieh-mihsel-nair veerob-kih*	umelecko priemyselné výrobky
necklace	*naahr-dyelnyeek*	náhrdelník
pottery	*keruh-mikah*	keramika

| ring | *prs-tyeny* | prsteň |
| rug | *pokroh-vets* | pokrovec |

Clothing

clothing	*odyeh-vih*	odevy
coat	*kah-baat*	kabát
dress	*shah-tih*	šaty
jacket	*sakoh*	sako
jumper	*sveh-ter*	sveter
shirt	*kosheh-lyah*	košeľa
shoes	*topaan-kih*	topánky
skirt	*suk-nyah*	sukňa
trousers	*nohah-vitseh*	nohavice

It's too ...
yeh toh pree-lish ...   Je to príliš ...

big	*vely-kair*	veľké
small	*mah-lair*	malé
short	*kraat-keh*	krátke
long	*dl-hair*	dlhé
tight	*ooz-keh*	úzke
loose	*voly-nair*	voľné

| It doesn't fit. | *nyeh-sedyee toh* | Nesedí to. |

Materials

cotton	*bavl-nah*	bavlna
handmade	*ruch-naa veeroh-bah*	ručná výroba
leather	*kozha*	koža
of brass	*moh-sadz*	mosadz

of gold	*zlatoh*	zlato
of silver	*stryieh-broh*	striebro
silk	*hod-vaab*	hodváb
wool	*vl-nah*	vlna

Colours

black	*chyier-nah*	čierna
blue	*behlah-saa/ mod-raa*	belasá/modrá
brown	*hnyeh-daa*	hnedá
green	*zeleh-naa*	zelená
orange	*oruhn-zhohvaa*	oranžová
pink	*ruzhoh-vaa*	ružová
purple	*nakhoh-vaa/ fiya-lovaa*	nachová/fialová
red	*cherveh-naa*	červená
white	*byieh-lah*	biela
yellow	*zhl-taa*	žltá

Toiletries

comb	*hreh-beny*	hrebeň
condoms	*prezer-vahtee-vih/ kon-doh-mih*	prezervatívy/ kondómy
deodorant	*dezoh-dorant*	dezodorant
hairbrush	*kefah nah vlasih*	kefa na vlasy
moisturising cream	*hidrah-touch-nee krairm*	hydratačný krém
razor (blade)	*zhilet-kah*	žiletka
sanitary napkins	*vlozh-kih*	vložky
shampoo	*sham-pohn*	šampón

shaving cream	*krairm nah holeh-nyieh*	krém na holenie
soap	*midloh*	mydlo
sunblock cream	*opa-lyovah-tsee krairm s fil-trom*	opaľovací krém s filtrom
tampons	*tahm-pohnih*	tampóny
tissues	*vrets-kohw-kih*	vreckovky
toilet paper	*toalet-nee/zaakhoh-dovee pah-pyier*	toaletný/záchodový papier
toothbrush	*zub-naa kef-kah*	zubná kefka
toothpaste	*zub-naa pahs-tah*	zubná pasta

Stationery & Publications

map	*mahpah*	mapa
newspaper	*novih-nih*	noviny
newspaper in English	*novih-nih v anglich-tyinyeh*	noviny v angličtine
novels in English	*beleh-tryiah v anglich-tinyeh*	beletria v angličtine
paper	*pah-pyier*	papier
pen (ballpoint)	*vech-nair peh-roh*	večné pero
scissors	*nozhnih-tse*	nožnice

Photography

How much is it to process this film?

| *koly-koh stoh-yee vivoh-lanyieh tokh-toh fill-muh?* | Koľko stojí vyvolanie tohto filmu? |

When will it be ready?
    kedih toh buh-dyeh   Kedy to bude hotové?
    hotoh-vair?
I'd like a film for this camera.
    maa-tyeh film doh tokh-toh Máte film do tohto
    fotoh-ahpah-raa-tuh?   fotoaparátu?

B&W (film)	*chyier-noh-byielih film*	čiernobiely film
camera	*fotoh-ahpah-raat*	fotoaparát
colour (film)	*fareb-nee film*	farebný film
film	*film*	film
flash	*blesk*	blesk
lens	*obyek-teev*	objektív
light meter	*ekspoh-zih-mehter*	expozimeter

Smoking

A packet of cigarettes, please.
    bahlee-chek tsiga-ryiet Balíček cigariet, prosím.
    proh-seem
Are these cigarettes strong/
mild?
    soo toh sil-nair/ yem-nair Sú to silné/jemné cigarety?
    tsiga-retih?
Do you have a light?
    muo-zhetyeh mih   Môžete mi pripáliť?
    pripaa-lity?

cigarette papers	*tsiga-retoh-vair pah-pyieh-reh*	cigaretové papiere

cigarettes	*tsiga-retih*	cigarety
filtered	*tsiga-retih s fil-trom*	cigarety s filtrom
lighter	*zapah-lyoh-vach*	zapaľovač
matches	*zaa-palkih*	zápalky
menthol	*mentoloh-vair*	mentolové cigarety
	tsiga-retih	
pipe	*fy-kah*	fajka
tobacco (pipe)	*fy-koh-vee tabak*	fajkový tabak

Sizes & Comparisons

small	*mah-lee* (m)	malý
	mah-laa (f)	malá
	mah-lair (neut)	malé
big	*vely-kee* (m)	veľký
	vely-kaa (f)	veľká
	vely-kair (neut)	veľké
heavy	*tyazh-kee* (m)	ťažký
	tyazh-kaa (f)	ťažká
	tyazh-kair (neut)	ťažké
light	*lyakh-kee* (m)	ľahký
	lyakh-kaa (f)	ľahká
	lyakh-kair (neut)	ľahké
more	*vyiats*	viac
less	*meh-nyeay*	menej
too much/many	*pree-lish velyah*	príliš veľa
many	*mnohoh/ velyah*	mnoho/veľa
enough	*dosty*	dosť
also	*tyiezh*	tiež
a little bit	*troh-khah*	trocha

Health

Where is ...?
gdyeh yeh ...?   Kde je ... ?

the doctor	*dok-tor/lekaar*	doktor´/lekár
the hospital	*nyemots-nyitsah*	nemocnica
the chemist	*lekaar-nyik*	lekárnik
the dentist	*zoob-nee lekaar*	zubný lekár

I am sick.
som kho-ree (m)   Som chorý.
som kho-raa (f)   Som chorá.

My friend is sick.
muoy pryiah-tyely yeh   Môj priateľ je chorý.
kho-ree (m)
moh-yah pryiah-tyely-   Moja priateľka je chorá.
kah yeh kho-raa (f)

Could I see a female doctor?
muo-zhem hoh-vohrity zoh   Môžem hovoriť so ženou-
zhe-nohw-lekaar-kohw?   lekárkou?

What's the matter?
cho vaas traa-pih?   Čo Vás trápi?

Where does it hurt?
gdyeh toh boh-lee?   Kde Vás to bolí?

It hurts here.
tuh mah boh-lee   Tu ma bolí.

My ... hurts.
boh-lee mah ...   Bolí ma ...

Parts of the Body

ankle	*chleh-nok*	členok
arm	*rukah*	ruka (rameno a dlaň)
back	*khr-baat*	chrbát
chest	*hrudyi*	hruď
ear	*ukhoh*	ucho
eye	*okoh*	oko
finger	*prst*	prst
foot	*nohah/ kho-dyid-loh*	noha/chodidlo
hand	*rukah*	ruka (len časť sdlaňou)
head	*hlah-vah*	hlava
heart	*srd-tse*	srdce
leg	*noh-hah*	noha (celá)
mouth	*oos-tah*	ústa
nose	*nos*	nos
ribs	*reh-braa*	rebrá
skin	*koh-zha/ pokozh-kah*	koža/pokožka
spine	*khrb-tyih-tsa*	chrbtica
stomach	*zhaloo-dok*	žalúdok
teeth	*zoobih*	zuby
throat	*hrd-loh*	hrdlo

Ailments

I have ...

an allergy	*maam aler-ghiuh*	Mám alergiu.

a blister	*maam otlahk*	Mám otlak.
a burn	*maam popaa-leh-nyinuh*	Mám popáleninu.
a cold	*maam naad-khuh*	Mám nádchu.
constipation	*maam zaap-khuh*	Mám zápchu.
a cough	*maam kah-shely*	Mám kašeľ.
diarrhoea	*maam hnach-kuh*	Mám hnačku.
fever	*maam horooch-kuh*	Mám horúčku.
a headache	*bohlee mah hla-vah*	Bolí ma hlava.
hepatitis	*maam zhl-touch-kuh*	Mám žltačku.
indigestion	*maam pokah-zenee zhaloo-dok*	Mám pokazený žalúdok.
an infection	*maam naa-kaz-livoo khoroh-buh*	Mám nákazlivú chorobu.
influenza	*maam khreep-kuh*	Mám chrípku.
lice	*maam fshih*	Mám vši.
low/high blood pressure	*maam nyeez-kih/ visoh-kee krv-nee tlak*	Mám nízky/vysoký krvný tlak
a pain	*maam boles-tyih*	Mám bolesti.
sore throat	*bohlee mah hrd-loh*	Bolí ma hrdlo.
sprained my ...	*vitkohl* (m)/*vitklah* (f) *som sih ...*	Vytkol/Vytkla som si ...
a stomachache	*bohlee mah zhaloo-dok*	Bolí ma žalúdok.
sunburn	*maam ooh-pahl*	Mám úpal.
a veneral disease	*maam pohlav-noo khoro-buh*	Mám pohlavnú chorobu.
worms	*maam chrev-neekh parah-zitohw*	Mám črevných parazitov.

Some Useful Words & Phrases

I'm ...

maam ...		Mám ...
diabetic	*tsuk-rof-kuh*	cukrovku
epileptic	*epi-lepsyiuh*	epilepsiu
asthmatic	*asth-muh*	astmu

I'm allergic to

som aler-ghits-kee nah ... (m)	Som alergický na ...
som aler-ghits-kaa nah ... (f)	Som alergická na ...
antibiotics	*antih-biyoh-tihkaa*	antibiotiká
penicillin	*penih-tsileen*	penicilín

I'm pregnant.
> *som tyehot-naa*   Som tehotná.

I'm on the pill.
> *pohw-zheevam hormoh-naal-nuh anti-kon-tseptsyiuh*   Používam hormonálnu antikoncepciu.

I haven't had my period for (two) months.
> *uzh (dvah) mehsyiah-tse som nyeh-malah men-shtru-aatsyiuh*   Už (dva) mesiace som nemala menštruáciu.

I have my own syringe.
> *maam vlast-noo in-yekch-noo stryieh-kach-kuh*   Mám vlastnú injekčnú striekačku.

SLOVAK

I feel better/worse.

tsee-tyim sah lep-shyieh/   Cítim sa lepšie/horšie.
hor-shyieh

accident	*nyeh-hodah*	nehoda
addiction	*nar-koh-maanyiah/*	narkománia/
	toksi-koh-maanyiah	toxikománia
antibiotics	*anti-biyoh-tihkaa*	antibiotiká
antiseptic	*anti-septih-khum*	antiseptikum
aspirin	*aspih-reen*	aspirín
bandage	*ob-vaz*	obväz
bite (animal)	*poh-hriz-nutyieh*	pohryznutie
bite (insect)	*ushtyip-nutyieh*	uštipnutie
blood pressure	*krv-nee tlak*	krvný tlak
blood test	*krv-naa skoosh-kah*	krvná skúška
contraceptives	*proh-stryied-kih*	prostriedky proti
	protih pocha-tyiuh	počatiu
injection	*in-yek-tsyiah*	injekcia
injury	*porah-nyeh-nyieh*	poranenie
itch	*svr-beh-nyieh*	svrbenie
medicine	*lyiek*	liek
menstruation	*men-shtru-aatsyiah*	menštruácia
nausea	*zhaloo-dochnaa nyeh-*	žalúdočná
	voly-nosty	nevoľnosť
oxygen	*kis-leak*	kyslík
vitamins	*vitah-meanih*	vitamíny

At the Chemist

I need medication for ...

potreh-buyem lyiek nah ...   Potrebujem liek na ...

I have a prescription.
  maam lekaar-skih pred-pis   Mám lekársky predpis
  (reh-tsept)   (recept).

At the Dentist
I have a toothache.
  boh-lyiah mah zoobih   Bolia ma zuby.
I've lost a filling.
  vih-padlah mih plom-bah   Vypadla mi plomba.
I've broken a tooth.
  zloh-mil sa mih zoob   Zlomil sa mi zub.
My gums hurt.
  boh-lyiah mah dyas-naa   Bolia ma ďasná.
I don't want it extracted.
  nyeh-khtsem sih toh   Nechcem si to nechať
  nyeh-khaty vih-trh-nooty   vytrhnúť.
Please give me an anaesthetic.
  uh-mrrt-vityeh mih toh   Umŕtvite mi to, prosím.
  proh-seem

Time & Dates
What time is it?
  koly-koh yeh hoh-dyeen ?   Koľko je hodín ?
It is ... o'clock
  yeh (jeh-dnah) hodih-nah   Je (jedna) hodina.
  soo (dveh, trih, shtih-rih) Sú (dve, tri, štyri) hodiny.
  hodyih-nih
  yeh (pety ...) hoh-dyeen   Je (päť ...) hodín.

in the morning	
dopoh-luh-dnyah/	dopoludnia/predpoludním
pred-poluh-dnyeem	
in the afternoon	
popoh-ludnyee	popoludní
in the evening	
veh-cher	večer
What date is it today ?	
koly-kairhoh yeh dnyes ?	Koľkého je dnes ?

Days of the Week

Monday	*pon-dyelok*	pondelok
Tuesday	*uh-torok*	utorok
Wednesday	*stre-dah*	streda
Thursday	*shtvr-tok*	štvrtok
Friday	*piah-tok*	piatok
Saturday	*soboh-tah*	sobota
Sunday	*nye-dye-lya*	nedeľa

Months

January	*yanooh-aar*	január
February	*februh-aar*	február
March	*maretz*	marec
April	*apreel*	apríl
May	*maai*	máj
June	*yoon*	jún
July	*yool*	júl
August	*ow-goost*	august
September	*septem-behr*	september

SLOVAK

October	*oktoh-behr*	október
November	*nohvem-behr*	november
December	*detzem-behr*	december

Seasons

summer	*letoh*	leto
autumn	*yeseny*	jeseň
winter	*zimah*	zima
spring	*yahr*	jar

Present

today	*dnyes*	dnes
this morning	*dnyes raa-noh*	dnes ráno
tonight	*dnyes veh-cher*	dnes večer
this week/year	*tentoh teezh-dyeny/ rok*	tento týždeň/rok
now	*teras*	teraz

Past

yesterday	*fcheh-rah*	včera
day before yesterday	*pred-fcheh-rom*	predvčerom
last night	*minuh-loo notz*	minulú noc
last week/year	*minuh-lee teezh-dyeny/ rok*	minulý týžden/rok

Future

tomorrow	*zai-trah*	zajtra
day after tomorrow	*poh-zai-trah*	pozajtra
tomorrow morning	*zai-trah raa-noh*	zajtra ráno
next week	*buhdoo-tzi teezh-dyeny*	budúci týždeň
next year	*buhdoo-tzi rok*	budúci rok

During the Day

afternoon	*popoh-ludnyie*	popoludnie
dawn,	*ooh-svit*	úsvit
day	*dyeny*	deň
early	*skoh-roh*	skoro
early morning	*skoh-roh raa-noh*	skoro ráno
midnight	*pol-notz*	polnoc
morning	*raa-noh*	ráno
night	*notz*	noc
noon	*poluh-dnyie*	poludnie
sunrise	*vee-khod sln-kah*	východ slnka
sunset	*zaa-pad sln-kah*	západ slnka

Numbers & Amounts

0	*noolah*	nula
1	*yeh-den*	jeden
2	*dvah*	dva
3	*trih*	tri
4	*shtih-rih*	štyri

5	*pety*	päť
6	*shesty*	šesť
7	*seh-dyem*	sedem
8	*oh-sem*	osem
9	*dye-vety*	deväť
10	*dye-sahty*	desať
20	*dvah-tsahty*	dvadsať
30	*trih-tsahty*	tridsať
40	*shtih-rih-tsahty*	štyridsať
50	*pety-dyeh-syiat*	päťdesiat
60	*shez-dyeh-syiat*	šesťdesiat
70	*seh-dyem-dyeh-syiat*	sedemdesiat
80	*oh-sem-dyeh-syiat*	osemdesiat
90	*dyeh-vaty-dyeh-syiat*	deväťdesiat
100	*stoh*	sto
1000	*tyih-seetz*	tisíc
one million	*milih-yawhn*	milión
1st	*pr-vee* (m)	prvý
	pr-vaa (f)	prvá
	pr-vair (neut)	prvé
2nd	*druh-hee* (m)	druhý
	druh-haa (f)	druhá
	druh-hair (neut)	druhé
3rd	*treh-tyee* (m)	tretí
	treh-tyiah (f)	tretia
	treh-tyieh (neut)	tretie
¼	*shtvr-tyih-nah*	štvrtina
⅓	*treh-tyih-nah*	tretina
½	*poloh-vitzah*	polovica
¾	*trih shtvr-tyeh*	tri štvrte

Some Useful Words

double	*dvoy-moh*	dvojmo
a dozen	*tuhtzet*	tucet
Enough!	*dosty!/stah-cheeh !*	dosť!/stačí!
few	*maa-loh*	málo
less	*meh-nyay*	menej
many	*mnohoh/veh-lyah*	mnoho/veľa
more	*vyiah-tzyey*	viacej
once	*yeden-kraat/yeden raz*	jedenkrát/jeden raz
a pair	*paar*	pár
percent	*per-tzen-toh*	percento
some	*nyieh-koly-koh*	niekoľko
too much	*pree-lish veh-lyah*	príliš veľa
twice	*dvah-kraat/dvah razih*	dvakrát/dva razy

Abbreviations

AIDS	AIDS
atď.	etc.
Austr.	Australia
ca (cca)	approx.
CK	travel agency
cm/m/km	cm/m /km(s)
g/kg	gm/kg
h. (hod.)/min./sek.	hr(s)/ min/sec
Juž. Afrika	RSA
n.l./pr. n.l.	AD/BC
NZ	NZ

OSN/EU	UN/EU
Sev. /Juž./ Záp. /Vých.	Nth/Sth /West/ East
Sk (slovenská koruna)	crown (unit of currency)
ŠPZ	Car Reg No
SR	Slovak Republic
t.č.	at present (now)
tel. č.	Ph. No.
t.j.	i.e.
t.r.	this year
Ul. /Nám./Nábr.	St /Sq/Quay
USA/Kan.	USA/Canada
V. Brit. (GB)	UK

Index

Czech

French

German

Hungarian

Italian

Slovak

Language Survival Kits

Complete your travel experience with a Lonely Planet phrasebook. Developed for the independent traveller, the phrasebooks enable you to communicate confidently in any practical situation – and get to know the local people and their culture.

Skipping lengthy details on where to get your drycleaning ironed, information in the phrasebooks covers bargaining, customs and protocol, how to address people and introduce yourself, explanations of local ways of telling the time, dealing with bureaucracy and bargaining, plus plenty of ways to share your interests and learn from locals.

Australian
Introduction to Australian English, Aboriginal and Torres Strait languages.
Arabic (Egyptian)
Arabic (Moroccan)
Brazilian
Burmese
Cantonese
Central Europe
Covers Czech, French, German, Hungarian, Italian and Slovak.
Eastern Europe
Covers Bulgarian, Czech, Hungarian, Polish, Romanian and Slovak.
Fijian
Hindi/Urdu
Indonesian
Japanese
Korean
Mandarin
Mediterranean Europe
Covers Albanian, Greek, Italian, Macedonian, Maltese, Serbian & Croatian and Slovene.

Nepali
Pidgin
Pilipino
Quechua
Russian
Scandinavian Europe
Covers Danish, Finnish, Icelandic, Norwegian and Swedish.
Spanish (Latin American)
Sri Lanka
Swahili
Thai
Thai Hill Tribes
Tibet
Turkish
Vietnamese
Western Europe
Useful words and phrases in Basque, Catalan, Dutch, French, German, Irish, Portugese and Spanish (Castilian).

Lonely Planet Audio Packs

The best way to learn a language is to hear it spoken in context. Set within a dramatic narrative, with local music and local speakers, is a wide range of words and phrases for the independent traveller – to help you talk to people you meet, make your way around more easily, and enjoy your stay.

Each pack includes a phrasebook and CD or cassette, and comes in an attractive, useful cloth bag. These bags are made by local communities using traditional methods, through Community Aid Abroad projects with the support of Lonely Planet.

Forthcoming Language Survival Kits
Greek, the USA (American English and dialects, Native American languages and Hawaiian), Baltic States (Estonian, Latvian and Lithuanian), Lao, Mongolian, Bengali, Sinhalese, Hebrew, Ukrainian

Forthcoming Audio Packs
Indonesian, Thai, Vietnamese, Mandarin, Cantonese

LONELY PLANET PUBLICATIONS
Australia: PO Box 617, Hawthorn, Victoria 3122
USA: 155 Filbert Street, Suite 251, Oakland CA 94607-2538
UK: 10 Barley Mow Passage, Chiswick, London W4 4PH
France: 71 bis, rue du Cardinal Lemoine – 75005 Paris

PLANET TALK

Lonely Planet's FREE quarterly newsletter

We love hearing from you and think you'd like to hear from us.

When...is the right time to see reindeer in Finland?
Where...can you hear the best palm-wine music in Ghana?
How...do you get from Asunción to Areguá by steam train?
What...should you leave behind to avoid hassles with customs in Iran?

*For the answer to these and
many other questions read
PLANET TALK.*

Every issue is packed with up-to-date travel news and advice including:

- *a letter from Lonely Planet founders Tony and Maureen Wheeler*
- *travel diary from a Lonely Planet author - find out what it's really like out on the road*
- *feature article on an important and topical travel issue*
- *a selection of recent letters from our readers*
- *the latest travel news from all over the world*
- *details on Lonely Planet's new and forthcoming releases*

To join our mailing list contact any Lonely Planet office.

LONELY PLANET PUBLICATIONS
Australia: PO Box 617, Hawthorn, Victoria 3122 (tel: 03-819 1877)
USA: 155 Filbert Street, Suite 251, Oakland, CA 94607 (tel: 510-893 8555)
UK: 10 Barley Mow Passage, Chiswick, London W4 4PH (tel: 081-742 3161)
FRANCE: 71 bis, rue du Cardinal Lemoine – 75005 Paris (tel: 1-46 34 00 58)

Also available Lonely Planet T-Shirts. 100% heavy weight cotton (S, M, L, XL)